A RIDE IN THE SUN

A RIDE IN THE SUN

Combat with a South Vietnamese Cavalry Troop in the Mekong Delta

By LTC (ret: USNG)
LARRY K. COLE

A RIDE IN THE SUN
Copyright © 2017 by LTC (ret: USNG) Larry K. Cole

All rights reserved. No part of this book may be reproduced in any form or by any means—whether electronic, digital, mechanical, or otherwise—without permission in writing from the publisher, except by a reviewer, who may quote brief passages in a review.

World Ahead Press is a division of WND Books. The views and opinions expressed in this book are those of the author and do not necessarily reflect the official policy or position or WND Books.

Paperback ISBN: 978-1-944212-74-2
eBook ISBN: 978-1-944212-75-9

Printed in the United States of America
16 17 18 19 20 21 LSI 9 8 7 6 5 4 3 2 1

DEDICATION

To My Family

PREFACE

Larry Cole's outstanding chronicle of his tour as an US Advisor to the Army of Vietnam is an excellent overview of the more than two decades of hard work by countless individuals who provided advice and assistance to indigenous forces within and on the borders of the Republic of South Vietnam. Their legacy of achievement is little known and largely overlooked by many historians of the period. Yet the service of these young officers and NCOs operating in small teams living and fighting as a part of the Vietnamese forces is a story that needed to be captured. Larry Cole has done this in infinite detail while taking the reader into the rice paddies and jungle battle fields and providing his personal perspective of the battle sights, sounds and emotions experienced. He candidly shares the fears of all soldiers going into combat for the first time regarding whether he will measure up. Or will he be overcome by the anxiety of the action and fail to do what he had been taught?

In addition, he clearly explains the loneliness faced by small advisory teams especially during the first few weeks and months of their tour as they attempt to establish a relationship with their Vietnamese counterparts. While frustrated by efforts to advise being initially rebuffed, it is interesting to see a mutual respect grow as he explains how the Vietnamese officers NCO and soldier gain a special status in his mind as he sees their willingness to endure unbelievable hardships and deprivations for their nation.

His up close and personal account of the savagery of the Vietcong attacks during Tet 1968, where in addition to many unit loses, he experiences the emotions associated with losing close friends and how that impacted on his ability to continue to do his job.

Finally, Larry provides an unvarnished viewpoint on the pros and cons of the war from the vantage point of young officers and NCOs who were isolated within ARVN formations with limited capability to see the big picture. While sharing many opinions and thoughts regarding how maybe the war should have been fought, the book provides a perspective of counter insurgency fought at the basic level and should be very useful and instructive for our current generations of Advise and Assist warriors.

H. G. (PETE) TAYLOR
Lieutenant General
US Army, Retired

FOREWORD

The original draft of *A Ride in the Sun* was written in 1988, 20 years after the fact. The exception was the depiction of the Battle of My Tho, which was written within a year of the action, while attending the Armor Advanced Course at Fort Knox in 1969. Memories, however were vivid, and with the help of my friend Ken Lord the names of places are believed to be acurate. The characters are real, but some names were changed where permission to use real names could not be obtained. The draft was set aside for years due to business conflicts; but is now revived for my family in the hope that it will shed light on a small part of the Vietnam War that many have forgotten. Hopefully, future soldiers will fine some lessons learned or reinforce current military instruction.

Surprisingly, duty with the Vietnamese was not as bad an assignment as some authorities have made it out to have been. Nor were the regular South Vietnamese soldiers (differentiated from Regional Forces and from Provincial Forces soldiers) as bad as some reporters have depicted them. Actually, I came to admire them, especially the officers. *A Ride in the Sun* takes readers through a totally different war of an Army National Guard officer who advised (or better said, coordinated indirect fire support) a South Vietnamese Regular Army (ARVN) unit in the Mekong Delta.

A Ride in the Sun describes the daily routine, living conditions, and combat actions as seen by an American soldier. Written in a conversational style with a liberal use of dialogue, the book will be accessible to the military novices without being too simple-minded for the professional.

For the novices, the book will offer clear descriptions of equipment and photographs which will enhance their understanding of living conditions and combat action. The uninitiated will vicariously experience combat through the vivid accounts, thoughts, and feelings of a soldier in combat. The battle for My Tho during TET-68 is covered in detail. Additionally, for the student who wants to learn of the military lifestyle in the mid-1960s several short vignettes about Army training in Germany and problems experienced by various soldiers in active units and in basic training are presented. These anecdotes are inserted at points in the narrative when they actually occurred in conversations between characters. For the historian or sociologist the book describes how the American advisors lived and socialized as well as provides insight into how the South Vietnamese soldier lived. Also, the characters' thoughts about the war, United States involvement, and anti-war demonstrators are addressed. For the military professional, the book will tell how operations were conducted and how they might have been conducted to obtain better results.

The narrative has not been embellished. What happened, happened as told.

For the non-military reader, a short explanation of a few terms might well be in order.

The team *Troop* refers to a company size unit in an armored cavalry unit. A similar size unit in the infantry is referred to as a *company*. In the artillery it is called a *battery*.

The term *track* refers to an armored vehicle that moved along on connected pads that forms a track like system. The M-113 in all its configurations was such a vehicle.

Trooper or troopers is how we referred to our soldiers.

In radio communications we use terms like *over* to end a comment to which we wanted a reply. We said *out* to end a conversation. *Roger* meant "I understand." *Wilco* was short for "I will do as told," *How me* was used to ask "how you hear me."

CONTENTS

	Preface	7
	Foreword	9
1.	Tan Hiep: 7 May 1968	15
2.	The Beginning: October 1967	29
3.	Team 75	54
4.	Cai Be: October 1967	78
5.	On the Road: October-November 1967	97
6.	Cai Lay: November 1967	110
7.	In the Paddies: November 1967	121
8.	Ranging Out: November 1967	135
9.	Thanksgiving: November 1967	153
10.	Long Dinh: December 1967	164
11.	Pre Tet: January 1968	193
12.	Tet—Charlie Attacks: 31 January 1968	215
13.	Counterattacks: 1-2 February 1968	240
14.	The Bridge: 2 February 1968	259
15.	Japan: February 1968	274

16. My Tho: 17 March 1968   296

17. Thruong Gong Dinh: 2 May 1968   309

18. The "Gofer": May-June 1968   327

19. Going Home: August 1968   336

Appendix One:
    Weekly Report 2–9 December 1967:   349

Appendix Two
    Weekly Report 14–20 January 1968   355

Appendix Three
    Viet Gong Battle Plan   359

CHAPTER ONE

TAN HIEP: 7 MAY 1968

Two days after the attack on Armor House, I was in the paddies again. Now I was acting as the Senior Advisor of the 6th Cavalry Squadron. We were operating with a battalion of the 11th Infantry and two Regional Forces companies. We had crossed the LD (line of departure) and moved into the paddies at 0730 hours. The going had been slow, then the Puffs (Regional Units) found Charlie. He was in a small village nestled in a narrow tree line on the edge of a vast inundated savannah of tall grass called the Plain of Reeds.

The M-113 was an aluminum cracker box designed to carry mechanized infantry and to float across European rivers. Its back was a ramp, which could be lowered and raised. There was a small door in the ramp to allow entry without lowering the ramp. There was a large hatch on top of the vehicle that could be folded back to allow the infantrymen to stand. Except when it rained, this door was always open. The armament on each vehicle varied, but most mounted a .50 cal machine gun in front of the commander's hatch and a 30-caliber machine gun on each side. In this configuration, American units called the M-113 an ACAV (Armored Cavalry Vehicle). We just referred to them as "tracks."

The morning sun beat down on us as the tracks slowly approached the tree line. I was beginning to sweat from the heat, and my t-shirt felt moist and heavy from my perspiration. I was more concerned with the heat than with the possibility of meeting up with Charlie. Suddenly, the chatter of automatic weapons fire resounded from within the trees. Colonel Thoan, the Squadron commander, halted our command track in the center of a paddy. I watched as the Troops' tracks maneuvered in the paddies for an assault on the jungle tree line. The infantry, wading in the mud between the tracks, began their advance. The tree line erupted with an avalanche of automatic weapons fire that drove the infantry into the mud. Within the trees, the roar and back blast of a recoilless rifle could be heard. A geyser of mud shot up near one of the tracks. The attack stalled as more automatic weapons and anti-tank fire tore into the stationary troops.

"Sierra Six, this is Charlie Two-six. I think we have a recoilless rifle in here, over."

"Roger, Two-six. What size is it?" I asked.

"This is Two-six, probably a .75. I can't tell for sure, over."

Reports coming in over the net indicated that Charlie was really dug-in. Lieutenant Lord and the Ruff Puff advisor finally recommended that they pull back and that I bring in the Air Force.

"Delta Tango, this is Sierra Six. Do we have many air assets available? Over," I called.

"Sierra Six, this is Tango. That's a roger. I can get you a FAC and at least two sorties, over." A FAC was a forward air controller who flew in a small aircraft with radios that netted with ground units, American planes, and South Vietnamese aircraft. The FAC in coordination with the ground commander directed air-strikes.

"Roger, Tango. We can use it. Who do I contact, over?"

"This is Tango, roger. Contact Skyhawk Two-one, over."

"This is Sierra Six, roger. Break, break. Skyhawk Two-one, this is Sierra Six, over."

"This is Skyhawk. What can I do for you, over?"

TAN HIEP: 7 MAY 1968

It was Major Gay, my old friend from the "Seminary." I was glad he would be over us. It's always good to work with someone you know.

"Roger, Skyhawk, from . . . Papa One-four . . . we're up nine period four, left one, over."

"This is Skyhawk. Roger. I'm on my way. Out."

I leaned over and said to Col Thoan, "Sir, I have air support on the way. If you'll have them pull back. "Col Thoan nodded his understanding and started to speak into his mic .

"Sierra six, this is Charlie Two-six. We're pulling back, over."

"Roger Two-six, out." The other Troop advisors reported they were also pulling back.

I leaned over to Colonel Thoan, "Sir, be sure to have the troops put out their orange panels." Colonel Thoan nodded his understanding and spoke into his mic.

Soon, I could hear the slow drum of an Air Force 0-2, a high-winged observation aircraft. The 0-2's fuselage housed two engines, one in front and a pusher in the rear. Extending to the rear, on each side of the plane's body, were silver booms that ran to twin tails connected by a horizontal stabilizer.

"Sierra six, this is Skyhawk. I have some of your tracks in sight. Where do you want us, over?"

This is Sierra. I'll turn you over to Charlie Two-six. He has a better feel than I do, over."

"This is Skyhawk, roger. Break, Break. Two-six, this is Skyhawk, over."

"This is Two-six. We have a bunker complex at coordinates four six six, ah five six two, over."

"This is Skyhawk. I think I have your tracks. Pop smoke so I can confirm, over."

"This is Two-six, roger, wait. Smoke is out, over."

"This is Skyhawk, roger. I identify purple, over."

"This is Two-six, roger. That's us, over."

"This is Skyhawk, roger. I'll mark the target, over."

"This is Two-six, roger, out."

The O-2 circled lazily in the hot morning sky. I was confident that Gay would soon identify Charlie's position and have a bit of death rained down on it.

The O-2 approached from the north in a shallow drive. A trail of gray-white smoke darted from under the O-2's left wing and streaked toward the thick jungle-like tree line.

When it struck, I heard, "Skyhawk, this is Two-six. You need to add one hundred and move east five-zero, out."

"This is Skyhawk, roger. Add one hundred, east five-zero. I'll try again."

The little O-2 circled around and dived in again. Again, he was off. Knowing Gay to be a light-hearted aviator, always quick with a joke or a smart remark, I decided to add a little levity to the conversation.

"Skyhawk, this is Sierra. Too much at the bar last night? You seem a little blurry-eyed this morning."

I didn't get the reaction I expected. "Knock it off, Sierra! This is no time for that bull! I'm busy!" Gay said in a bristling tone.

He was right. I was embarrassed. In the middle of a firefight, there was no time to be flippant. He may not have had a serious thought in his head at the club, but at the office he was all business and a professional—I hadn't been.

Finally, Skyhawk marked the target and brought in his "fast movers." They didn't seem to have much effect. After each pair of aircraft pulled away,

Charlie showed his contempt by lobbing a few 75 mm recoilless rifle rounds at our command track.

We sat fully exposed in the center of the paddy. Colonel Thoan seemed oblivious to the recoilless rifle rounds. At first, so did I; they were impacting to our left front and presented no immediate problem. But, as the morning wore on, the gunners began to find the range and moved them in closer. The morning crawled with the sun beating down and getting hotter.

After each airstrike, the task force (a combined armor and infantry unit of battalion size) tried to advance, only to be driven back by fires from well dug-in automatic and anti-tank weapons. After two unsuccessful tries to make the tree line, Colonel Thoan decided to shift his main effort further to the north. While the Air Force struck the jungle with bombs, the infantry and Cav backed off and moved north.

When Gay reported that he was finished for the day, the Ruff Puff and 2nd Troop were ordered to assault the village that lay astride a footpath in a narrow finger of jungle. The clamor of automatic weapons' fire, explosions from RPGs and the 75 mm recoilless seared the air. Charlie was putting up a stiff fight.

Lieutenant Lord's voice came on the net, "Sierra Six, this is Charlie Two-six. How about getting those damned Ruff Puff off their asses and moving, over?"

"Roger Two-six, out." We had good communications and had dropped the formality of normal communications procedure.

"Romeo Papa six, this is Sierra Six, over," I called.

"This is Romeo Papa, over."

"Roger, Papa. Can you get your people moving, over?" I asked.

"This is Papa. We're doing the best we can. We're receiving heavy fire from two bunkers and a couple of huts, over."

"This is Two-six, they can move if they're pushed," Lord said dropping all formality.

"We're doing the best we can. I'm trying to get them moving," the Ruff Puff advisor cut in without waiting.

"That's a crock a shit! They're afraid to try!" Lord snapped back with derision in his voice.

"Yeah," I thought, "there goes Lord, the aggressive armor officer charging ahead without fear of the devil himself!"

"Look, we're doing the best we can. Every time we raise our heads we draw fire," the RF advisor said in an annoyed tone.

"Shit! All you need up there is someone to kick some ass. We can take these bastards, Lord shot back.

"Look, why don't you come down here with me? If you can walk when I finish with you, you can try digging them out yourself," the RF advisor replied in anger.

"Break, Break!" I cut in. "This is Sierra six, that's enough! Y'all are here to fight Charlie, not each other, over!"

The net went dead. Neither officer answered.

A few months later, I'd meet the frustrated Ruff Puff advisor. I was at Fort Knox snow-birding (doing gofer jobs) until the start of my Armor Officer's Advance Course Class. A couple of officers and I were swapping stories and I related this one. Captain Joe Trowbridge asked with a smile if I knew the Ruff Puff advisor.

"No," I replied. "That was me," he replied with a laugh. I didn't believe him until he described a few landmarks around My Tho, the major city in our area.

Joe and I became good friends and desk mates during the Armor Advance Course. I've never met a finer gentleman. Easygoing and soft-spoken, he seemed to take everything in stride. Lord, however, had raised his dander that day. Dry season jungle heat makes for short tempers.

It's a good thing Lord didn't take Joe up on his offer. Joe had twenty or thirty pounds on him and had fought on the University of Arkansas boxing team. He had enough trophies to tell me that Lord wouldn't have stood a chance in a round of fisticuffs. Strange things happen in the heat of battle, though.

The battle for the village ebbed and flowed throughout the afternoon. The fighting was so heavy that the ARVN (pronounced R-van, South Vietnamese regular army soldiers) passed up their normal siesta. We alternated artillery and gunship strikes on Charlie's positions, but still he tenaciously held on. He knew he was dead if we forced him into the open.

Colonel Thoan and I watched from the paddy. The enemy recoilless rifle crew took pot shots at us between artillery barrages and gunship strikes. They were getting closer each time they fired. *Why doesn't the colonel move?* I wondered. You don't sit in one place when being shot at—you move! I had been taught to fire no more than two rounds without moving. *Always move when the bad guy knows your position and has your range. A moving target is harder to hit*, I thought. I remained silent. It would have seemed cowardly to suggest that we move.

A bright flash of light to my left front caught my eye. One of the tracks had taken a direct hit from the recoilless rifle. The crew was bailing out. All was confusion around the track. troopers ran through the paddies to the safety of other tracks. Other vehicles maneuvered to recover the disabled vehicle. I watched passively while other tracks carried the wounded to the rear.

Fortunately, my war wasn't as personal as the foot soldier's. I wasn't lying next to a tree or behind a log or behind a mound of earth exchanging rounds with an adversary fighting for his life and bent on killing me. Sweat might burn my eyes, but it was relatively clean sweat. It wasn't contaminated by caked filth that had filled my hair and covered my face from endless days in the paddies and jungles. I wasn't soaked to the skin from wading the canals. Ants didn't eat at my body, while I huddled on the ground for protection. I was getting over.

True, I was a target. I had no cover or protection save the troopers around me. Gone was my imaginary cocoon of protective machinegun fire. The crew of the Squadron command track couldn't fire their weapons. We were to the rear of friendly soldiers. Yet, we were within range of our antagonists and the recoilless rifle fire kept getting closer. I felt alone. I had no one of a common language to share my doubts and fears. I had only the friendly American voices coming through my radio's headset to break my thoughts about probable survival. Most of all, I wasn't in charge of my destiny. I could not react or command a reaction. I could only sit and watch and hope that my track was not hit and that decisions were made that would enable the Squadron to win with the fewest casualties. Still, I was getting over. I had showered the night before. I had had a good night's sleep and I started the day with a shave and a clean uniform. I couldn't complain.

Two 75 mm rounds hit a few feet from the track. The radioman sitting in front of me fell back into my arms. He had caught a piece of shrapnel in his left eye. Another trooper took his place. *Come on, colonel, those rounds are coming closer. The gunner is getting the range. Please move!* I urged in my mind.

More gunships came in. More casualties were carried to the rear. More 75 mm rounds came in. Its shrapnel cut down the second radioman. It was getting late; Charlie would make his move soon.

What am I doing here? Stupid question! This is what you wanted! Now you got it, I thought. The glory of being a soldier isn't so romantic when you're being shot at and men are being killed around you. I wanted to lead men to victory. I dreamed of being a hero. Ha! Is the price of glory in some unknown, god-forsaken rice paddy? Is it worth my life and my family's suffering without a husband and father, particularly in a war that we won't try to win and doesn't endanger my country?

Stop this; you have a duty.

Two 75 mm rounds hit next to the track. Something hit me in the side that burned. I wasn't wearing my flack vest. I had been too hot. I looked down at my left side. I was bleeding. I thought, *Well Colonel, you did it! You sat here until Charlie got me.* Again, I couldn't say anything. The others had lain in the track's floor without a sound until they were evacuated to the rear. I couldn't complain. I couldn't ask to be medevaced. Who would direct the gunships? I reached into the track for my web belt. Retrieving it, I took the attached first aid packet from its pouch and covered my wound, tying the bandage tight around my waist to stop the bleeding. The pain was

TAN HIEP: 7 MAY 1968

manageable. Colonel Thoan had the driver shift our position. *Now you move! Thanks! Thanks a lot!*

Charlie had us. He shifted his fires and continued to pour in the 75 mm rounds. He had recognized us as the command track. He wanted us. How could he have ignored us so long? Our track had six antennas protruding into the sky and more men on its top than any other two tracks in the area. We were easily identified as the control center.

Now enough is enough! I began to get concerned. Enough of this bravado stuff; I reached for my steel pot (helmet) and slid down into the track's cargo compartment. Fear had won. I wanted out. No matter how badly I wanted to, however, I couldn't leave. I couldn't show fear. I had to set an example of strength and determination. I wasn't about to let those little fellas see a big, bad American run. A memory of OCS (Officer Candidate School) shot before my eyes. I was sitting at my desk crying because of the continuous pressure and harassment from my Tac officer. I had thought I wanted to be an Army officer more than anything. Yet, my Tac had gotten to me. He had torn me down more than I thought anyone ever could. I was beaten and wanted to go home. Of course, I couldn't. I'd be a disgrace to my family and to my friends. I had to find the strength to stay. I couldn't quit. The same was true now. No, it was even truer now! As badly as I wanted to jump from the track and run, I couldn't. If I ran, I'd dishonor every American who had fought for our great country—not to mention my family. I could never look my sons in the eye if I ran. No, I couldn't, I *wouldn't* run.

Colonel Thoan finally got the message. He ordered the driver to back us out of range. We backed to a large embankment where the casualties had been carried. It was getting late. We had only an hour of daylight left. Charlie was getting serious about breaking out. The tempo of the battle increased. Another set of gunships reported on station.

"Sierra Six, this is Hunter One-six. What you got for us, over"

"Roger Hunter, we're getting the heaviest fire from my right front. I'll put you in there, over."

"Roger Sierra. Pop smoke, so I can identify you, over."

I knew that was coming and had the smoke grenade in my hand. "Roger, smoke's out, over."

"Roger, I identify purple, over."

"Roger, that's us. Charlie is about five degrees north in the tree line to our front. Recommend you come in from the east and over us, over."

"This is Hunter. Roger, out."

The gun-ship, a modified Huey (UH-l, utility helicopter), came whump, whump, whumping in and let go with a barrage of rockets. Then it banked sharply to the right and pulled out. The second Huey came in slower and seemed to sit stationary in the sky to our rear. I looked over my shoulder to watch his approach, engulfed in a stream of red trackers.

A surge of fear for the chopper swept over me. My heart was racing. I couldn't believe that the chopper didn't burst into a ball of flames. I expected at many moment to see a large orange explosion and helicopter parts flying in all directions. Surely, the pilot didn't know he was in the kill zone of a .50. If he knew, he'd pull off as fast as his rotors would carry him. I had to warn him.

"Hunter, Hunter, break off, break off. You're taking direct fire," I screamed into the radio's microphone. "There are tracers all around you," I yelled as he banked lazily to the right without firing. The red tracers continued to fly around the Huey's fuselage and through its rotating blades. Surely, Charlie couldn't have missed. If he did get a hit, he wasn't hit with anything that could bring the Huey down.

The gunner must have been firing a captured American .50 cal. I had never seen Charlie's tracers because we didn't fight at night, but Soviet weapons reportedly used green tracers, not red. Whatever, that Huey's crew had really had a close call.

Darkness began to fall. I turned my attention to getting the casualties out. I requested and received the support I needed. The dust-off pilots wouldn't refuse a request for help. They came in low and slow from the rear without drawing fire. It took three ships to get our wounded out. I was on the last one out. I had learned my lesson. I didn't want another infection. As I climbed into the Huey, I wondered if I'd manage another trip to Japan. How easily one became spoiled by the "good life."

As the Huey gained altitude, thoughts of another month in Japan passed quickly from mind. My thoughts were filled with concern for the ARVN soldiers who lay silently on the aircraft's floor. During the past few months, I had come to truly appreciate these men. They were good soldiers who had fought well on this day and had been bloodied. Most weren't badly wounded; but there were two seriously wounded, one with a head wound and one with his abdomen shot away. The soldier with the head wound was unconscious; the one with his stomach torn open lay staring at the Huey's ceiling. He must have been drugged with morphine. I wondered about their care when they were returned to ARVN's control. They deserved the best. Would they get it? I thought not. Theirs would be a long, painful, unsanitary recovery. If they recovered. They deserved better. Still, they lay in the chopper uncomplaining.

It was a short flight to Dong Tam. It seemed that the chopper had hardly gotten airborne when I felt a gentle sway before touch-down at its 9th Evac Hospital pad.

I was met by a medic when I jumped from the chopper. He ushered me into a treatment room in one of the inflatable, sand-bagged, rubber Quonset huts that sat a few feet from the helipad. In the treatment room, the medic told me to remove my uniform and to lie on the examining table. In a few minutes, a young doctor came in to look me over.

"This isn't too bad. I think we can take care of you here," he said. He went to a cabinet and removed a syringe.

An MSC (Medical Service Corp, the hospital administrators) captain came in. He asked the necessary questions to complete his paper work while the doctor filled the syringe with whatever he was going to use to deaden the pain.

His paperwork completed, the MSC left. The doctor inserted the needle in my wound two or three times, then he cut the wound open so that he could probe me with a large tweezers-like tool (forceps, I guess). He was going to work on me unassisted. That was okay with me. I had complete confidence in our doctors. They had proven that they knew what they were doing. Thanks to their efforts and training, we had the best survival rate of any army in the world. So, why worry? These guys are the best.

The doctor probed around in my side for a few minutes. He couldn't find the shrapnel. Muttering to himself, he laid his instrument down and inserted his index finger into my side. The MSC came back into the room and walked around to the doctor. They exchanged a few remarks about the doctor's difficulty. Curiosity got the better of me. I raised my head to watch and listen.

The MSC was a large, mustachioed, wrestler type. He came around to my left side and took my hand. He looked down at me with all the concern and pity he could muster. Patting my hand he said, "Don't worry. He's having a little trouble finding the shrapnel. We'll have you out of here soon." I wanted to laugh. I wasn't feeling a thing. I only wanted to watch. Just my luck, here I am wounded, and I get a pro football player type to console me. Where are the beautiful Florence Nightingales? Who said war was romantic? I did, however, appreciate his concern and effort. They were another demonstration of the lengths the medical people went to heal and to comfort the line soldiers.

The doctor finally found and retrieved the shrapnel. He put an IV in my arm and sewed me up.

"Okay, that should do it," the doctor said. "It's not too bad, but we need to keep you here a few days to make sure there's no infection."

Damn, no trip to Japan.

The MSC had a medic bring me a pair of hospital pajamas, house shoes, and a robe. Then he assigned me to a GP Medium Tent Ward (a general purpose, medium-sized tent that slept twelve people) with standard Army-issue steel cots. The beds were covered with the standard Army OD blanket.

I had hardly fallen asleep when I was awakened by the soft explosion of incoming mortar rounds. A medical orderly came running through the tent yelling for us to get up and move into a sand-bagged bunker behind the tent. We sat in the bunker for about thirty minutes, listening to the distance explosions. Sitting in the dark, I thought, *How silly this is. Those rounds are too far away to bother us. Let's get back to bed. If it's going to be like this, I'm ready to get back to the Squadron now. I'll get more rest.*

During the day, time passed slowly. There was nothing to do except lie in bed and think. My mind again drifted back over my past. My early years had been nomadic moving around the Texas Panhandle and Southwest Oklahoma following the restaurant development business or the oil fields finally settling in Odessa in West Texas. I met my wife, Nelwyn, while in high school. I joined the National Guard after my junior year in high school. While in high school I worked weekends and summers in the oilfield. After graduation I attended Texas A & M and dropped out almost immediately: no money, home sick, and love sick. Nelwyn and I were married in January 1957 and I worked odd jobs until becoming a policeman in Odessa. While on the Force, I stayed in the Guard and was given leaves of absent to attend Infantry OCS (Officer Candidate School) at Fort Benning, Georgia, and then the Armor Officer's Basic Course at Fort Knox, Kentucky. During this period, Nelwyn and I produced two sons and a daughter. I was commissioned a second lieutenant in the Guard in 1961 and worked my way up to Headquarters Troop Commander by 1963 when I applied for active duty and was accepted. My first assignment was as a tank platoon leader and then scout platoon leader in the 1st of the 37th Armor in Germany. From Germany I was stationed at Fort Polk, Louisiana at a Basic Training Company Commander.

What a change. During my first few months, I thought nothing exciting would happen to me. I was sure that Charlie had gone into hiding and that I wasn't going to see any action. The first few months had been a dull, boring, and frustrating time punctuated with a few moments of terror. Those last few months however, had been more excising and had allowed me to learn.

While I sat in the darkened bunker, my mind went back over my past few months in country.

CHAPTER TWO

THE BEGINNING: OCTOBER 1967

I had arrived in California the day before I was scheduled to fly out of Travis Air Force Base to Vietnam. In the first of many in-processing lines at the Oakland Army Terminal, I met Captains Lawson and Dunn and struck up a conversation. When we arrived at the billet's assignment desk, we asked to be assigned adjoining rooms for our overnight stay before busing to Travis for our flight to Nam.

Lawson, Dunn, and I decided to cross the bridge to San Francisco for dinner that evening. We wanted a night on the town and a good meal before flying to our destiny. We ate at Fisherman's Wharf, and then made the trek to Broadway Street and the Peppermint Lounge. We wanted to see firsthand if the Frisco nightlife was as wild as we had heard. It wasn't. We were disappointed at our reception as we walked the street, had a drink in several topless bars, and watched the people. We saw what we considered a few long hair weirdoes, but not one young damsel made an effort to sweep us off our feet. I guess our hair was too short.

Our flight was long, quiet, and tiring. Our only break was a two-hour layover in Hawaii to refuel, where we spent our time admiring young ladies in miniskirts. Lawson, Dunn, and I passed the time playing poker for matches, discussing current Army issues, and relating hearsay experiences about the fighting.

I related one of my most memorable experiences. During my last month at Fort Polk, I sat on a court-martial board of a recruit that would not follow orders and was disrespectful toward officers, particularly the brigade chaplain, on several occasions when the chaplain counseled him for refusing to get out of bed or attend training. The recruit must have been intelligent, as he had been pre-qualified to attend flight schools after completing basic.

The Board consisted of six officers: a major, two captains, and two lieutenants. This was during the time when unit officers conducted courts-martial at brigade level and below. We met in an old World War Two, one story, wood-frame building with no air conditioning. We were all wearing starched khaki uniforms; which in the high humidity and 95-plus degree temperatures in Louisiana made everyone involved most uncomfortable. So, the president of the board asked that a large container of iced Kool-Aid be brought into the court room for refreshments during the proceedings.

The first motions of the defense were to challenge the two senior members off of the broad, which left me as the president. During the proceedings, the defendant was smiling, jovial, and quite relaxed. He seemed assured that he would be acquitted of all charges. At some point, the defense raised a legal point on which neither the prosecution nor I knew how to rule, so I called a recess and sent the prosecutor out to find an answer to the question.

For some reason, it took a long time for the prosecutor to find someone to address the issue in question. While we waited, the defendant began to serve everyone in the room Kool-Aid. He was smiling and most cordial as he served each person in the room several times.

When the prosecutor returned, he gave an explanation of the point in question and I ruled against the defense. As the trial moved along, it was clear that the defendant was guilty, but we played out the game to the deliberation phase. After all the testimony was in, I had the defendant leave the room and the board deliberated. We found the young man guilty and decided on a punishment of six and six (six months in the stockade without pay) the maximum we could give.

When the young soldier returned to the court room, he reported to me with a broad smile, sure he would be cleared of all charges. But when he heard the finding of the court and the sentence his jaw dropped and he stood in silence for a few seconds. Then he turned slowly toward the table where the Kool-Aid container sat and moved toward it. Everyone in the room sat motionlessly as he picked up the container and moved back in front of me. He smiled, raised the container as high as he could and poured it over me from head to foot. I came out of my chair, and was halfway across the table when someone stopped me. We stood looking into each other's eyes for a few seconds and then we both burst out laughing. The MPs took him away. I had to go home and change my uniform.

I went on leave within a few days so I did not attend his trial for his assault on me; but a few days into my leave, I received a call from the JAG (Army attorney) at Fort Polk and was asked to give a statement over the phone. The JAG officer told me that the young man gave the MPs a hard time as he signed into the stockade and received some rough treatment. I have often wondered what happened to him.

When we tired of poker, Dunn and Lawson played Hearts. I couldn't join in these games because I didn't know how to play, and didn't particularly want to tax my brain to learn. The other passengers passed the time in much the same way. Some read; others played cards; some engaged in quiet conversations; a few slept; but most seemed to be thinking about what awaited them. For me most of the trip was spent thinking of things past. I wasn't overly concerned about the future other than my assignment.

During my pre-deployment leave, I had gone through a period of anxiety about surviving combat and about being able to fulfill my responsibilities. After several prayers, I found peace on the survival issue. Now, I was concerned about not letting down my fellow soldiers under fire. But I didn't dwell on the negative. I had been in the Army for over four years and was confident in my abilities. Time would tell if I could apply my knowledge and fulfill my responsibilities. Many subjects must have turned over in my mind. I can recall only two that I dwelt on: physical conditioning and basic training of the soldier.

My last assignment had been as a commander of a basic training company at Fort Polk. In that assignment, I had become acutely aware of the physical condition of the average American male when entering the service. New recruits were generally in poor physical condition and many were grossly overweight. I found it strange that the Army spent eight weeks fine-tuning recruits' bodies to withstand the rigors of combat, only to let them return home for two weeks to impress family and friends and to party. When they left basic, they were highly confident, lean machines. After leave, they were back, out of condition, to undergo eight weeks of advanced training before being allowed another leave on the way to Nam. There must have been a better way, but it probably would have been politically unacceptable.

Though the scenario for the new soldier was bad, the scenario for non-commissioned officers and officers was worse. In most cases, these soldiers received no physical conditioning before rotation to Nam. The possible exception were those who attended the Army's Special Warfare School at Fort Bragg, North Carolina, before leaving for Nam. I didn't know about their training. I had been assigned directly to an ARVN without the benefit of special training. But, knowing the Army, Special Warfare graduates most probably received a leave before flying to combat.

I knew I was in relatively poor physical condition and somewhat overweight. In my last assignment, I had marched and exercised daily with the recruits. I had played handball as often as I could. Still, during my leave, with the best of intentions, I hadn't maintained the little conditioning I had achieved.

THE BEGINNING: OCTOBER 1967

While I considered how foolish it was to fine-tune a machine only to allow it to fall apart from rust before it ran its most important race, I began to consider the basic qualifications I'd expect a soldier to have when he reported for combat duty. First, I'd expect him to be disciplined. He had to be depended upon to follow orders! Second, he should be in good physical condition. Conditioning was essential if he was to attain my final two requirements. Third, I'd want him to be able to fire his weapon and hit a target. Lastly, I'd expect him to be knowledgeable in battlefield survival skills. There was nothing new on my list. Each of the areas had been taught in my basic training company. Still, I was uncertain that we (the Army and I) had fully prepared our men for the challenges that awaited them. I wanted a quick fix that would overcome any past failures on my part. Later experience would confirm that I was re-inventing the wheel. The intellectual exercise, however, helped pass the otherwise BORRR-ING time between a few hands of seven-card stud or five-card draw.

My orders assigned me to MACV, the Military Assistance Command, Vietnam. This was a general assignment. Once in country (Vietnam), I'd be reassigned in accordance with the needs of the command. I could receive any one of a variety of assignments. Being an armor officer, I wanted an assignment with a Vietnamese cavalry unit. My second choice was assignment to an ARVN tank unit. I preferred a cavalry unit because of the romanticism associated with the cavalry (Cav) of the American West. Also, ARVN Cav units had gained an excellent fighting reputation. I didn't want an assignment with either a Regional Forces or a Popular Forces Military Assistance Team (MAT) team . These were infantry assignments. I had learned long ago as an automatic rifleman in the National Guard and in Infantry OCS, there was a better way to close with the enemy than to walk or run. I liked to ride and the feel of power furnished by a tank. OKAY, OKAY! Stop counting the flowers on the ceiling!

I looked up from my companions' game of Hearts when our stewardess announced our arrival over Saigon. There was a flurry of excitement as passengers adjusted their positions to look out the plane's windows. They were anxious for a first glimpse of Saigon. I didn't try to look. I was seated on the aisle. It was almost 10 o' clock at night. *Saigon is in a war zone,* I thought, Besides, the stewardesses were more interesting than a spangle of lights from 30,000 feet.

On the ground, the Boeing 707 taxied to its parking ramp. The stewardesses began our briefing. We were to remain seated for a briefing when the plane came to a stop. We weren't to remove our seat belts until the plane stopped. The plane would be disinfected before we could deplane. *Disinfect the plane? Who are they trying to kid! Vietnam is the country with a disease problem, not us,*" I thought. *They can't seriously believe that we're transporting germs after the vaccinations we were given before we left the States.*

When the plane stopped and the front door opened, a Vietnamese gentleman came aboard to welcome us and to spray the cabin with a fine mist from an aerosol can. I don't know why he bothered. His short bust of spray was so fine that I hardly noticed each spurt as he quickly walked the aisle.

After the one-man Vietnamese welcoming committee, an Army sergeant came on board.

"Good evening, gentlemen. I'm Sergeant Wright from the MACV transportation office. Welcome to Vietnam.

"We have buses outside to transport you to your overnight billets. Personnel reporting to American units will board buses one through three when told to deplane. You'll RON (remain overnight) at the Replacement Center at Camp Alpha to await transportation to your units. You could complete your processing and depart sometime tomorrow, or certainly within two days at the most.

"Personnel assigned to MACV will board bus number four. Officers will be taken to Kopler Compound in downtown Saigon. Enlisted personnel will go to the Hoalu Hotel. You'll complete your in-country processing and receive your final assignments at those locations. Your baggage will be placed under the plane. You can collect it before getting on your bus. There's space in the rear of each bus to stow your gear."

There wasn't much baggage. We had been authorized only fifty-five pounds of luggage and a carry-on. Most of us had only a duffel bag. In my bag, I had packed fatigues, books, underwear, and two changes of civilian casual wear.

"Personnel assigned to American units may deplane at this time."

When MAGV personnel were told to deplane, my two friends and I exited the plane, rummaged for our duffel bags, and boarded a forty-five passenger OD (olive drab) Army bus with screened windows. The night was cool and calm. There was little activity on the darkened tarmac. Other than the headlights of the buses, only a few flickering lights could be seen in the distance.

Kopler Hotel photo by Larry Cole

When I got on the bus, I looked for an aisle seat. It had finally dawned on me that I was in a combat zone. I didn't want to be an easy target for a sniper. Looking through the screened windows, I thought of the many newspaper reports I had read about Viet Cong terrorists throwing hand grenades through a restaurant, bar, car, or bus window. I wondered if the bus would get to the billets without being attacked. That screen wasn't on the windows for ornamentation.

Hoalu Hotel photo by Larry Cole

We traversed a maze of fifty-five gallon oil drums filled with concrete to get off Ton San Nhut Air Base. Few details of the city could be distinguished as we traveled the unlighted streets. The street we took into the heart of the city was lined with trees. In better times, it was probably a beautiful boulevard. Now the gutters were filled with debris and the trees were poorly maintained—some appeared to be dying. Buildings were silhouettes against the moonless night. The only structure that offered any identity was a horseracing track over-grown with vegetation.

THE BEGINNING: OCTOBER 1967

After about a fifteen-minute ride, which seemed much longer, the bus turned a corner and stopped in front of a double wrought-iron gate (Kopler Hotel). Two Vietnamese guards stood in a shelter to the right of the gate. White fifty-five gallon drums partly blocked a smaller gate between the double gate and the guard's shelter. Among the white drums was a single red fifty-five gallon barrel sitting at a forty-five degree angle. This barrel was used by armed soldiers to clear their weapons before entering the compound. The Hotel Hoalu was down the street on the next corner.

The driver opened the bus door and turned in his seat. "Kopler Compound, all officers will get off here."

An enlisted man met us at the bus and guided us through a small courtyard to the back of a two-story building sitting in the front left section of the yard. In the building, we were led into a small office where we met the "CQ" (Charge of Quarters). He was a sergeant.

When we were all gathered, the CQ greeted us. "Good evening, gentlemen. Welcome to Kopler Compound. Kopler was a French Hotel during their colonial days. The Army has leased it to use as a billet for rotating officers. The billets are in the building behind this building."

An officer in the group interrupted. "Pardon me, Sarge. How long will we be here?"

"Five days," the sergeant replied. "This building houses administrative offices and a mess hall on this floor. Classrooms are on the second floor."

Another officer asked. "When will we receive our orders?"

"In about three days," replied the sergeant. "While you're here, you'll be issued your TA-50 (field equipment) and receive classes on the Army's in-country organization, the current situation, communications processes, and survival tips."

Looking around the room, the sergeant pointed to his right and said, "Breakfast is from 0600 to 0700 hours."

"The mess is down the hall to the left. You're to report to Chief (Chief Warrant Officer) Stone at 0800 to begin your in-processing. If there are no questions, I'll assign your rooms as you sign in." He motioned toward a large opened book on the desk.

When Lawson signed in, he asked if he, Dunn, and I could be assigned to the same room. The sergeant studied his room ledger. "Sure, sir, I have a four-man room open on the fifth floor."

Entering the foyer of the six-story main building, culture shock struck. The foyer's walls were a dirty white, trimmed in light blue. To our right front was an old elevator that looked like it couldn't lift one person, much less three with their baggage. It was the type seen in French movies that resembled a small basket within a latticed cylinder. There was barely enough room for the three of us.

To our relief, the vibrating, noisy elevator lifted us to the fifth floor with ease.

Our room was small and spartan. It barely accommodated four Army steel cots, stacked two high on each side of the room. The beds were made with a pillow, sheets, and two Army OD blankets, standard configuration regardless of the climate. A four-bladed fan hung from the ceiling. Directly ahead, a rear door opened onto a balcony. There was no lavatory. Sleep was a long time coming in the humid night.

The next morning we found the combination shower, wash basin, and toilet down the hall. It was a small community facility. The three conveniences were compressed into an area no larger than a normal American shower stall. It, however, served its purpose. The fixtures must have been pre-1940 French. The water closet was the type with an overhead tank and a long pull chain. The commode's antique qualities fascinated me. Reflections of Humphrey Bogart in the movie *Casablanca* flashed in my mind as I studied the contraption. This is what the French considered an adequate bath? It seemed a little lacking to me.

After breakfast, we reported to Chief Stone to begin our processing. There wasn't much to do. I completed the necessary forms quickly. I only needed to draw my TA-50 and take my pay records to Finance. Chief Stone told me I had to go by Army bus to the MACV finance section in Cholon to apply for a soldier's deposit savings account and to check on my wife's allotment. "While you're in the area, you may as well check out the PX. It's in Cholon too," the Chief recommended.

I had no idea where Cholon was in relation to Kopler Compound. I only knew that Cholon was the Chinese section of Saigon. I was apprehensive about venturing around Saigon not knowing where I was going. I concealed my concern, however; it wouldn't have been macho to appear timid.

The Chief gave me directions to the bus stop before I went to the supply room to draw my TA-50 (jungle fatigues, jungle hat, boots with steel sole liners, poncho, poncho liner, air mattress, canteen, cup, and cover, web belt, and load-bearing suspenders that attached to the web belt). I'd draw my weapon the day I left for the field. After stowing my gear, I took my jungle fatigue's blouses and hat to the tailor shop in the compound's courtyard. I needed to have patches (name tag, rank, branch insignia, and US Army) sewn on the blouses. The patches had to be embroidered, sew-ons to qualify me as a well-dressed officer. My jungle hat had to have my rank insignia embroidered on the front and my name embroidered across the back before I'd be in style. After accomplishing these important details, I headed for Finance.

The street, alive with pedestrians, was just wide enough to accommodate a single American car or two small Renault taxis. Across the street was a line of small military specialty shops, tailor shops, and gift shops. The gift shops specialized in brass items for wives, mothers, or girlfriends. I made a mental note to check them out later. I turned right and headed down the street, wide-eyed and unarmed.

At the end of the block, a broad boulevard intersected the street. The larger street was heavy with small blue and yellow Renault taxis and motor scooter traffic. The air was purple from engine exhaust, which hung heavy in the still, hot, humid air. The seven story Hoalu Hotel sat diagonally across the intersection. I was impressed. It was a beautiful street scene, even with the smog. Both sides of the street were lined with shops. The buildings were two and three stories high with shops on the ground floor. The upper floors were apparently living quarters. They were built of either concrete or concrete blocks; they were painted white or gray. The paint on most buildings was peeling and some buildings were partly covered with black mildew. Along the roofs' edges were small hedges and flower boxes. Miniature trees reached skyward from some roofs. I made it

Saigon Street Scene photo by Larry Cole

across the boulevard and continued to the bus stop. The pedestrian traffic became heavier. About a half block down the street, I noticed an older Vietnamese man lying in the middle of the sidewalk. His eyes were closed and his head was in a pool of blood. No one paid him any attention. My first thought was, *Is he dead?* Next, I wondered

Saigon Housing photo by Larry Cole

what had happened to him. He must not have paid his VC taxes. At any rate, I wasn't going to pay him any "never mind." I had heard that in Asia it was customary for a Samaritan to become responsible for an injured person if he helped him. If he died, his benefactor buried him. I didn't know if this was true or not, but I wasn't going to take any chances. Whoever hit him might still be in the area and take exception to my helping. I really didn't want to be killed on the streets of Saigon my first day in-country. Though I had convinced myself I'd survive Vietnam, I was wavering. I didn't want to test fate . . . at least not just yet. I picked up my pace and moved on. As I passed him, a woman rushed to him from an adjacent shop. I've often wondered how, why, and who hit him and if he was dead. It sure looked that way. I've often wondered if I should've stopped. At the time, I was unfamiliar with my new environment, and I had a bus to catch. I hurried on to the bus stop. I was adapting already.

The bus ride was uneventful. The streets we traveled were narrow and filled with potholes. Trash and garage filled the gutters. At many intersections there were open garbage piles of varying sizes. There was a lot of road construction, filling the small holes and repairing larger sections of the streets. The heavy traffic was a mixture of vehicles, small horse-drawn carts, petty-cabs, six-passenger tri-wheeled buses carrying from six to ten people, motorcycles with lovely ladies seated sidesaddle behind an operator who weaved their vehicles dangerously and adroitly through the other traffic; and the ever-present Renault taxis. The most popular vehicles were the various varieties of cycloes, a large tricycle powered by a small engine or the driver's legs. A seat that held two or three passengers was placed either in front of or behind the driver. There was no order to the traffic flow. Each driver charged toward his or her destination seemingly oblivious of the surroundings. Each driver thought he or she had the right-of-way.

I completed my processing at Finance with no problem. When I finished, I caught the bus on the next round for the Cholon PX. The PX was in a large building that resembled a warehouse. At the entrance were the customary concrete-filled fifty-gallon oil dumps. Barbed concertina wire, stacked three layers high, circled the building. I looked over the various departments to see what merchandise was available. The place was well stocked. It had everything a soldier needed and a few things he didn't. I was surprised at the radio, stereo, and television inventory. Brand-name cameras and Rolex watches were also in ready supply. I thought, *The war couldn't be all bad if the* troops *had a place and the time to use those goodies.* My only purchase was a 16-millimeter camera that I could carry in my shirt pocket. In Germany, I had gotten into the habit of taking 35-millimeter slides of the places I visited so that I could show the family where I had been and what

I had seen. With camera in hand, I headed back to Kopler Compound.

Cholon PX photo by Larry Cole

Saigon Shanty Town photo by Larry Cole

View of Saigon photo by Larry Cole

I was relieved as I walked from the bus stop to Kopler Compound. I had completed my first solo trip into the wild and frightening world of Vietnam without incident. That evening, my two captain friends and I decided to have dinner at the Rex Hotel. The Rex housed the main officer's club in Saigon. It had gained a good Army-wide reputation among officers as *the* place to go in Saigon. Being the curious types and enjoying the finer things of life, we wanted to try the place. We hailed one of the small taxis outside the compound and crammed in. Fortunately, Lawson was a small fella—maybe a 160 pounder at most—or we'd never have fit into the taxi. Captain Dunn put his six foot-two, 220-pound frame in the back seat with Lawson. At six foot-four and 235 pounds, I filled the front passenger seat all by my lonesome.

I anticipated a hair-rising ride; I had heard several stories about the aggressive Vietnamese drivers. The traffic was heavy. The driver drove fast and offensively, but we arrived safely, with only a few close calls.

The Rex was located on the side of a small horseshoe-shaped plaza. The mouth of the plaza was cordoned-off with fifty-gallon barrels and guards. In the center of the plaza was an imposing statue of two Vietnamese infantrymen charging the hordes. One infantryman carried a World War II machine gun; the other followed closely with a radio on his back.

We paid our cab fare and caught the elevator to the club on the hotel's top floor. I was struck by the elegance of the dining room, tables set with white table cloths, bright lights, chandeliers, music, and a festive atmosphere. The ambience wasn't what I expected. There was a good mix of male and female guests. The men were mostly field-grade officers in Class B uniform (dress trousers and open dress shirt, no coat). A few were casually dressed in civilian clothing. The ladies, a mixture of Americans, Asians, and Eurasians, were dressed for cocktails and dinner.

Surveying the room, I thought this was a rather leisurely way to serve a combat tour.

We ordered cocktails and steaks. While we waited, we watched the crowd and discussed the outstanding qualities of the ladies. We made small talk, again discussing stories and rumors we had heard about the war. After dinner, we went out onto the balcony to watch the street scene and to admire the statue. As we looked down on the street, we could have been watching the plebeians of any peaceful bustling metropolis. The only evidence to the contrary was the barbed wire and oil drums at the mouth of the plaza.

Our tranquility was shaken when Dunn noticed a bright red stream originating from a spot in the black sky and disappearing in the distance behind Saigon's rooftops.

"Look," he said, pointing upward into the night sky. "That must be Spooky."

"Spooky," or "Puff the Magic Dragon," was either an Air Force C-47 or C-130 cargo aircraft. The C-47 was a lumbering World War II cargo aircraft that was also used as a troop transport as well as to drop paratroopers. The C-130 was the Air Force's latest turbo-prop-driven cargo aircraft. Both planes were armed with a six-barrel,

20-millimeter Gatling gun mounted in their side door. The planes were used by the Air Force to support engaged ground troop. Some C-130s were even fitted with a 105-millimeter howitzer in one of the doors.

"I'd hate to be on the receiving end of that," I said. "Yeah, that thing puts two or three rounds in a square foot, I've been told," Dunn replied.

The stream danced in the sky as its origin slowly circled in the heavens. There was no distinguishable sound from the red steam as we watched it twist and descend toward the rooftops.

"It must give you a good feeling to know you have that kind of support available," remarked Lawson.

"Maybe so," I said. "But it's getting mighty personal when you have to call for that."

A second stream appeared. What a contrast. Here we were safe and sound, dining in the best of surroundings, and some poor souls were out there terrified, fighting for their lives.

"Well, you guys can have all that you want," said Lawson as he turned to go back into the dining room. "I'll stay right here in Saigon." Luckily, Lawson was a finance officer. His orders assigned him directly to the MACV headquarters finance section. He wouldn't have to leave Saigon during his tour, lucky guy, and he'd get combat pay too.

The next day was spent in briefings on the Vietnamese military organization. There were four corps areas, beginning in the north and running south to the Delta. The northernmost corps was I (Eye) Corps. It bordered the Demilitarized Zone (DMZ). II Corps was next, and then the III Corps was around Saigon. The Mekong Delta comprised the IV Corps. The military forces consisted of the Regular Army (ARVN) and two organizations similar to our National Guard, the Regional Forces and the Popular Forces. The Regional Forces (RF) were organized as companies that operated throughout their home district. Popular Forces (PF) were organized as platoons and worked in or near their village or hamlet. Both organizations were referred to as "Ruff Puffs."

We were briefed on the Vietnamese government's organization, which consisted of forty-four provinces. A province was roughly the political equivalent to one of our states. There were approximately eleven provinces per corps area. The provinces were further subdivided into districts. Below districts were villages and hamlets. Hamlets were the lowest level of organized government.

I remember a briefing on the initial in-country training American units gave their new people before sending them to line units. As I recall, personnel going to an American unit received a week of intensified training on the type of combat operations they'd participate in, how to search a hooch (house), and how to locate booby traps along a trail.

Of course, we received the normal briefing on how well the hearts and minds of the natives were being won to democracy. This briefing included a summary of the rules of engagement. Succinctly, we couldn't fire unless fired on. We couldn't fire preparatory artillery rounds. If, during the search of a village, we found an arms cache or booby trap, we could take no action against the people. We couldn't recon by fire (fire at suspected enemy positions before we received fire). These weren't the best of rules to fight a war by. There were exceptions, but you had to go through channels for approval. That took time and cost unnecessary lives. Areas that Province Chiefs identified as VC were declared free-fire zones. Anything that moved after dark was considered VC.

I faintly recalled getting some general tips on how to survive in the countryside. The briefings could be likened to drinking water from a fire hose: too much information to swallow at one time. They were the typical Army effort to inform its people and to look after their welfare. Like most soldiers, we weren't interested at the time. Only a month later, when trudging through jungles or rice patties, would we realize that we should've listened.

That evening, I decided to eat at the NCO Club atop the Hoalu Hotel. I wanted to see if two NCOs that had been in my company at Fort Polk were there. According to their orders, they were to report a few days before I was. They'd still be in-processing. If they were at the club, I'd have no problem seeing them. Officers had an open invitation at NCO clubs. Sure enough, when I walked in, I spotted them at a table on the balcony overlooking the street.

Staff Sergeant (SSG) Hollis saw me as I walked toward the table and waved me over. The two sergeants had eaten but offered to keep me company while I ate. We discussed the normal soldierly subjects, joked about our favorite recruits, recalled humorous stories from Fort Polk, and talked about their new assignments. One of them asked about Sergeant First Class Wells.

Two weeks before I left the company for Vietnam, I got a letter from a woman in Michigan claiming to be Sergeant Wells' wife. She claimed that Wells had sent her home to Michigan two years earlier. He had stopped her allotment and other support a year ago. She wanted help in getting support payments.

Similar situations arose with regularity in each unit I had been in. The twist in Wells' case was that he was living in a Leesville trailer park with a woman and three kids. A review of his records showed that he claimed them as dependents and that he was being paid a basic allowance for quarters with dependents. To support the payment, there was a copy of a marriage license in his records. The name on the license was the same as the woman he was living with.

When I called Wells in to get his side of the story, he told me that he had divorced the Michigan woman two years before and that he had married his current trailer mate a year later. He couldn't provide copies of the divorce decree to support his story. He told me he'd have to write his attorney in Michigan to get copies of the legal papers. The way he acted caused me to doubt his story. I didn't think he could produce the Michigan divorce papers. If he had filed for a divorce, I doubted that it was final. I believed that the Army had a bigamist on its hands.

I had to plead ignorance to the sergeant's question. My orders had moved me on to bigger and better things before I could find out the true story. At any rate, the problem had provided my first sergeant and me with a couple of days' entertainment jumping through hoops. I turned the problem over to the new commander and headed for Vietnam by way of Texas.

When I finished my dinner, we shook hands, wished each other well, and made our way to our billets. I never heard from either NCO again. I often wonder what happened to them.

The next morning I completed my briefings. That afternoon I received my orders. I was delighted. I was assigned to a Cavalry Squadron in IV Corps, the Mekong Delta. I'd get to wear one of those nice little ARVN armor badges and maybe a CIB (Combat Infantryman's Badge). An armor officer could receive the CIB if he served twenty-four hours in combat in an infantry MOS (military occupation specialty) at brigade or lower level. An ARVN Cav unit was organized as mechanized infantry and called cavalry. If a colonel or general wanted to be a good sport and stretch a point, he could authorize the award to ARVN Cav advisors.

The CIB was the most treasured award in the Army, or at least in the combat arms. Not too many people went deliberately looking for the Medal of Honor or the Purple Heart. The CIB on a soldier's breast said, "I was brave enough to get shot at for my country," and most importantly, "I played target and made it back." Only the Purple Heart said more: "I got hit."

That afternoon, after packing my gear, I visited the shops across from the compound. Walking along the street, alternating between window-shopping and people watching, I saw a captain I thought I knew. When he saw me, I could tell from the look on his face that he knew me. We had gone through OCS together. I couldn't remember his name. We hadn't been buddies or in the same platoon. We had only passed in the halls. I looked at his nametag.

"Howdy Ford, what a surprise."

"Hi, Cole"

"What in the world are you doing here?" I asked. He was a National Guardsman like me. I wondered how he came to be on active duty.

"The Army needs company-grade officers, I guess. My Guard unit got a notice about six months ago asking interested company-grade officers to apply for active duty."

"So, you did and here you are," I said.

"Yeah, I've been in-country about a month. How about you? How long you been on active duty?" Ford asked.

"Just over four years. I applied in '63."

"Where all've you been?" he asked.

"Originally, I went to Germany and then to Fort Polk."

"Do you know if any of the other guys are on active duty?" he asked.

"No, I don't know of anyone."

"Say, I'm sorry, but I got to move on. I've got a catch my ride," Ford said. "It was good runnin' into you."

"Yeah, where are you assigned?" I asked.

"Just north of Saigon, near Long Binh," he replied. We shook hands as he turned to walk away. "Good luck, hope to see you again," I said.

"Same here," he answered over his shoulder as he walked down the street.

I stood watching him disappear into the crowd and thought what a small family the Army is. After my first year in Germany, wherever I went I met someone I had served with before. It was a good feeling to get to a new station and find an old friend or acquaintance there to help you get settled.

I completed my tour of the shops without buying anything. The rest of the afternoon was spent getting ready to move out and viewing Saigon from my balcony. From one end of the balcony, I looked down on the red tile roofs of numerous hovels. There was no organization to their location. There was no recognizable entry into them other than a small serpentine crack between the buildings. Further out, I could see two or three lines of railroad tracks bordered by a wide field of high, bright green grass. Along a fence separating the field from the street, was a line of shanties built of any materials the people could scrounge, such as cardboard, tin, and wood planking. The shanties were three-sided, resembling a lean-to, with ceilings four to five feet high. The fronts were open, with at most a piece of tarp hanging from the roof serving as a removable wall and entrance. Looking down, a wave of profound, sentimental sorrow washed over me for the people milling around the shanties. I wondered how they could live under such conditions. The fact that they chose such filthy, inadequate shelter and little food over life in the communist countryside reinforced the American decision to provide aid. How could we not help these people who gave up everything to live in freedom?

From the other end of the balcony, the scene was more attractive. I could see the Hoalu Hotel. There were roof gardens and the family laundry was hung out to dry on some roofs. What a contrast! From this vantage point, the city was beautiful, even with the heavy purple haze.

The next morning, I drew my carbine (an obsolete World War II rifle) and boarded a bus for Tan Son Nhut. I looked at my weapon and thought how stupid we Americans are. Here we are the wealthiest nation in the world and we give our allies obsolete weapons to defend themselves, democracy, and freedom. On the other hand, the Soviets provide their surrogates with the best small arms available to the Russian Army. When are we going too wise up and give the Vietnamese the weapons they need to be equal on the battlefield? A rifleman armed with a World War II carbine was no match for a rifleman with an AK-47 (the standard Russian assault rifle), even if it was a Chinese reproduction.

My stay in Saigon had been pleasant. Though it was during the rainy season, it hadn't rained that I remember. Best of all, the hot, humid days hadn't bothered me, probably because I had just come from Fort Polk, where the climate was similar to that of Saigon. And the nights were cool enough that I could get a good night's sleep.

At Tan Son Nhut, I boarded one of the Army's last Caribous, a two-engine Canadian-built aircraft with high wings and retractable landing gear. The rear of its small fuselage sloped sharply skyward to support a high tail section. A ramp the width of the fuselage offered a rear entry into the plane. The Caribou had been designed for short takeoffs and landings on unimproved landing stripes. The Army used it to move troops and supplies around the battlefield. The Air Force objected to the Army moving into its territory by using fixed-wing aircraft, so the Secretary of Defense brokered a deal whereby the Air Force got the mission, and the Caribou, to support the Army with fixed-wing aircraft and the Army got the helicopter to use as it wanted. My Caribou had not yet been transferred to the Air Force.

I was on my way to Dong Tam; the 9th Infantry Division's base camp and the home of its in the Mekong Delta.

Dong Tam photo by Larry Cole

THE BEGINNING: OCTOBER 1967

The Delta photo by Larry Cole

CHAPTER THREE

TEAM 75

The Caribou was crowded and noisy. Fortunately, the flight to Dong Tam was short. The plane vibrated continually as it lumbered along, struggling to stay in the air. Replacements who were hitching a ride sat in fold-down canvas seats along the sides of the aircraft. Baggage was stacked among the mail and cargo in the center of the fuselage. The flight was uneventful. The plane's engine noise made conversation impossible, so we each sat with our own thoughts. As we descended to a lower altitude on our approach to Dong Tam, there was a distinct change in the comfortable cabin atmosphere. The air became hot and humid.

When the Caribou touched down on the steel-matted runway, I could hear the sound of firing artillery over the reversed pitch of the propellers. The bulky Caribou slowed with such force that the passengers were thrown forward against their safety belts. Before the plane stopped, the pilot advanced the throttle and taxied toward the end of the runway. The rear ramp began to lower as the aircraft bounced along the steel matting. At the end of the runway, the pilot wheeled the plane around in the direction from which it had come and then stopped. At the end of the rear ramp, I was met by a young Spec Four (Specialist Fourth Class) who directed me to an old 3/4-ton Army truck. After he helped me load my baggage in the back of the truck, he collected the mail and a few other small items destined for the Advisory Team.

While I waited, I watched the artillery crew's fire. They were in a steady rhythm as the five guns fired in rotation. The sound of the cannon's discharge was similar to a slow firing machinegun, only louder. As we pulled away, I couldn't take my eyes from the battery. I wondered what the target was. They could be firing in support of an operation or they could be firing H&I (harassing and interdiction) rounds. I didn't ask the driver. He probably wouldn't have had any better idea than I did.

Watching the battery fire brought back memories of an artillery live fire demonstration I saw during OCS at Fort Benning, Georgia. I could picture the Georgia hill erupting and disappearing in a cloud of dirt, while I watched. At the time, I thought I never wanted to be on the wrong end of anything so awesome. Later, when I walked the hillside, there was so much black, jagged shrapnel on the ground that I wondered how anyone could survive such a barrage. Then I remembered they do somehow. Nevertheless, a cold chill went up my back as I watched the deadliest killers on the battlefield go about their labor. I wondered how the VC on the other end was reacting. I watched the barebacked cannoneers load and fire until we turned off the airstrip and headed into Dong Tam.

Only a few months before, Dong Tam had been a marsh. The engineers had dredged the Mekong River for mud to fill the marsh on which the base was built. The dredging operation left a harbor for the Army's Riverine Flotilla of small landing craft. The Dong Tam cantonment, built around the harbor, served as the armada's base of operations. The cantonment area was a beehive of activity. Everywhere I looked barebacked construction engineers worked on wooden barracks and administrative buildings.

As we drove through the cantonment, I remembered that one of my lieutenants, Second Lieutenant Barry Hemphill, at Fort Polk had received orders assigning him to the 9th Division. I wondered if he was at Dong Tam. I'd try to run him down later. We left Dong

Tam behind and moved along a narrow dirt road toward My Tho, nine klicks (kilometers) to the east.

The road was bounded on the south by what I thought was jungle. Actually, it was a thick growth of banana trees, nipa palm trees and other vegetation that lined the many canals and rivers of the Delta. To the north were open rice paddies partitioned by small dikes and hedgerows. The road was dirty and bumpy. The light traffic encouraged the driver to speed along at what I thought a dangerously fast speed. I said nothing, however, as he swerved to miss pot holes and a few carts. He knew the road, I didn't. We made small talk, while we rocked and bucked along. The normal questions were exchanged, Where are you from in the States? What was your last duty assignment? How long you been in-country?

Shortly after leaving Dong Tam, I heard small arms fire to the north. The driver paid no attention. I looked across the paddies. There was no activity other than a few farmers working the fields who showed no concern. They continued their work as though the shots were a normal occurrence. I guess they probably were. We continued our journey without incident.

On the western outskirts of My Tho, we turned north along a narrow street lined with shops and residences toward Team 75's headquarters, located in a compound that sat on the east side of Highway Six-A and the west bank of the Rach Bao Dinh River. The compound took its name from its pre-war use. It had been a Catholic seminary before the war, so when the Army leased it, it was christened "The Seminary" by the troops. What irony!

The Seminary's main building was a white, two-story masonry structure with a red slate roof. From the highway, it looked L shaped. Another section, however, ran from the toe of the *L* toward the canal. The compound was protected by a high, white masonry wall across the front and a barbed-wire fence on the other sides. Outside the walls and fence were barbed-wire entanglements with mines. A double gate entry sat at the southwest corner of the wall. Guard posts were placed at each corner atop the wall. A machine gun crew manned each position. A 4.2-inch mortar position was placed in the northwest corner of the compound. Altogether, the defenses appeared adequate, but they certainly were not really much of a deterrent. Not being an infantryman and not having been trained to defend forts, I really couldn't judge the adequacy of the defenses, but I thought that I could blow the place away with a light section of tanks (two tanks). But to my knowledge, the VC didn't have tanks in the Delta. I quickly decided this would be a safe place to hang my spurs.

Slowing to turn off the highway, we yielded to a jeep filled with four green berets exiting the compound. The jeep came speeding out the gate and turned north up the highway. The berets presented an air of owning the road.

"What're they doing here?" I asked.

"Oh they come down out of the Plain of Reeds for supplies," answered the driver. "We have people from all over the area coming in to use the PX."

"PX! You have a PX here?"

"Yeah, it's small, but we have most of the things you need—toilet articles, underwear, radios, watches, tapes, records—those sorts a things."

When we passed through the gate, a Vietnamese guard followed us with his eyes but made no attempt to stop us. We drove along a drive that ran along the south side of the compound past a combination basketball and volleyball court, to the back of the building.

The driver helped me unload my gear and set it in a hall just inside the building. Leading the way, he escorted me down a cloistered hall to the Adjutant's office. On our right, we passed rooms of various sizes. The doors were open revealing Army steel cots stacked two high around the walls, placed alternately with metal wall lockers. Mosquito nets hung from each bed. Footlockers were placed under some beds. In the center of the rooms were various combinations of coffee tables, end tables, poker tables, chairs, couches, and footlockers. The rooms looked comfortable and offered the necessary conveniences for relaxation.

"Who lives in these?" I asked, motioning to one of the rooms. "Those are the Division staff advisor's rooms," the driver replied. I nodded and smiled. Not a bad way to live, I thought, a little crowded, but not bad. They seemed to have all the comforts. These accommodations weren't what I expected. I had thought advisors lived in little huts under the same conditions as the Vietnamese. These people were living high on the hog. This is a small palace compared to what I had expected.

At the end of the cloister, we found the staff offices. Small signs hanging over each door identified the offices: G-3 (Operations), G-2 (Intelligence), and the Communications Officer offices on the right; the Adjutant's and Commander's offices on the left.

At the Adjutant's door, I knocked and stepped to a small desk. A narrow-shouldered major looked up from his paperwork with an expressionless stare. Written on his desk plaque was John L. Gooden, Major Infantry. His eyes moved to my nametag as he stood.

"Yeah, Captain Cole," he said, smiling as he extended his hand. "Good to have you aboard. Have a seat."

"How was the flight?" Gooden asked as he sat down behind his desk.

Fine, "I replied. "The plane was an old Caribou. The noise wasn't too bad, but the vibration made me wonder if it'd hold together, especially on takeoff."

The major nodded agreement.

"Well, you'll be going to the Cav. It's a good outfit. It sees a lot of action. Major Evans is the senior advisor. He's in with the colonel right now. I'll get you with him when he comes out.

"Fine."

"You'll be here about three days, and then you'll go wherever Major Evans puts you. While you're here at the Seminary, you'll be briefed on the area and some dos and don'ts. The G-3 will arrange your briefings and Major Evans can show you around. Any questions?"

"No, not now. I'm too new to know what to ask," I replied.

"Okay, just relax; they'll be out in a few minutes." Major Gooden returned to his work. I sat waiting for only a few moments.

When the door opened, a short, stocky, gray-haired colonel came into the Adjutant's office. A slightly taller, stoutly built major followed him.

I stood as the colonel approached. "Captain Cole, good to have you. I'm Colonel Jones. This is Major Evans; he'll be your boss."

"Good afternoon, sir. I'm glad to be here," I lied. Turning to Major Evans I nodded and said, "Sir."

"I'll leave you with Major Evans for now. John will get you on my calendar, if possible, before you go to the field. We'll get acquainted then." The colonel turned and went back into his office.

Major Evans extended his hand and said with a smile, "Good to have you." He turned to Major Gooden, "John, do you need him for anything more?"

"No, he's all yours. I'll tell Colonel Watts (the G-3 Advisor) he's here. You can drop by in the morning and get the briefing schedule," Gooden replied.

"Fine, I'll take him on down to the unit. He can stay with us until I can get him out to a Troop. Turning to me, "Where are your bags?"

"They're down the hall."

"Let's go," he said as he headed for the door. As we drove into My Tho, Maj. Evans began his briefing, "The Cav has two compounds in My Tho. The Troop compound is on the east side of town. We're staying at 6th Squadron Headquarters Compound. It's in downtown My Tho. We're in one of the maintenance buildings until we can get moved. It isn't much, but we've a roof over our heads. We eat and shower at the Seminary."

"Where are we moving to?" I asked.

"I'm working on leasing a villa in My Tho," he replied. "We'll be the only advisors living in town. We'll be away from the Seminary so we can do our own thing," he continued. "Until I get the lease approved we'll have to stay in the Cav Compound."

"How long will that be?" I asked.

"Oh, a couple a weeks at the most, he said. After we get you settled, we'll go over and take a look at the place. It's in a small area with some other homes leased by Americans."

"Who're they?"

"In the house next door are some civilian construction contractors. The house across the street is used by Military Intelligence types," he answered. "I don't think we'll have a problem with security. There are enough Americans around and the Squadron is going to provide us with guards."

"How long do you think I'll be here?" I asked. "Three, four days, however long it takes to get you briefed. We'll chopper you out to 1st Troop when we're finished here, he said. "The Squadron has three troops. Our main mission is to keep Highway Four open. We keep one Troop here in My Tho and two Troops on the road. One Troop is at Cai Be and the other is at Long Dinh. We rotate each month."

"Which Troop will I be going to?"

"First Troop, my old outfit, they're at Cai Be now. Captain Vinh will be your counterpart," he replied. A counterpart was the South Vietnamese officer or non-commissioned officer that an American advised. "You have two sergeants: Sergeant First Class Maia for maintenance and Sergeant Lockett for weapons. Also, you have two Xenon searchlight crews attached to you," Evans continued.

"What do we have searchlights for?" I asked.

"We're testing them. They were sent over from the artillery. The original idea was for them to illuminate the battlefield by bouncing their beam off the cloud cover...," Evans began to explain.

"Oh, yeah. I've read about that."

"Well, it didn't work, so the artillery gave them to us to see if we could find a way to use them," Evans continued.

"Have you?" I asked.

"Not really. We use them for night security on the road and have tried to use them with ambushes. We hadn't been too successful, though," Evans replied.

My Tho's traffic was heavy. The street was crowded with motor scooters, Renaults, petty cabs, bicycles, and pony-drawn carts. From what I could see, the city was beautiful in comparison to Saigon. The street was lined with blooming trees of varying colors and multi-colored flowers. The people were moving about as though there were no war. The scene was one of a busy, bustling city. The only evidence of the war was the military traffic. We passed a large market and bus station, negotiated a traffic circle, and passed through an intersection with churches on two corners before we got to 6th Squadron Compound.

We passed through an open gate with pale yellow stone columns trimmed in light blue onto a dirt quadrangle twice the width of the street. On the left was a pale yellow two-story building that looked like a residence.

"That's the officer's club. It's not in use right now because of its condition. Colonel Die plans to have it fixed up, but he hasn't gotten around to it yet," Evans said.

Next to the club were two large single-story rectangular buildings that looked like warehouses. Across the dusty quadrangle were two more large rectangular buildings. We stopped at the first building past the club.

"This is home," Major Evans said as he swung his feet out of the jeep; "the driver will get your bags. Come on."

I alighted from the back of the jeep and followed Evans. "Third Troop is in town this month," Evans said, walking toward a door. "Captain Arthur is its Advisor."

I had known a Lieutenant Arthur in Germany and wondered if this might be the same officer.

We entered a narrow door into the building. The forward section of the building was furnished with three rows of Army folding cots and wooden footlockers. The cots were fitted with wooden poles from which hung mosquito nets. Three soldiers sat in a small circle on the last row of cots. I saw that one was indeed the officer I knew.

"Hello Cole, small world," Arthur said as he stood and extended his hand. "You're right. I never expected to run into anyone from Crailsheim here," I greeted him.

"Oh, do you two know each other?" asked Major Evans. "Yes sir, we were stationed on the same post in Germany," Arthur explained. "We were in different battalions, but we got to know each other at the club and around post," I added.

"Well, I need to see the Squadron commander about a few things. I'll leave you two to swap stories," Evans said as he turned to leave. "Oh Mark, you might get Larry one of our M-16s. That carbine isn't much use on the road."

"Will do," Arthur replied. Then turning to me, "Take any cot that's not in use."

I picked out a cot and motioned for Evans's driver to put my bags beside it. Arthur walked to a metal wall locker and took out a black M-16 rifle. "Here you go. This is a lot better than that thing," he said, handing me the rifle.

"Where did y'all get M-16s?" I asked.

"Ah, the major scrounged them up somewhere," Arthur replied.

I didn't pursue the question. I figured it was better that I didn't know. "Give me your carbine. We'll keep it in the locker until you get ready to turn it in," Arthur said.

With the carbine secured, Arthur and I sat down to reminisce about Germany and to update each other on mutual acquaintances. I had left Germany before Arthur. After I left, our two armor battalions were moved to Ansbach. Arthur told me about the move. When he left Germany, he had been sent TDY (temporary duty) to the Special Warfare School and the Army's Language School at Monterey, California, on the way to Nam. He had been in country about six months.

"You know Cole, I never understood how you managed in Germany. I don't think I could have lived between two lieutenant colonels and stayed out of trouble," Arthur said turning the discussion to the personal side.

In Germany, my family and I had been assigned quarters in a stairwell with the two armor battalion commanders. Arthur's boss lived over us and my boss lived under us. This wasn't the best of arrangement for a first lieutenant, which was my rank at the time. I walked on eggshells; afraid I'd upset my colonel. If he got down on me for whatever reason, my career was shot. I couldn't afford to make him mad or disturb him.

"Yeah, I know what you mean," I said. "I was in hot water with Wolfe all the time. I couldn't do anything without him getting on my case. Your boss, what was his name?"

"Mills," Arthur said.

"Yeah, Colonel Mills wasn't bad, he always had a good word and a smile for me. But Colonel Wolfe was another story."

"Yeah, he seemed like a hard nose."

"I remember one morning after one of our parties, Colonel Mills met me in the stairwell as we were leaving for work. He gave me a big smile and a thumbs-up and said, 'good show.' That made me feel a little better, particularly since Wolfe had called me the night before around 10:00 to tell me it was time to stop the noise and go to bed."

"What happened?" Arthur asked.

"Oh, we had invited Jim and Rose Mosley and Joe Morris over for dinner. Morris brought his guitar, so after we had eaten, we started a hootenanny. By 10:00 we were having a really good time. Jim got to laughin' about something and leaned too far back in his chair and fell over backwards. After Rose stopped screaming and the rest of us stopped laughing, the phone rang. It was old Wolfe. "

"What 'd he say?" Arthur asked.

"Just said, 'Cole that's enough. It's time to go to bed.'"

"Did he ever say anything else to you about it?" asked Arthur.

"No, but from then on I could tell he didn't have much use for me."

"How did you get in the same stairwell with them?" Arthur asked.

"Because I had three kids, two boys and a girl. I was authorized a three-bedroom apartment. When I first brought the wife and kids over, there were no three-bedroom quarters available in the officer's section, so we had to take NCO quarters. The first three-bedroom quarters to come available in the officer's section were in the field grade area. We took them and billeting wouldn't make us move. They said we had been inconvenienced enough. Wolfe tried to have us moved, but billeting wouldn't go along." I explained.

Major Evans returned from his meeting with Colonel Die, interrupting our memories.

"Tell you what," Evans began. "Let's drive over to the new Armor House, so you can see where we're moving. Then we'll go to the Seminary for dinner. After dinner, we'll show you the club. Then we'll go down to Fruit Juice Roll for a look at My Tho's night life."

"Sounds good," I lied again. I was apprehensive about a night on the town. Being nosy and a people watcher, I wanted to see what went on in the bars. I imagined beautiful, longhaired maidens vying for my favors and drunken soldiers fighting over women and which units were the best. I imagined all the action of a John Wayne movie.

I didn't necessarily want to be part of the action; I just wanted to see what was going on. Overriding my curiosity, however, was a concern of being grenaded by a VC while enjoying good company and a drink.

"Mark, we'll meet you at the Seminary," Evans said as we left. The Armor House was in western My Tho on the north side of a dirt street.

A new house, it was enclosed by a masonry wall with two double gates. It was a two story duplex with a balcony across its front. The tall, white structure looked out of place surrounded by less imposing homes.

"The landlord is going to put a door in the second floor wall so we can move from one side to the other without going outside," Evans explained while we sat in front of the house. "We'll put the EM [enlisted men] on one side and the officers on the other."

"How many rooms?" I began.

"Twelve. We'll have two kitchens and two showers." We admired the house for a few moments from the street, and then we headed for the Seminary.

Armor House photo by Larry Cole

Armor House Reading Room photo by Larry Cole

Amor House Bar photo by Larry Cole

At the Seminary, Major Evans made his excuses to visit with various members of the division's advisory staff, leaving me to my own devices for introductions and entertainment.

Fruit Juice Row photo by Larry Cole

It was late in the afternoon. A jungle volleyball game, where anything goes, so long as a player doesn't tear down the net, had just started on the court. Not knowing anyone, I didn't invite myself into the game. I watched until Mark Arthur found me. We made small talk and commented on the game until Major Evans joined us.

The mess hall was located on the ground floor in the center section of the Seminary. We queued up in a short chow line. When we got to the door, we paid, signed a meal roster, and headed for a table.

The mess was a large room furnished with tables covered with red and white checkered tablecloth and set with four places. Along the rear wall, tables were joined to form a single, long table for the division staff advisors. Visiting officers, which was our category, could sit at the individual tables or at the staff table. The individual table section was divided into an enlisted section and a NCO. We chose the NCO section.

After dinner, we went upstairs to the club. It was in a well-furnished room over the mess. It had a small bar and several areas with round or long coffee tables surrounded by overstuffed chairs and couches. A bell hung over the bar, used to announce that an officer had been caught at the bar wearing his cap. When the offender was seen and the bell rung, he was obliged to buy everyone in the bar a drink. The room was dimly lit with candles on the tables. It had the feel of a comfortable civilian lounge.

Major Evans introduced me to the few officers at the bar as we worked our way to a table in a far corner. We ordered drinks and sat back to discuss the war. I ordered my usual rum and Coke. I wasn't an experienced drinker and didn't know what else to order. I had started to drink socially in Germany after ol' Colonel Wolfe told me to relax and join the crowd if I wanted to be a successful Army officer. After that counseling session, I began drinking wine or rum and Coke at social gatherings. I couldn't stomach beer, but I kept it in the refrigerator for fellow officers when they came by the apartment.

"Larry, I checked in with Colonel Watts. He'll have someone brief you in the morning," Evans began.

"Fine, how do I get out here?" I asked.

"You can come in for breakfast with me and then hang around until 8:00 for Watts," Evans answered.

"Okay. "

"Larry, you shouldn't have any problem with the Troop. As I said, First Troop was my old Troop."

"How long you been gone?" I asked.

"Just over a month. I left to take the Squadron," Evans answered.

"They've been without an officer all that time?" I asked.

"Right; they were in My Tho until the first of the month. I could look after them," Evans said. "Anyway, Captain Vinh is an old hand. He has been fighting this war for over six years. There isn't anything you can tell him about armor operations in the Delta."

"What am I supposed to do then?" I asked.

"You go along for the ride and report what happens to me."

"That doesn't sound too challenging," I replied.

"Well, there's a little more to the job than that. Mainly, you'll be Vinh's fire support coordinator. Although Vinh speaks good English, the Vietnamese are hard to understand over the radio. So, you coordinate the air strikes and the artillery. Also, you'll need to send me a weekly report on the Troop's daily activities."

"It's a good job," Mark Arthur chimed in. "You'll enjoy working with the Cav once you get used to them. They're the best troops in the Vietnamese Army."

"Yeah, I think so too," Evans added. "Just bide your time. Don't be critical. There's a good reason for most of the things they do. Vinh will come to you when he wants something. You ready to hit the town?"

"Yeah, I guess so," I answered.

"Oh, one other thing…" Evans paused.

"What's that?" I asked.

"Vinh is married to the Squadron commander's daughter. He's the fair-haired boy of the Squadron."

Great, I thought as we left the club. That's all I need: to get a fella that can do no wrong and who has the ear of the commander. I won't be able to advise him on anything. He'll just get the old man to go along with anything he wants.

Fruit Juice Row, the local red light district, was on Bao Dinh Street. The street ran north and south along the west side of the Bao Dinh River, which fed into the Mekong River. The west side of the street was lined with hotels and shops; the east side was a long line of bars that hung out over the river. The bars were single story, concrete block structures. The front of each establishment consisted of a half wall and door. The upper portion of the front wall was an open wire-mesh window.

It was a quiet night. Neither the street nor the bars were crowded. We walked the street for a short distance trying to decide which bar to patronize. The place we chose was representative of the others on the street, sparsely furnished with crude tables and chairs. We chose a table along the back wall. Looking down on the river, all I could see was sampans and houseboats rocking in filthy brown water. The little boats were stacked side by side ten or twelve deep against the river's bank out into the river. Most of the sampans had a tarp over their center portion that served as a tent for living quarters. As I looked down on the massed flotilla, I thought how miserable it must be to live in such crowded and filthy conditions. Where did they bathe? Where did they cook? Where did they sleep? How could three, four, five people sleep in a small sampan? How could mom and dad make love with the kid sleeping next to them? I asked the questions but got no answers. What a mess! I was grateful to God that my family didn't have to live under similar conditions. I could now truly appreciate the United States' standard of living and how fortunate Americans were to live in a country that gave its civilians the opportunity to own a home and have a good job.

We didn't stay at the bar long. It was getting close to curfew. Our tour was uneventful. The girls didn't push us to buy drinks, and we weren't propositioned. Boy, had I been misled. This wasn't the Vietnam I had heard about back at Fort Polk. It was just as well; we weren't armed. We didn't need to find any excitement.

The next morning, I reported to the G-3 Advisor's office to begin my briefings. A Captain Watson took me upstairs to a large room with a big map of the Mekong Delta nailed to one wall. Captain Watson's briefing was another of those fire-hydrant experiences. With pointer in hand, he began his spiel, pointing on the map to each area he discussed.

"As you know," Watson began, "we're located in IV Corp. The Corp's Headquarters is here in Can Tho. Colonel Nelson is the Senior Corp Advisor; the Corp Commander is Major General Thanh.

"Team 75 advises the 7th ARVN Division. The Division's Headquarters is here in downtown My Tho. The Division

Compound is located next to an old sports complex and soccer field. Our principle Area of Operation [AO] is Dinh Tuong Province, in which My Tho is the principal city. Occasionally, we drop down into Kien Hoa Province south of the river [the Mekong] and extend north into Kien Phong Province and the Plain of Reeds.

"The division's mission is to keep Highway Four open. Highway Four is the main transportation route from the Delta to Saigon. The Delta is Vietnam's main agricultural area, and Highway Four serves as the main route for transporting the Delta's produce to Saigon.

"To accomplish its mission, the Division has three regiments -the 10th, 11th, and 12th- supported by artillery, engineers, the 6th Cav, and a Ranger battalion, the 32nd. One brigade is here in My Tho, one operates out of Long Dinh, and the other out of Cai Be.

"Currently, the Cav is providing road security between Check Points Two-four [CP-24] and One-four [CP-14]. "He pointed to the ferry crossing on the Mekong at My Thuan and to Long Tuong at the intersection of Highways Four and Six-A north of My Tho.

"Team 75 has a parallel structure to the Division's. We have advisors with each Division staff section, at each regimental headquarters and with each battalion. The Cav has advisors at Squadron and Troop levels.

"My Tho is also the headquarters of Advisory Team 63. Team 63 is the Provincial Advisory Team. Their headquarters is in downtown My Tho on North Hung Vuong Street. Are you familiar with the Province Team's organization and mission?" Watson asked.

"Yeah, we were briefed on the Provincial set-up at Kopler, "I replied. "Good. Colonel Daniel is the Senior Province Advisory. You'll meet him and other provincial advisors as you go along. They use our mess and club, and you'll be going on operations with them. Do you know the difference between the RF and the PF?" Watson asked.

"I think so. The RF are regional Troops similar to our National Guard. The PF are local Troops that stay in or around their villages." I answered.

"Close enough," he replied. "The other unit you need to be aware of is the 9th Division in Dong Tam." Watson continued.

"Do we work much with them?" I asked.

"No. They operate alone. They work mostly from the canals. They don't do much in the paddies or along the roads. We do get some artillery support from them though." Watson said.

"We (Team 75) control all fire support for ARVN activities in the province. We operate a TOC (tactical operations center) at the Division's Headquarters on a twenty-four hour basis. Our main function is to control and coordinate all supporting fires within the province. We have to maintain communications with the 9th Division and all district teams. The TOC is manned by a seven man team: An operations officer who maintains contact with the 7th and 9th Division TOC's to track the tactical situation; an intelligence officer who maintains contact with the various intelligence sources; a fire support coordinator who controls the supporting artillery, gunships, and air support in the province; an operations NCO and an intelligence NCO to maintain the situation maps; and two radio operators. These teams are on duty twelve hours and off twelve hours." Watson said.

Captain Watson's briefing ended with a few details about recent actions in which team members had participated and with a listing of the various principal team members and their jobs. He finished within an hour.

After the briefing, I borrowed Captain Arthur's jeep and went to Dong Tam to see if I could find Lieutenant Hemphill. I wanted to find out how he was doing as an infantry platoon leader. He hadn't been much of a training officer at Fort Polk as I remembered. He was nineteen and just out of OCS when he was assigned to my company. His tac officer in OCS must have thought he had leadership ability or he wouldn't have been commissioned. I, however, had my doubts. He had the intelligence to be an officer, but he was still extremely immature. Because of his small stature and boyish looks, he didn't radiate confidence. These were the same qualities of Audie Murphy, our most decorated soldier during World War II, but I didn't think Hemphill would turn out to be a fearless tiger like Murphy. I had to counsel him twice about "putting the make" on recruit's girl friends when they came to visit on family days. One weekend he had gone so far as to take a young lady visitor back home to Texas after she paid her respects to her soldier. Fortunately for him, he was back for duty on time Monday morning. He had to drive all night to made it back to Polk. As I had been told by my tac officer, that's good soldiering if you don't get caught. But Hemphill had gotten caught, and it was reflected on his efficiency report as an inability to exercise good judgment.

    I located Hemphill's unit after asking a few questions. When I got to the unit, I found Barry in the supply room. The visit was short; I brought him up to date on the old company's activities after he left. He told me about the operations he had been on. Evidently, his new commander didn't hold him in particularly high esteem either. He had been moved to the supply officer's job after his second Riverine assault (an attack from a canal using special navy boats). Barry hadn't said he had been relieved, but it just wasn't normal to make such a re-assignment early in a tour. I didn't push the subject, but he must have screwed up. A year later, I read in *The Army Times* that he was reported missing, not as a result of enemy action.

    It was late when I returned to the Seminary. While waiting for chow, I managed an invitation to the evening volleyball game. I had a great time. We played hard. Heated arguments erupted over close line shots and a fist extending over the net. Anyone watching would have thought that we were playing for a world championship, not because of the quality of play but from our enthusiasm. After dinner, Major Evans, Captain Arthur, and I made the rounds on Fruit Juice Roll with the same results as the night before.

    The next day, I made my rounds at the Seminary to get acquainted with the other officers and to visit the PX. I found the officers to be well situated. They were equipped with stereo components, tapes and records, and radios and tape players in each room. Numerous magazines and both fiction and nonfiction novels lay on the tables. Houseboys and girls were busy making beds, cleaning, returning laundry, and shining boots. No! This wasn't a bad way to fight a war. Where else could you have a batsman (military for valet) and a maid to look after your every need before charging off into battle?

The PX was stocked with small radios, greeting cards, underwear, Seiko and Rolex watches, tapes, records, and toilet articles. If you couldn't find what you wanted, you could order it (stereo components, china, silverware, and other gift items) from the PX in Japan. I wouldn't be deprived. I bought a small tape recorder so I could mail tapes home instead of letters. Writing took too much time. Also, I bought a green nylon hammock. I had been told that the only way to sleep was in a hammock.

After lunch, on the way to the division compound for a tour of the division TOC and staff offices, Major Evans told me that I would move out that evening. I was to be at the airfield at 1900 hours to catch a chopper to Cai Be. I'd spend the night with the district team at Cai Be and then be picked up by my team the next morning.

"But I haven't had my interview with the colonel."

"He's tied up with the Corps Commander and won't be able to see you. It's no big deal," Evans assured me.

After visiting the various offices at the division compound, we looked over a large display of captured weapons. All types of weapons were on display. The display was visited by both the division and corps commanders. After leaving the division compound, I spent the rest of the day getting ready for the field. Major Evans had given me two map sheets, which had to be taped together. They covered some 578 square miles of the Delta. I studied them while I taped them together with Scotch tape. I didn't recognize a single feature or town pointed out during my earlier briefing. After I finished with the maps, I packed my rucksack with extra underwear, socks, uniforms, and boots. Shaving gear and C-rations went in the side pockets. The poncho, poncho liner, and air mattress were strapped to the bottom. When I was satisfied that I had the bare essentials for survival, I cleaned my weapon and waited.

Major Evans delivered me to the airfield on time. I was finally on my way to the greatest test of my life. As the Huey lifted out of the dust caused by its own motor blades, I waved to Major Evans. He was standing in the dust anchoring his black beret to his head with his left hand. I wondered what awaited me. Would I be up to the challenge or would I fail? Strangely, I was neither afraid nor apprehensive. Mostly, I was just relieved to be getting on with the mission.

I was on the mail run. The Huey made several stops. I sat next to the large open door in the passenger's compartment. A crewman manned a pedestal-mounted M-60 machinegun behind me. I watch the paddles as we flew from one stop to the next. I wondered why there wasn't any movement in the fields. Where was everybody? I guessed that it was time to change the guard. The farmers must have left the fields to take up their role of Viet Cong terrorist, or maybe they had gone home to be out of the way of any actions that might erupt at dusk. Soon, it grew dark. Only a few lights penetrated the darkness like the eyes of demons. I waited, straining my eyes for VC tracers raising out of the paddies. They never came.

After what seemed a lifetime, we slowly descended onto a small landing pad surrounded by a single roll of barbed concertina wire. A single, waving red light guided the pilot's landing. The chopper swayed gently as it tore the ground. Touch Down! I felt as though I had cheated death. When I jumped from the chopper, Sergeant First Class Rodriguez greeted me.

Sergeant Rodriguez led me through an opening in the concertina toward a small building whose blackened silhouette looked more like a ramshackle old hovel inhabited by hobos instead of American soldiers. I had no idea where I was in relation to My Tho or anywhere else. For all I knew, I was at the end of the earth. I felt lost, but I was glad to be on the ground.

"I told Sergeant Maia this afternoon that you'd be in tonight," Rodriguez said as we walked toward the team house. "He'll be in to pick you up in the morning after the road has been cleared."

"Fine. What about clearing the road?" I asked.

"Charlie either blows the road or mines it nearly every night. The Cav has to clear their section every morning. " Rodriguez explained.

"Yeah, okay, I understand," I interrupted.

"Captain Ackerman and Sergeant Borgmann are on an operation tonight. You can use the captain's cot tonight," Rodriguez said.

"Thanks, I appreciate it. Y'all been having much activity?" I asked as we reached the hooch's sandbagged porch.

"Naw, not much, just a few mortar attacks. We get about three a week." The porch entrance led into a sitting room. The room was furnished with a couch and two overstuffed chairs. Against one wall was a rickety table with a radio sitting on it. Over the radio, taped to the wall, was a map of the area. The end tables next to the chairs were covered with back issues of *Playboy* and other girlie magazines. We passed through the sitting room into a dining area and then a kitchen. The dining room table accommodated eight people. Straight back chairs that didn't match the table or each other surrounded it. There was a stove and refrigerator. A rear door led from the kitchen to a large sleeping room filled with mosquito net-covered cots. There wasn't anything fancy about the arrangements. This team wasn't living so well as the Division's advisors, but they weren't uncomfortable.

Sergeant Rodriguez introduced me to two sergeants who were sitting on their cots. I dropped my rucksack by the bed Rodriguez pointed me to and leaned my rifle against the wall. Sergeant Rodriguez went back to the sitting room to continue his radio watch. The two sergeants and I exchanged greetings and the normal questions, then they returned to their paperbacks.

Though it was early, I was tired and ready for bed. I hit the sack and waited for the first dreaded mortar round to land. I didn't wait long. I was asleep almost as soon as my head hit the pillow.

CHAPTER FOUR

CAI BE: OCTOBER 1967

Sergeant Rodriguez rustled me from the sack at 0600 hours. I was lucky. My first night had been quiet. Rodriguez fed me an excellent breakfast of bacon and eggs and then showed me around his little compound. There wasn't much to see. The team's hut sat a few feet from the road that joined Cai Be with Highway Four. The front of the compound was open to the road. Three rolls of concertina wire and a low dike cordoned off the rear. A small privy sat at the rear periphery. A platform for a fifty-caliber machinegun merged with the perimeter's rear dike. The .50 cal wasn't in position. Rodriguez told me that the team mounted it only when needed.

The compound offered little defense. If the team were attacked, it'd be at the mercy of the VC. It couldn't hope to hold out long.

"Y'all ever been attacked?" I asked as we entered the team house to wait for Sergeant Maia.

"No, nothin' more than an occasional mortar attack. Charlie drops in a couple a rounds."

"How often?" I asked.

"Couple a times a week."

Around 0830, I heard a jeep come speeding off the road and slide to a stop near the porch. I was in the sitting room. I stepped out on the porch to see Sergeant First Class Maia alight from the jeep's front passenger seat with a big smile. Sergeant Lockett, who crawled over the fold-down passenger seat followed him.

"Howdy, sir, I'm Sergeant Maia and this is Sergeant Lockett," Maia said extending his hand and motioning with his head to the young sergeant.

"Howdy, glad to meet . . ."

"Where's your gear?" Maia asked. "We'll get you loaded up and out to the Troop. We're down the road at Papa Two-one. Captain Vinh is expecting you."

We fetched my rucksack and piled into the "made in Japan" jeep. It looked a good deal like an American jeep, but there were differences: It had more road clearance; it was narrower than its American counterpart; the hood was higher; the front seats had more padding, thank goodness; and the front passenger seat folded down. Its most distinguishing features were its top and the rear side curtains. I was surprised about the top, because units I had served with before didn't allow jeep tops. It was believed that tops impaired observation, the ability to engage the enemy, and the ability to dismount. Also, with the windshield up, the sun's reflection could disclose a vehicle's position. For these reasons, American soldiers froze during the European winters and fried under the Texas sun, all in the interest of learning to survive in combat. I was of the opinion that I didn't need to practice being miserable; I could do that well enough when the time came. Little did I realize the time was at hand. During the next three and a half months, the jeep would be my home. The top and side curtains made it bearable.

Maia introduced me to the Vietnamese driver, Ba, as we climbed into the jeep. Maia and Lockett got in the back. They sat on a large wooden box that filled the passenger compartment to the top of the jeep's wheel wells.

We turned north from the compound and headed toward Highway Four along a narrow macadam road. The road was in good condition. Traffic was light. Ba floored the accelerator as we came out of the turn.

Maia leaned over the seat and said, "They only know two speeds, full out and stop." I nodded agreement but said nothing. I was watching the road and the tree line. The nipa palms came to the edge of the road. The trees and tall grass afforded perfect concealment. Our safe passage was dependent on the VC's whim. We could be ambushed at any point.

When we reached the Highway Four intersection we turned west. "This is Papa Two-zero," Maia pointed out. "We spend a lot a time here." The Papa Two-zero and Papa Two-one designations were part of a checkpoint system used for quick location reference. The reference points were written on maps and in operation orders as P-20, P-21, P-22, and so on. and were referred to as Papa Two-zero, Papa Two-two, and so on in conversation. The Cav operated along Highway Four between Papa One-four and Papa Two-four.

Papa Two-zero was only a Y in the road. The tail of the Y led to Cai Be. One side of the fork led west and then south to Vinh Long. The other fork led north and then east to My Tho and Saigon. In the center of the Y was an Esso service station. Several thatched huts

Papa 20 photo by Larry Cole

and a few masonry buildings sat along the road in either direction from the intersection. Rice paddies were nestled between the structures.

Coke Stop-Papa 20 photo by Larry Cole

Public Restroom, Papa 20 photo by Larry Cole

"What's that?" I asked, pointing to a small stand set about four feet from the edge of one of the paddy's dikes. The stand set on two small poles. The platform was surrounded by a two-foot high piece of tin sheeting. A two-inch by twelve-inch plank connected the stand with the dike.

Tom Brings Coffee photo by Larry Cole

"That's one of the local latrines," Lockett answered. A few feet from the stand stood an old man fishing with a twelve-foot pole in the same paddy as the latrine.

"You mean to tell me they eat the fish from that paddy?" I asked in disbelief.

"Sure," replied Lockett. "The fish have a hell of a fight for the feces when someone takes a crap. Sometimes they make such a splash that you get your bottom washed. You don't even have to wipe you're . . ."

"Yeah, it's the real life cycle, Maia added. "The fish eat the feces and the people eat the fish, which starts the cycle again."

"Well, I'm not eating any fish," I declared.

"You may go hungry then," Maia replied.

"Isn't there anything else to eat?"

"Oh, rat and chicken," Maia replied.

"Don' t we get any C-rations?"

"Not often," answered Lockett.

When we arrived at Papa Two-one, we found 1st Troop's headquarters section strung out along the road. There was no system to how the vehicles were dispersed. Actually, there wasn't room to take up firing positions and allow traffic to pass. There wasn't any way to conceal the APCs (Armored Personnel Carriers) either. Rice paddies or buildings bordered both sides of the road. The road's shoulders had only enough room for the section's APCs, trucks, and jeeps to pull off the macadam in a single file. A soldier sat behind a .50 cal machinegun in the commander's hatch of each APC, or "track" as we called them. A few soldiers performed maintenance on various vehicles and some sat at a Coca-Cola stand drinking coke or Ba Muoi Ba, the Vietnam beer. Ba Muoi Ba—translated as "thirty-three—was bottled in a brown, long neck bottle with a tiger head label. I never learned how the manufacturer chose the name. Maybe it was the thirty-third formula he tried.

Ba stopped at the command track. Maia introduced me to Captain Vinh and Lieutenant Tran, the Troop's XO (executive officer). The introductions were short and cool. Vinh politely looked me over. His face showed no emotion. I'm sure he was thinking, *Another big shot American captain who thinks he knows it all. He thinks he's going to tell me how to fight a war he knows nothing about.* The reception was what I expected, and I'm sure I added to its coolness. I spoke no Vietnamese. I couldn't even offer a greeting in his language. What could I to say? We were from extremely different worlds. Our backgrounds and cultures were vastly different. We had nothing in common. He was the experienced veteran; I was the untested novice. He was from the rice paddies of the Mekong Delta and I was from God's country, the oil fields of West Texas. I made my exit as quickly as possible. I wanted to meet the searchlight crews and to talk with Sergeant Maia about the Troop, its personnel, and its performance.

During my brief exchange with Vinh, Ba moved the jeep down the road and parked it in front of a trailer. When we arrived at the jeep, Lockett had the searchlight team leader, Sergeant Williams, and his five-man section assembled behind the trailer. After introductions, Sergeant Maia and I crossed an undulating single-plank bridge to a cola shop to get acquainted and to discuss the team and the Troop. I had to watch my footing to keep from falling into the narrow water-filled ditch between the road and the shop.

The shop was a thatched hut with a packed mud floor. There was no front wall. The thatched sidewalls were four feet high and open at the top. The upper section of the front wall was hinged to the roof and pulled up to form an awning. The back wall was lined from floor to ceiling with shelves filled with Vietnamese Coca Cola and Ba Muoi Ba.

"What do y'all do around here to pass the time?" I asked as we sat down at a wooden table with two homemade wooden stools.

"Sit beside the road . . ." Maia started.

"No, seriously," I interrupted.

"Really, most of our time is spent fighting the dust," Maia replied. We go out on operation a couple times a week."

"What are the operations like? What do you do?" I asked.

"Mostly just rides in the sun. We haven't had much contact lately."

"What's the worst type . . ." I started.

"Night road-runner," Maia replied. "We did a few when I first got here."

"What type operation is that?"

"We just get out on the road sometime between 2200 and midnight and run up and down daring Charlie to hit us." Maia replied.

"Were you ever. . ." I asked.

"Yeah, a couple of times. The last time, Charlie was climbing up on the tracks." Maia said.

A lump came into my throat and I had a hollow feeling in my stomach. This sounds like hand-to-hand combat. I didn't like that idea; that's getting too personal for my liking. I don't know if I can look anyone in the eye and pull a trigger. And how about knives, did they use knives? I hate knives. I wasn't going to ask these questions, I didn't want to appear concerned.

"How did it turn out?" I asked.

"Pretty good. We kicked Charlie pretty good. After that, he has pretty much left us alone."

"Why is that?" I asked.

"We've got too much firepower. Charlie don't like to mess with us." I felt somewhat reassured.

"How about Vinh? What's he like?"

"He's pretty good. He knows what he's doing. You don't have to worry about him. He's a little slow about getting acquainted. He'll come to you in his own good time." Maia said. "And don't worry about having to eat with him. He has been through several advisors and understands that we have trouble with their food. He doesn't insist that you eat with him. He'll ask you in a couple a days."

I was relieved. I was a picky eater—meat and potatoes were my dish. I couldn't stomach fish and didn't care for chicken since I had tried to eat a half raw one at Boy Scout camp many years before. I'd fulfill my obligation if asked, but I wasn't looking forward to eating a Vietnamese meal. I had heard several stories about advisors being served dog, cat, rat, and nu' o mam, the Vietnamese national fish sauce.

"How about food. Do we have any C's?" I inquired.

"A few, we keep them in the jeep's trailer." Maia answered.

"What else do you keep in the trailer?" I asked.

"We keep our cots, mosquito nets, and extra clothes in there." Maia replied.

"What's in the box in the jeep?"

"Some paperback books, stationery, anything we don't want to get wet," He said.

"Where's the rest of the Troop?" I asked.

"Oh, each platoon is given responsibility for a section of road. They move out each morning to various positions and sit. They may move a couple a times, but mostly they just sit. Occasionally, a platoon will provide convoy escort for resupply convoys passing thought." Maia answered.

"Whadda they do at night?" I asked.

"They all assemble at the CP. They come in just before dark and then we move some time after dark, so Charlie won't know where we're at." Maia said.

"How do we from up?"

"Single file along the shoulder of the road," Maia explained.

"How do we use the searchlights?"

"We set one at each end of the Troop and they use their infrared to watch the tree lines. If they see anything that looks like Charlie, they go white light."

"So, they're up all night?" I asked.

"Right," replied Maia.

We finished our cokes and walked down the road to look at the tracks. First Troop was equipped with the M-113 APC. We had no tanks—the roads, bridges, and paddies wouldn't support their weight. So, we played tank with an APC. To help with canal crossings, several vehicles carried lengths of balk span (aluminum bridge sections). These sections were use when the tracks couldn't used their amphibian ability because of added weight or when a canal's banks were so steep that tracks couldn't enter without taking on water—which was most of the time. Few canals offered slopes that allowed for safe entry into the water.

Because of the M-113's light weight, it could move through the rice paddies with relative ease. The only place it couldn't go was the heavily wooded areas bordering the canals. It didn't have the weight to knock over the larger trees. It couldn't swim wide channels because of the added weight—additional weapons and ammunition. Still, it offered the ARVN excellent mobility and overwhelming firepower.

While we visited, the men relaxed and, like most soldiers, did as little as they could get by with. It was getting hot and most of them were searching for shade. They were in good spirits. Each one we spoke with greeted us with a smile and a friendly handshake—not much grip but enthusiastic. Around 1100 hours, Sergeant Maia went to the jeep's trailer and broke out two cots.

"It's siesta time," he said. "We don't do anything between 11:00 and 2:00—gets too hot."

The remainder of the day was used to look over the jeep and to continue my education about First Troop's operational procedures. I went by the searchlight jeeps to get acquainted with the crews. Sergeant Williams was from Alabama, Specialist Young from Tennessee, PFC Laney from Chicago, PFC Ward from Kentucky, PFC Lord from Kansas, and PFC Hunt from Oklahoma. None of them was over twenty years old. My first impression was that they were good troops, and I was mostly right. Only Sergeant Williams would disappoint me. Sergeant Lockett was in his early twenties. He was married; his wife was at home in Michigan.

After dark, we moved the Troop down the road a few klicks and parked for the night. Seventeen tracks, three jeeps, and two trucks were strung out along the shoulder of the road.

That night, I reported the Troop's location to subsector in code, a nightly ritual. We had to keep them informed of our location so that the artillery wouldn't accidentally drop H & I fires on our position. Sergeant Maia and I spent an hour with the searchlights, taking turns observing the paddies and tree lines through the infrared sights. Nothing was moving.

"What are the sleeping arrangements?" I asked as we looked over the paddies.

"I sleep with the mechanics, Maia replied.

"And Lockett?" I asked.

"With the mortars," Maia gestured in that direction.

"Do y'all sleep in the tracks or what?" I asked.

"Depends," answered Maia. "When we're out in the open like tonight, we usually use hammocks. If we're in a village where we can go inside, we use the cots.

"What if it rains?"

"If we're on the road, we just pull a poncho over us or get in one of the tracks," Maia said.

As I started for the jeep Maia said, "Sir, I wouldn't take off your boots if I were you. We may get mortared and have to move off in a hurry."

"Okay, I won't."

It was the rainy season, and it looked like rain. I decided to sleep in my new hammock and to lay my poncho over me if it rained. I strung the hammock between the jeep and the command track and began my struggle to get in the elusive sheet of nylon. The hammock was attached between two vehicles by ropes at each end. When the ropes were pulled tight, the hammock became a thin sliver of cloth. No matter how I approached it, it moved away from me. Finally, I managed to get in the green cocoon. Because of my 230 pounds, the hammock sagged, so badly that I was bent into a *V*. The nylon wrapped around me, covering my head and shoulders, pinning my arms to my side, and forcing my knees and ankles together. My buttocks were only inches from the road. I was miserable but determined to sleep in the torture chamber. If the others could sleep in a Vietnamese hammock, so could I.

I lay in the gently swaying hammock, my hands folded over my stomach, my ankles as high as my head and locked together, listening to the artillery's H & I fire. I wondered if I'd see the next sun rise. I envisioned a mortar attack followed by a human wave assault from the paddies. The occasional passing of a guard and the vigilance of the searchlight crew didn't relieve my anxiety. I felt helpless; this was the first time I felt my life depended on the proficiency of others. I was apprehensive. I didn't know these troops. Based on stories I had heard in the States about how lax the ARVN were about security, I didn't trust them to remain alert. I made it through the night, although I didn't get much sleep. I was waiting for the sun when it rose over the nipa palms.

The next few days were much like the first. We sat beside the road watching traffic and eating dust or sat in the cola shops drinking Vietnamese cola, a flat, less acid reproduction of its American cousin. We might move a few times each day or we might not. Generally, the moves were administrative, so I rode in the jeep. We broke the monotony by reading paperbacks or writing letters. I had time after all. Each day during siesta, we sunned for two hours. I was beginning to think that we were never going on an operation.

Finally, after siesta of the fourth or fifth day, Vinh told me that we were going on a short operation. We were to conduct a search-and-destroy mission on a small village north of the highway.

We mounted the tracks and headed east along the highway. I radioed our move to subsector at Cai Be as we rolled out. We moved at a leisurely pace. The command track followed the lead platoon. Though the command track was equipped with the same weapons as the other tracks, it stood out because of its radio antennas. Captain Vinh had two AN-VRC-47s (we called them Anger 47s), one for the Squadron command net and one for the company command net. Then we had one for the AM radio used for long distance communications with the Squadron in My Tho. The Vietnamese artillery observer had his own radio with an auxiliary receiver, and I had an AN-VRC 53, which could be discounted and used as a back packed PRC 77, another antenna. Altogether, there were six antennas waving from the top of our track. The command track carried more crewmen than the others. Besides the normal crew of eleven, we had the artillery observer, sometimes the first sergeant, Vinh, and me.

We rode on top of the vehicles. In the US Army, during peacetime, riding on top of a vehicle would have been a serious safety violation. In combat, however, riding on top was standard procedure and essential to staying alive if the track hit a mine. If that happened, the troopers on top would be thrown clear. If inside, they could be killed or seriously wounded from the explosion, concussion, or flying objects within the track. Vinh rode on the left side of the track directly behind the driver. I rode behind Vinh. We were the only two crewmen with seats. The maintenance section had rigged two jeep seats to the top of the track for our comfort.

After a short distance, we turned off the highway and headed north across the rice paddies. The water in the paddies was about a foot deep. The paddies were partitioned into varying sizes by two-foot high dikes. Some dikes were planted with small trees forming hedgerows. We moved slowly through the paddies in column. No one worked the fields. It was deadly quiet except for the slow, even hum of the track's engine, broken occasionally by a high pitched whine when a driver accelerated to force his vehicle over a dike. After an hour of bouncing over dikes, we crossed an improved dirt road. When the last vehicle cleared the road, the Troop moved into a line formation. It was a joy to watch the tracks accelerate and come on line. Each vehicle created a small wave as it moved through the water. Granted, they weren't tanks, but they looked awesome nonetheless. When the tracks came on line, the assault was on. A feeling of invulnerability swept through me. I was almost as excited as when I led a tank platoon in a training assault. It was the old armor maneuver of "high diddle diddle right down the middle—how dare you try to stop me?"

At the edge of the paddies, we halted at a tree line. The troopers, except the driver's and gunners, dismounted and entered the trees.

A village lay hidden in the trees beyond. Vinh and I stayed on the track After about thirty minutes, the troopers returned to the tracks. The operation had produced my first of many rides in the sun resulting in, as we said in the oil patch, a dry hole. Nothing happened.

Daisy-chaining in the paddies photo by Larry Cole

Daisy -chaining through a Canal photo by Larry Cole

Daisy-chaining photo by Larry Cole

In the Attack photo by Larry Cole

We headed back for the road. The operation had been nothing more than a training exercise. The village had been deserted except for a few old men, women, and children. If Charlie had been there, he had seen us coming and moved out along the canal behind the village. When we reached the dirt road, Vinh turned the Troop east in column and moved out sharply at increased speed. I wondered where we were going but didn't ask any questions. I was glad to be out of the paddies and dikes. I checked my map, the road we were on intersected with another road, which led back to Highway Four. Maybe Vinh wanted out of the paddies and an easy ride home too.

Sure enough, when the Troop's lead track reached the intersection it turned south toward the main road. When the Troop completed its turn, I leaned back in my seat and relaxed—enjoying the ride and the passing mosaic of scenic paddies. Still, no one worked the fields. We had made it through the operation without any action and most important, no casualties—we'd see the moon rise.

Without warning, there was a thunderous explosion behind me. I felt its concussion on my back. I turned to see the track behind me settle to the ground in a cloud of dust and grind to a halt. Before I could comprehend what had happened, a torrent of automatic weapons fire broke loose over the paddies. Every weapon in the Troop was firing. The noise was deafening. The water in the paddies erupted from the impact of the rounds. The trees along a far hedgerow to the east swayed and shed their leaves as .50 caliber rounds passed through them.

I didn't feel anything. There was no fear. I must have been in shock. All I could think of was that my track had just passed over a mine. Why had we not hit it? I was so preoccupied with the question that I didn't think to join the defensive fire. A cold chill went up my spine and caught in my throat. Death had passed me by, but why? Why? I can still see that track settle to earth from time to time and still ask the same question. There's no answer. After what seemed an eternity, but probably no more than thirty seconds, the firing stopped as abruptly as it had begun and the recovery operation began.

When I got to the rear of the disabled track, the Troop medics were working on the wounded. None had been seriously injured. There were only a few cuts and bruises. Riding on top of the vehicle had saved them.

Sergeant Maia strolled up as though nothing had happened. "Let's look along the side of the road to see if we can find any wires." he suggested.

"You think it was controlled detonated?" I asked.

"Don't know, It may've been."

We searched both sides of the road while the track's crew worked to put the right track together. We couldn't find any wires leading to the trees or into the paddy to our west. The mine must have been pressure-detonated. If it had been controlled-detonated, the command track, my track, would have been the target. Charlie, like any antagonist, targeted leadership. Our track had those six radio antennae protruding from its top signifying a command vehicle. We looked like a porcupine moving along the road in comparison to the other vehicles. We were an easily identifiable target. Charlie would have had no difficulty deciding when to twist his detonator.

The mine must have been small, probably homemade. There wasn't much damage to the track or the crew. If it had been a standard American or Soviet anti-tank mine, the track would have been damaged too badly to have remained in service. Most of the crew would have been killed as well. It took the crew and maintenance section about an hour to fix the track so that it could move under its own power. We were back on Highway Four before dark.

It had been an excellent operation for a starter. I hadn't learned much about conducting a search-and-destroy operation or how to move a Cav Troop through the paddies, but I had learned that I could never relax in Nam. I'd never know when we might be hit. An operation was never over. It was a lesson that had been drummed into me by every article and report I had read. It had been taught in every class I had attended on guerrilla warfare. Unfortunately, it was a lesson quickly forgotten. Soldiers can stay alert only so long. After a time, they get tired, the adrenaline subsides, they relax, they get careless, and they do things they shouldn't do or they don't do things they should. Charlie was expert at waiting and picking the time when his enemy was least prepared and the most off guard. I knew that I'd relax again and come up short of the mark.

After we made our night displacement, Vinh's runner came to invite me to dinner. Though the day's operation was fruitless, Vinh must have considered me blooded. I didn't look forward to the dining experience, but I had to go. I accepted the invitation with resignation. It was my duty to uphold the honor and tradition of the US Army and to establish a good rapport with my counterpart. I hoped I could meet the challenge without throwing-up, embarrassing my fellow Americans and myself.

"Don't worry," Sergeant Maia said, as I started for my test. "He'll probably have chicken. It may be too spicy for you, but it's usually not bad."

"I just hope he doesn't offer me any nu'o mam. I don't think I can handle that." I said. I had heard at least fifty horror stories about how nauseating the fishy sauce was to the American palate.

The meal was served in a thatched hut which Vinh had chosen as his quarters for the evening. The hut sat across a ditch beside the road. I had to negotiate a wobbly, single plank bridge to cross the ditch. In the darkness, I was afraid I'd lose my balance and fall into the black gelatinous mud beneath the bridge.

A single kerosene lamp without a chimney lit the hut. I couldn't make out the furnishings of the room. The lighting was so poorly dispersed I could barely identify Vinh and Tran sitting at a wooden table. An old woman placed a large pot on the table as I entered. When I sat down, I couldn't see over the rim of the pot, so its contents were a mystery. I wanted to keep it that way. The last thing I wanted was to look into that pot and see a chicken's head with open eyes staring at me.

Vinh dished up a plate of whatever we were having and handed it to me. From what I could see, it looked like a thin Cajun gumbo. The plate was filled with vegetables, small pieces of meat, and red, watery gravy. The concoction was spicy but palatable. I picked at my food until I had emptied the plate of vegetables and meat. I didn't know what to do about the gravy. At home, I'd have shown my lack of manners and sopped it with bread. But this wasn't sopping gravy. Though I didn't have an appetite, I asked for seconds to ensure that my host and the chef thought I enjoyed a delightful meal.

Uncomfortable with each other, we didn't talk much during the meal, still feeling our way. At least I was. The gist of our conversation was an exchange about our families and where I was from in the States. Vinh didn't mention his father-in-law, but he told me his wife lived in My Tho. I don't recall if they had children or not. I would never be invited to his home or meet his family, so it didn't matter. Tran didn't talk; he ate and listened.

After what I thought a respectable time, I excused myself. I sauntered back to the jeep for another bout with the hammock and to be serenaded to sleep by the H & I fire. Maybe, if I were lucky, Spooky would be out. Then I'd have the added attraction of watching his red dance of death.

The next few days were spent getting acquainted with Sergeant Maia and learning about the area. Sergeant Maia was the picture of the professional noncommissioned officer. He looked to be near fifty years old, lean and looked mean with a full head of white hair cut in a flattop. Though he looked mean, he was really a considerate and caring person. I liked and respected him. He was on his last enlistment. When he finished his tour, he was going to retire at Fort Hood and live in Central Texas.

CHAPTER FIVE

ON THE ROAD: OCTOBER-NOVEMBER 1967

The next few weeks were spent adjusting to a gypsy's life. The days, though it was the rainy season, were dusty; they were also hot, humid, and monotonous. The days and weeks became routine, and I began to relax. I came to the conclusion that we weren't going to be mortared every night. Before long, I could drop off to sleep without worrying about seeing the sun rise and sleep soundly all night. I even occasionally took off my boots when I sacked out.

The action wasn't as in articles I had read about combat action in Nam. I expected to be in a fire fighting daily. I expected to be ambushed regularly. I thought I'd have to work my way through punji stakes and booby traps in each village we searched. I thought I'd have to run a gauntlet of B-40 (a Russian anti-armor weapon used by the VC, also called RPGs) fire each time the Troop moved. That wasn't the case. We mostly ranged up and down the highway, seldom moving into the paddies on operation. Aside from the mining incident, we were involved in only two minor actions during my first month with the Troop. Once, when returning from convoy escort, a sniper fired on the Troop as it sped toward Cai Be. When I noticed the shots, they didn't seem to be directed at the command track. Then one round passed so close to my head that I heard it cut the air. Again, like during the ambush, I wasn't frightened until the danger had passed. On the other occasion, Charlie threw a hand grenade into a village where we stopped for the night. After the grenade's explosion, there was much excitement. We lit the village with the searchlights and searched for an hour without finding who threw the grenade. There were no casualties among either the villagers or the troopers.

My daily routine changed little when the Troop provided road security. The day began with a cup of instant coffee brewed over Sergeant Maia's small, one burner Army stove, with water from the Troop's water trailer. After coffee, I heated more water for shaving and bathing from my steel pot. After I brushed my teeth, I was ready to meet the day.

An hour or so after sunrise, Vinh dispatched the separate platoons to various security positions. Each platoon's mission or task as we referred to them, en route to its position was to clear the road of propaganda signs, road blocks, or mines which Charlie had placed during the night. Once in place, their task was to keep Charlie from blowing craters in the highway—an impossible task. In their positions, some troopers kept watch, some worked on vehicles, some visited local shops, some played cards, and some visited with their families who followed along with the Troop.

The headquarters section remained in its night position or relocated into a hamlet near one of the platoons. On some days, Vinh moved both the headquarters and the platoons several times. The idea was to keep Charlie off balance, but it didn't work too well. The road was blown twice during the day while the Troop was in the Cai Be area. Charlie could always find an unguarded spot to disrupt traffic. Luckily, on those occasions, the explosions were well away from one of the Troop's positions and resulted in only minor damage.

An additional tasking was an occasional job serving as convoy escort. These missions were usually scheduled during the afternoon and might be accomplished as a Troop or by separate platoons. Either way, they were great taskings because Charlie chose not to ambush us, discounting the snipers, and they broke the monotony, gave me new terrain to see and made the day pass quicker.

When the headquarters was positioned in a hamlet, Sergeants Maia, Lockett, and I made a grand tour of the two or three shops along the road, while the searchlight crews slept. We'd find a coke shop and discuss home; the war in general; how the Troop conducted operations; the pacification program, which we knew nothing about; and where we planned to go on R&R. After we talked ourselves out, we separated a short distance to find some shade and read The *Stars and Stripes* (when available), read letters from home (when delivered), write letters, or clear our weapons. In my case, I had an additional chore of making daily notes about my impressions of the Troop's operations and its activities.

By noon, I was ready for a meager lunch. My daily diet consisted of a Coke and part of a C-ration meal for lunch and a bowl of rice with Vinh for dinner. I was carefully watching what I ate because of an experience I had with the headquarters section. The Troop had escorted a convoy to Cai Lay one afternoon. While we waited to pick up another convoy going back to Cai Be, a crewman broke out the rice pot. He set the charred aluminum pot of cold, crispy leftover rice on the track's back deck and dug in with a small aluminum spoon. When he passed the pot to me, I spooned up a mouth full of rice and passed the pot to Maia. I noticed some small pieces of meat mixed in with the rice but said nothing. The rice was glue-like and bland. After three portions, curiosity got the best of me.

"What are the chunks of meat?" I asked Sergeant Maia. "Rat," he replied with a smile.

I lost my appetite. I didn't embarrass myself by throwing up, but that was the end of the meal. This was the same day we were sniped at on the road; it wasn't one of my better days.

Also, I was watching how much I ate because the advisory team was short of rations. For some reason, we weren't being resupplied as we should. To stretch our rations, I issued each man one C-ration meal a day. This meal was supplemented with whatever could be found in the shops or in the Troop. I nursed a meal for two or three days by adding Coke to the menu. One day I ate the meat, the next day I ate the fruit, the third day I ate the bread ration—fruit cake, pound cake or cheese and crackers. If I got hungry between meals I drank a Coke when on the road, or water when in the paddies.

Surprisingly, the team suffered few ill effects from drinking the ARVN's water—I was the only member to have a mild diarrhea attack. This was probably because we drank water only from the Troop's water trailer. Since the team drank the water freely, I never asked Vinh where it came from. A possibility was that the supply sergeant picked up potable water at the American airfield when he made his resupply runs to Vinh Long every two or three days.

Just before dark, the Troop reassembled into a column along the road, leaving Charlie with a free rein for the night. After dark, I shared a bowl of rice with Vinh; then I spent some time with the searchlight crews before calling it a day. Occasionally, I passed a little time with Maia and Lockett while the troopers strung their hammocks between the tracks.

After a few weeks of this routine, I lost so much weight that my clothes were getting loose. I became so hungry that I was beginning to think that rat might taste good after all. It was only a passing thought that was pushed aside quickly. My stomach became queasy at the thought. Besides, I needed to lose the weight and the rice and Cokes were keeping me going.

The first improvement in my standard of living came when I took the jeep as my residence.

My first few nights in the hammock left me with an aching back. I could hardly straighten up after a night in the green cocoon.

I tried the cot for a few nights but couldn't get a decent night's sleep because of the nightly rain. I'd pull my poncho over me, but I still got drenched. I'd get up, put on my rain suit and walk the road until the rain stopped. No good. I was so hot in the rain suit that I saturated my jungle fatigues with sweat. Then I had a vision of brilliance. I'd sleep in the jeep. It had a covered top and fold down seats. All I had to do was fold down the passenger seat and place my air-mattress cat-a-cornered across the seat and the supply box in the back. I tried it. The mattress stuck through the door-well about a foot, but that was no problem. I could cover my feet with my poncho when it rained. The first night I tried my new accommodations, I slept like a king in his palace. When it next rained, I slept through the storm like a baby, wrapped in my poncho and poncho liner.

My alternate accommodations was a cot in a Buddhist temple when we spent the night at Papa Two-one or Papa Two-two. This arrangement resulted in one small inconvenience. The chants of the priest and the ringing of gongs awakened me each morning.

Whatever our daily routine on the road, we mostly watched the traffic and the people. Regardless of age or sex, the populace wore the traditional black pants, white blouse or shirt, and sandals. Few people wore the conical straw hats so often seen in the movies or on travel posters. Contrary to what I had been told, neither sex went topless in our area. Even in the paddies, the farmers wore shirts. Clothes were their only protection from the sun and mosquitoes. On special occasions, the young ladies dressed in the Ao dais (a long white silk skirt which hung to the ground and split on both sides to the waist). Either black or white long pants were worn under the Ao dais' skirt. It was a wonder how the ladies kept their white clothing clean. They were always spotless, despite the mud and filth around them.

Also, I was amazed at how well the people survived without the conveniences we Americans took for granted. There was no running water. There was no electricity. There were no telephones.

There were no social services or medical facilities. Still, these people survived, multiplied and seemed happy.

Each hamlet or village was a beehive of activity. Bartering for food was the major commercial endeavor. Men, women, and children of all ages shuffled about with a heavily laden pogie stick over one shoulder carrying all kinds of goods. The amount of weight the children could carry amazed me. I felt sorry for the old, stoop-shouldered mama sans going to market with what looked like fifty pound bundles on each end of their pogey sticks. They shuffled along the road, barely placing one foot in front of the other, with betel nut spittle oozing from both sides on their mouths. When they spoke with acquaintances, their blackened, rotting teeth were clearly visible.

"What's that red juice?" I asked Sergeant Maia the first time I saw a mama san with red juice dripping from her chin.

"That's betel nut," he replied.

"They chew it like we chew tobacco?" I asked.

"Not really," Maia told me. Betel nut is an anesthetic. They chew it to relieve the pain from their teeth." Later, I'd learn it was also use as a stimulant and as an appetite suppressant.

Each village we visited had a number of attractive young ladies. Surprisingly, we seldom discussed their attributes. Officers didn't discuss such things with enlisted men—familiarity breeds contempt, we were told. Yet, to my knowledge, none of the Team had an affair with a village beauty. The searchlight crews had the opportunity to bed down when the Troop was on operation, but I never heard about any social contact if it happened. Sergeants Maia, Lockett, and I were almost inseparable, so I'm sure they didn't sample the local wares.

I can't speak for the others, but it was difficult to get excited about bedding a local lovely. It was enjoyable to watch a young lady approach in her black silk pajamas pants and white silk blouse with raven black hair flowing down her back to her derriere. But, when I looked down at her bare, mud-covered feet and ankles, my libidinal urges quickly subsided.

My sergeants and I were nursing Cokes at one of our favorite hangouts when I saw an attractive young lady stop to make a purchase. She had a large purple bruise on each side of her neck.

"What in the world caused those bruises on her neck?" I asked nodding toward the girl.

"Ah, those are hickeys, "Sergeant Lockett answered. "How did she get them?" I asked in surprised naiveté. "The Viets suck each other's necks while making love," Sergeant Maia answered with a smile.

"What? That looks painful to me."

"It may be, but when they get excited, I guess they don't notice". Maia said.

"Why don't they cover them?"

"They're badges of honor or success, I guess. Sir, are you really that naive? Every kid in high school knows about hickeys," Lockett said with a shocked smile.

Well, naive or not, it was the first time I had seen a hickey on a girl's neck. From then on, I never tired of checking the number and size of hickeys on both the men and women. The large number sported by some individuals fascinated me. The Viets didn't try to cover their marks of conquest and no one, except me, seemed to take note of them. Later, I learned the bruises weren't all caused by sexual activity. The Vietnamese used a heated drinking glass as a suction cup to draw blood to the skin's surface as a treatment for some illnesses, much like we used bleeding during America's colonial days. This was probably the real reason for the bruises.

One of the Troop's frequent stops was Papa Two-one. After a few stops, I made a new friend. He was an eight- or nine-year old boy. I never learned his name. When we stopped at the checkpoint, which was often, he would search me out and shyly watch from a distance. His small, slender body and sad eyes reminded me of refugee children I had seen in documentary movies about World War II. My heart went out to him. I wanted to do something to make his life better and to show him that Americans and I were his friends. I wanted to show him in some way that we were trying to help his people, not to destroy or to force a particular way of life on them. But, since I couldn't speak Vietnamese I could communicate only through a smile and a gift. I offered him my bread ration, which he was reluctant to accept at first. After a few days, however, I was bouncing him on my knee and trying to teach him English. Though we didn't get far with the lessons, I enjoyed trying to teach him. It helped break up the day. Also, he reminded me of my children and how fortunate they were not to suffer his deprivations.

Along with watching the people, I entertained myself by watching the ARVN infantry pass by from time to time. The infantry battalions and regiments operated much like the cavalry. They, like we, rotated through the 7th Division's different operational areas. The battalion stationed in the Cai Be area during October was the 3rd Battalion, 11th Infantry. Its advisor was Captain Wood. A large man at over six feet tall and 200 pounds, he stood out among the Vietnamese. He had played first team offensive tackle for the West Point football team.

When Wood's unit passed, he would stop for a while to discuss the war and happenings in the States as seen through *The Stars and Stripes*. His short visits were always welcomed and enjoyable. They helped break the monotony of the road by having someone new to talk with and to exchange ideas.

I was amazed at the amount of equipment the ARVN Infantrymen carried. They each carried a field pack larger than anything I had seen an American soldier carry. The US Army was on a kick to reduce the weight its soldiers carried. Under this policy, American infantry carried a small rump pack with an optional bedroll. The pack and bedroll were dropped at an assembly area before going into combat. This wasn't so with the ARVN. They carried everything they owned in a large pack that must have weighed fifty pounds or more. Their basic weapon was the World War II, M-1 Garand, which added another ten pounds to their load. The poor fellas armed with the BAR (Browning Automatic Rifle, another WW II weapon) carried an additional five or six pounds. The most overloaded were the mortar men, carrying sixty-millimeter mortars with base plates, and the machine-gunners. Considering the weight of the ammunition they carried, I couldn't see how they kept from becoming swallowed up in the paddies. Despite their heavy burdens, they filed by all smiles and waving.

Whatever the routine, the day's major event was to take our daily malaria pill, and the major project was to find some shade. The sun was unmerciful. Even during siesta, we sunned no more than thirty minutes. The heat and the sun caused my first disciplinary problem. My two sergeants and the searchlight crews wanted to go topless during the day. Though it was hot and humid (the reason they gave) the real object of, going shirtless was to get a good tan. I thought barebacked men roving a village or sitting beside the highway were unseemly for American soldiers. Further, they would appear to be undisciplined. The villagers were fully dressed when in public. The ARVN soldiers, when in the villages or on the highway,

Vietnamese Infantryman photo by Larry Cole

were in full uniform. I thought we could and should meet the same standard. I wanted my men to represent the United States and the Army in the best possible light. Half-dressed American soldiers

My visitor photo by Larry Cole

Local Fisherman photo by Larry Cole

roaming the villages didn't present the picture I wanted. Further, in my opinion, they would insult the villagers by roaming around half dressed.

Laundry Day photo by Larry Cole

Proper wearing of the uniform was a matter of maintaining group identity and discipline. Members of armies had worn uniforms for centuries to show unity and pride of unit. The Army had set a standard; it was my duty to ensure that it was met. I had been taught that if discipline were allowed to decline, proficiency would decline. When proficiency declined, soldiers were killed unnecessarily. Lord Mountbatten had required his troops to shave daily, despite hazardous or miserable conditions, as a basis for maintaining discipline. General Patton, as a foundation for discipline, had required his soldiers to wear the steel helmet at all times in combat and to wear a specified uniform when off duty. Both leaders attributed their success in combat to the maintenance of discipline, even in the seemingly minor areas.

The responsibility of winning battles wouldn't come my way during my tour. But I could ensure that my charges properly represented America. Also, as the senior member of the team, I was responsible for the others lives. I couldn't face a soldier's family if I hadn't done everything or hadn't upheld standards, which would increase his chances of survival. If I allowed discipline to slip, I might allow weapon maintenance or any number of other areas to slip. If a weapon didn't fire when needed, a life could be lost. It was the old story of a battle lost for the want of a nail. It was my responsibility to prevent mediocrity and to maintain discipline. I didn't want lives on my conscious because I hadn't fulfilled my responsibility.

Sergeants Maia, Williams, and I discussed my policy for the better part of three days. The two sergeants used every excuse imaginable to justify not wearing a blouse.

"Sir, it's too hot, we'll have a heat casualty," Sergeant Williams argued.

"No we won't," I replied. "We aren't moving around enough to produce a heat stroke or a casualty. We've got to set a good example for the Vietnamese."

"The Vietnamese don't care," Maia said. "They crap in the paddies for the World to see."

"We have to stay in uniform; it's regulations." I said.

"We're out here on our own. No one will know if we're out of uniform. Besides, people in American units don't stay in uniform," Williams argued. He was right. The *Stars and Stripes* was filled with pictures of American soldiers in the paddies and in the jungles in all types of uniforms and degrees of dress and undress. I remembered seeing one photograph of a shirtless and helmetless American platoon crossing a rice paddy. One of the soldiers even had a transistorized radio ear plug in his ear. Hopefully, the platoon wouldn't receive fire from his sector. If it did, the only thing the soldier could have heard was "Good Morning Vietnam" or whatever AFN (Armed Forces Network) program he was listening to.

"Sarge, I can't help what other units do. I'm not responsible for them," I told Maia. "Their officers aren't doing their job; I've got to maintain discipline."

Finally, one night, while Maia and I leaned on the hood of my jeep discussing my policy, I relented. It's said that a principle of setting policy is to make no policy that can't be enforced. Though I could bring charges against anyone in the team who disobeyed me, the procedure would have been lengthy and would have lowered morale. In a small group, anything that lowered morale would have been counterproductive. Therefore, I really had no way to enforce the policy. So as in politics, we compromised. I decided to allow the team to strip down during siesta to sunbathe. Maia thought this would satisfy the men and put down the uprising. This was the first of many compromises I would make in the interest of morale.

As we started to turn in, the peaceful night was suddenly lit by several white flashes and rocked by thunderous explosions in the distance toward Cai Lay. The rhythmic chatter of machine-guns pierced the night loud and clear. We stood and gazed toward the action in shock. After what seemed an eternity, I asked, "Who do you think it is?"

"Must be mech (mechanized infantry) from the 9th," Maia said. "I thought all they had at Dong Tam were Riverine units," I replied.

"Sometimes a mech unit comes down from up north to conduct road runner operations, Maia said. "They're the only ones with the guts to run the roads at night."

I felt helpless standing in the road watching a steady spray of tracers arch lazily toward the stars. A knot of mixed fear and relief caught in my throat. I could be under those dancing arches of death, but I was a safe spectator instead. Still, I wanted to rush to the relief of my fellow Americans, although to charge up the road could be suicidal. I was sick of spirit because I could do nothing to help the troops in the ambush.

The shooting stopped as abruptly as it had begun. Then it hit me. Vinh and the troopers had shown no interest in the action; there was no incoming artillery; there were no gunships, or Spooky. The ambush must have been initiated by 9th Division troops or by ARVN. The blasts must have been claymore mines being detonated. We had gotten to Charlie. He'd be looking for revenge. My baptism was at hand.

CHAPTER SIX

CAI LAY: NOVEMBER 1967

We were in a night position between Papa Two-zero and Cai Be when I was shaken from a sound sleep.

"Dai uy, Dai uy (captain, captain), VC, VC, " Ba shouted when I raised my head to acknowledge that I was awake.

I could hear engines starting and men shouting. Something serious was happening. I jumped from the jeep, landed on a dead run, and headed for the command track--fortunately I hadn't taken off my boots. I entered the track through the rear ramp door and stood up through the top hatch behind Vinh. He was on the radio issuing a steady stream of orders. He was too busy to answer questions. I switched on my radio, put on the headset and keyed the mic.

"Bravo Three-six Oscar, this is Charlie One-six, over," I yelled into the mic as the track bucked and lunged forward.

"Charlie One-six, this is Bravo Three-five, over," Captain Ackermann, the executive officer of the Cai Be sector headquarters, answered.

"This is One-six, what's happening, over?" I asked.

"This is Five, Charlie is trying to blow the bridge at ah one three one, ah four five niner, over.

"Roger, Five. What size force has he got, over?" I asked.

"This is Five, don't know. We just got the call from the outpost. I'll need a SITREP (Situation Report) when you get there, over," Ackermann answered.

"Roger, out." I replied.

I clung to the radio mount with one hand and fought to put on my flak jacket with the other hand as the track raced north along the road. I didn't have any idea where the bridge was. I had to get dressed and in my seat before I could check the coordinates. When dressed, I grabbed my rifle and climbed on top the track. Falling into my seat, I laid my rifle across my lap, we reached Papa Two-zero and swung west toward the bridge. It was located only about one kilometer west of Papa Two-zero.

Our track came to a stop several meters behind the forward platoon. There was a steady fusillade of machinegun fire from the Troop. Red tracers ricocheted into the night. The .30 cal machine guns on both sides of the track opened fire. The noise was deafening, even with the ear-pieces of my radio's headset over both my ears. I could hear only the radio's squelch (a loud rushing noise) and the machineguns.

"Bravo Three-five, this is Charlie One-six, over," I said after a few minutes.

"This is Five, what you got? Over."

"This is One-six, I don't know. I can't see anything," I said

"Roger, One-six. How about the bridge, over?" Ackermann asked.

"This is One-six; I think it's still in. I haven't heard an explosion and there's a platoon down there."

"Roger, One-six. Let me know as soon as you can, out."

I watched Vinh and the tracers until I saw Vinh take his handset from his ear. I tapped him on the shoulder and asked. "Is the bridge still in?" He nodded his head yes.

"Bravo Three-five, this is One-six, over."

"This is Five, over."

"This is One-six; counterpart says the bridge is still intact, over."

"Roger, One-six. Keep me informed. Let me know if you need anything, out," Ackermann replied.

I leaned back in my seat; stretched out my legs as best I could, folded my arms across my chest, and believe it or not, relaxed. This was better than a Fourth of July fireworks display. It seemed that the Troop was doing all the shooting. I felt as though I were at a movie, watching a battle scene on a wide, silver screen instead of being in the middle of one. I felt I was safe and secure from danger. I had just started to enjoy the show when I looked to my left into the paddy. *Damn!* I thought as my heart jumped out of my chest. Little geyser spouts of water were jumping from the paddy into the air. *This is for real! They are shooting at us!* I swung my legs to the right and dropped down into the track. With my head stuck through the cargo hatch, I peeked around my seat like Jerry would peek around a corner looking for Tom in a Tom and Jerry Cartoon. I warily watched the incoming rounds land short in the water. I jerked my left ear-piece from my ear and slid it up on the side of my head. *Boy, I'll never put both ear-pieces on again. I can't hear anything with both ears covered,* I thought to myself. *Why hadn't Maia told me?*

I continued to watch the shooting for a few minutes from the hatch. The paddy geysers didn't move closer. I couldn't hear any rounds whistling over head. Vinh was still fully exposed, talking on the radio. If he could sit in the open, so could I. I climbed back into my seat.

Shortly, the firing died down and then stopped. Vinh continued to direct the Troop by radio. The tracks began to turn in the road and assemble for our return to our night position. Vinh turned in his seat and said, "We must go to Cai Lay. The VC attack."

Oh, no, I thought, *It's twenty klicks to Cai Lay. The bridge was a diversion; there's no telling what Charlie has waiting for us between here and there. We'll be easy ambush bait.*

I had about recovered my composure when the radio's squelch was broken. It was a call from Captain Ackermann.

"One-six, this is Bravo Three-five, over."

"This is One-six. Over."

"This is Five," Ackermann said. "Cai Lay has just come under heavy attack. Your counterpart should have received orders by now to break contact and relieve Cai Lay, over."

I looked at my watch. It was 0210 hours.

"Roger, Three-five. He just told me. Who's my contact in Cai Lay?" I inquired.

"This is Five. Bravo Two-six, over.

"Roger, Five," I replied. "I'll try to raise him when we're about ten klicks out. Is he on this freq? Over."

"Roger that, One-six," Ackermann answered. "Good luck. I'll continue to monitor in case you run into anything."

The Troop formed up and raced east toward Papa Two-zero. At the intersection, we picked up the wheel vehicles and headed north toward Cai Lay.

We had traveled only five kilometers when the column came to a stop. The road had been blown in two places. troopers from the lead vehicle dismounted and waded into the craters to determine their depth and their bottom's composition.

Vinh had one platoon dismount and search the sides of the road and the paddies for mines. After a thirty-minute delay, Vinh decide that the Troop could drive through the craters. Slowly each track moved through the obstacles. Vinh supervised the crossing of each vehicle. The wheeled vehicles had to be pulled through each muddy crater. Over an hour was lost negotiating the obstacles.

The Troop continued its move more slowly toward Cai Lay. Vinh was concerned about mines. In the dark, the men couldn't see to detect freshly dug mine holes or remote control wires. The lead vehicle would move ahead a short distance to check the road. When the all clear was given, the Troop would advance. The procedure was repeated until the lead vehicle closed on several large mounds in the road. Vinh dismounted a squad with a mine detector to check for mines. The squad swept the mounds and determined there were no mines. Another half-hour was lost. The dummy minefield had served its purpose.

I was searching the tree line to my left with all my consciousness when my radio came to life.

"Charlie One-six, Charlie One-six this is Bravo Two-six, over." Two-six sounded excited.

"This is One-six, over." I answered.

"This is Two-six, what's your location?" the excited voice asked.

"This is One-six; we're about twelve klicks out. What's your situation, over?"

"Roger One-six, Charlie is running free in town. The sector headquarters is under attack and our compound is receiving some fire. What's your ETA, over?"

"This is One-six, I don't have an ETA. We've run into craters and mines," I answered.

"Roger One-six, tell your counterpart to pick it up, we need you here, over."

"Roger Two-six, we'll be there as soon as we can, out," I answered.

I returned to my search of the tree line and road. I pushed the action in Cai Lay to the back of my mind. I was more concerned with the Troop's safe passage. I was lost in my search when I was thrown forward in the seat. The Troop had been stopped by another obstacle.

I had to let Two-six know that the Troop would be delayed. "Bravo Two-six, this is Charlie One-six, over." I said into the radio's mic.

"This is Two-six, over."

"This is One-six; we've hit another crater, over."

"This is Six, how long will it take to by-pass, over?"

"This is One-six, I don't know yet, over."

"Roger One-six, get your counterpart on the move. Charlie is increasing the pressure. He's at the sector compound walls. The incoming is getting heavier, over," Two-six said excitedly.

"Roger, over," I said. Two-six didn't answer.

I turned my attention to the obstacle. *Who does he think I am?* I thought, *I can't tell Vinh what to do. Besides, he's doing his best. If I interrupted, I'd only slow the effort.*

The obstacle was perfectly located. There were deep canals on either side of the road making it difficult to move into the paddies and by-pass the craters. Slowly, the lead tracks moved into the paddies on both sides of the road and around the obstacle. Some drivers had trouble negotiating the canal and became hung up. A daisy chain was formed to pull the remaining vehicles through the canal and paddies. It was a slow process attaching the tow cables in the dark water. The wheel vehicles slowed the Troop's progress even more than before.

While the Troop worked to by-pass the crater, I received several calls from Two-six. He became more and more frantic. He kept up a running account of the VC assault. He pleaded for us to hurry. I felt helpless while I watched the cavalrymen work to get each track around the crater. Americans were in trouble and I couldn't influence the action. I began to pace the road and asked Vinh how long. I didn't know what awaited the Troop in Cai Lay, but I believed it could handle whatever Charlie threw at us. If nothing else, Charlie would have to engage us, which would relieve the pressure on the town's defenders and their advisors.

It took almost two hours to negotiate the obstacle. When the Troop began to move, Two-six had become hysterical in his raving for the Troop to hurry. I could tell that he expressed true fear when he called. As the last vehicle pulled onto the road from the paddies, I received my last call from Two-six.

"Charlie One-six, this is Bravo Two-six. Hurry, they are coming over the wall. We're receiving direct fire, over."

"Roger Two-six. We've cleared the obstacle and moving, over." I received no reply. A wave of depression swept over me. We'll be too late.

Vinh must have received a similar message because the Troop raced toward Cai Lay at top speed. Day began to break as the Troop charged toward the battle. The sun came over the horizon when Vinh turned in his seat and said, "VC are withdrawing to the north. We follow."

On the outskirts of Cai Lay, Vinh ordered the Troop into the paddies. The Troop moved across the paddies and dikes faster than it had ever moved before. I became caught up in the excitement of the chase. Hopefully, we'd make Charlie pay for his folly. Artillery rounds fell to our front. There were only a few rounds, which fell at random, but ARVN was finally using artillery.

Shortly the Troop joined scattered elements of an ARVN infantry unit moving through the paddies and along the dikes. There was no sign of Charlie. At mid-morning, the Troop broke off the pursuit and headed for Cai Lay.

The Troop drove into the center of town and parked. Sergeants Maia and Lockett began helping the various crews make their after-operations maintenance checks. While the Troop recovered from the night's march, Vinh and I went to the subsector headquarters to coordinate future missions. I followed Vinh for a while as he coordinated with the District Chief, an ARVN lieutenant colonel, and various staff officers. I was interested in the headquarters organization and the arrangement of the offices, maps, and charts. When Vinh became involved in a long conversation with an officer, I walked out onto the headquarters' front porch where I found the district chief sitting in a padded rocking chair studying a map set on a US Army issue four-legged easel. He appeared relaxed while he alternately studied the map and looked off into space. He didn't present the demeanor of a man who had spent the night directing a ferocious battle for the survival of the town. The map was posted neatly with symbols of the units in pursuit of the retreating VC. I studied the map closely. The blue symbols identifying the ARVN units were shifting north in a horse shoe formation toward the Plain of Reeds. ARVN wouldn't trap Charlie today. I walked back to the Troop, but couldn't find Maia or Lockett. I decided to go by the advisor's compound to present my regards and to see what damage Charlie had caused. Entering the gate, I saw no widespread destruction; actually, I had trouble identifying evidence of a battle. There was some debris in the courtyard, which the advisors were busy cleaning up.

A small, clean-shaven major in pressed jungle fatigues came across the yard to meet me.

"Hi, I'm Major Ruff, the senior advisor," he said extending his hand with a big smile.

So, this was the frightened Bravo Two-six. He doesn't look too worse for wear, considering what he went through last night, I thought.

"Morning, Sir, I'm Captain Cole. Did anyone get hit last night?"

"No, we were lucky. Charlie got into the compound, pumped off a few rounds and left," Ruff said over his shoulder as he entered the team house. I followed. The room we entered was better furnished than the team house in Cai Be. It was clean and neat. It didn't appear that a battle had been fought from it the night before.

"Have a seat. You're welcome to the magazines," Major Ruff said as he walked into the dining room and toward the kitchen.

It was near noon and I could smell dinner cooking. My mouth watered. My nostrils opened wide to take in the scent of the cooking food. My stomach turned over, aching from hunger and desire. I hadn't eaten a decent meal in over a week. My last food had been canned cheese and crackers at noon the day before.

Major Ruff had a discussion with someone in the kitchen. I couldn't understand what they discussed. I leafed through a magazine until Major Ruff passed through the room on his way back into the yard. He didn't acknowledge my presence when he passed. I followed him into the yard.

"Sir, I'm sorry we couldn't get here sooner."

"Ah, that's fine. As it turned out, we didn't need you." Ruff said. As we walked toward a small hut, I thought he was mighty calm considering his frantic calls for help during the night. He was acting as though he had passed a pleasant evening at the opera instead of fighting for his life.

"Well, sir, I need to get back to the Troop. I just wanted to drop by to see how y'all got through the night and if there was anything I could do for you," I said.

Ruff stopped and looked up into my eyes for a long moment. "You may be able to do us a favor. Charlie put a bullet through the can we used to keep oil for our generator. All the oil drained out. Could you ask your counterpart to give us four or five gallons of oil?" Ruff asked.

"I'll try, sir. I haven't been with the Troop long, and I haven't gotten to know my counterpart too well, but I'll ask," I replied.

I didn't want to ask Vinh for the oil. I had told Ruff the truth. I didn't consider myself to be on good enough terms with Vinh to ask him for a favor. But I was hungry. I rationalized that if I could get the oil, Ruff would invite me to eat lunch with his team. I headed for the Troop.

I found Vinh next to the command track. When I asked for the oil, Vinh looked at me in disgust. I could tell that he didn't want to part with the oil. After a few moments, he said that I could have a five-gallon can of oil. One of the troopers brought me the can of oil and I carried it back to the compound. I found Major Ruff and an NCO next to the small hut in the courtyard working over the generator.

Stopping next to Ruff I said, "Sir, I got the oil for you."

"Ah, thanks just set it there," he said pointing to a spot next to him.

He returned to his work. He didn't introduce the sergeant who never looked up from his work.

I set the oil where Ruff wanted it and went to the team house. I was going to hang around for my lunch invitation. From the sitting room, I saw that the table was set. They were having roast beef with mashed potatoes and green beans. The aroma in the house was heavenly. I looked through a few magazines, while I waited. When I became bored with the magazines, I roamed the room looking at the pictures on the wall. Next to the door, I noticed a small sign that stated the team's meal policy. The sign said there was a $1.25 per meal charge for guests. I didn't pay much attention to the sign. I considered it a CYA sign for the benefit of inspectors who might drop-in from higher headquarters. Officers were required to pay for their meals but no one in the field charged. Besides, my Troop had come to this team's rescue and I had scrounged the oil. Ruff owed me. He wouldn't ask me to pay. If he did, I'd tell him that I thought I had earned the meal and wouldn't pay.

I waited until Major Ruff and the sergeant came into the room. They didn't speak on their way to the dining room. I waited, but an invitation wasn't forthcoming. I was too proud to ask to join them. When it became evident that I wasn't going to be invited to eat, I became angry. I waited awhile longer in the hope that someone in the group would be neighborly enough to invite me in--they didn't. Finally, I left in a rage!

I may not have had good reason to be angry. The Troop had arrived late. It wasn't responsible for Charlie's withdrawal. The VC most probably would have withdrawn at dawn, regardless of the Troop's location. I felt, however, that an invitation was deserved if for no other reason than that I was a fellow American. I may not have gotten so angry if Major Ruff had invited me to eat and to pay. As it was, he had manipulated me.

Back at the Troop I found Maia and Lockett working with the troopers getting ready to move out. When we mounted up to move back to Cai Be, Maia joined me on the command track. I told him my story.

"Not very considerate of the son-of-a . . ."

"Yeah I agree," I interrupted.

"Any other team would have asked us to eat with them." Maia said.

"I hope you're right." I replied. "I'd hate to think that everyone is as sorry as that . . ."

"Naw they ain't."

"I'll tell you one thing, he needn't ask me for anything again. I wouldn't give him the sweat from my crotch if he were dying of thirst in the desert." I said. I was still hopping mad! I had missed lunch with the Troop. For once there were no leftovers. It'd be night before I could eat some rice.

CHAPTER SEVEN

IN THE PADDIES: NOVEMBER 1967

When on operation we roamed the paddies in search of an elusive phantom. Wisely, there was no pattern to when we charged into the fields. This precaution, however, didn't seem to hide the fact that we were not earnestly looking for Charlie. Whatever we tried, he stayed out of our way. As the days wore on, the paddies and the sun become more our enemies than Charlie. Each operation was a never-ending struggle against the mud, dikes, canals, and heat of the Delta.

On occasion, getting off the road and into the paddies was an exercise in futility. On my first day-long operation, we were given a mission north of the highway. When the first vehicle turned off the road, it slipped into a deep canal that bordered the road. The bank next to the road was sloped, allowing the track to slowly settle to the canal's bottom. The opposite bank was so steep the track couldn't climb out. The vehicle was trapped in the canal with water reaching to within a foot of its top. The driver could drive along the canal; but he couldn't turn or back out because of the track's construction. The front of the vehicle was designed so that the tracks could catch on a slope, log, or whatever and pull it up and over, provided the obstacle wasn't over two feet high. At the rear, the tracks were set too far forward to provide this feature. When the driver tried to back out of the canal, the back of the track dug into the bank before the tracks could catch and pull it out. The driver tried to turn the vehicle and drive out the way he entered but couldn't. When he tried to turn, the vehicle climbed partially up the canal's side and almost capsized.

The Troop sat on the road while the lead vehicle maneuvered to exit the canal. The trapped vehicle moved along the canal trying to negotiate the banks at several points without success. A second track was ordered into the canal to push the first vehicle up the opposite bank with a section of aluminum balk span. After several tries, the lead vehicle was pushed up the bank to an angle that almost caused it to capsize.

Now it couldn't move forward. A trooper jumped into the muddy water and dove several times to connect a tow cable to the front of the recovery vehicle and to the back of the stuck track. When attached, the recovery track pulled the other vehicle from the bank to a level position on the canal's bottom. Both carriers were now trapped.

Vinh gave up and sent his demolition expert into the canal to blow a hole in the canal's bank. Two small C-four charges were needed to prepare the bank. Two hours after the first vehicle entered the canal, a hole was blown in its wall and the Troop moved into the paddies.

I watched the exercise with curiosity and frustration. I wasn't asked for advice and I offered none. I was surprised that Vinh or someone in the Troop didn't know the condition of the bank at that location. The Troop had operated in this area for several years and should have known the location of each tree and the condition of every road and canal. If they didn't, Vinh should have sent a reconnaissance party to determine the best place to enter the paddies. In his defense, he would have needed a Navy frogman to determine the condition of the canal at the Troop's entry point. Because of the inundated paddies, their water level was even with the canals. From the road, it was impossible to see that the canal was there, much less that it presented an obstacle.

Once the Troop was off the road, the paddy battle was joined. The Troop moved through the paddies single file, in column formation, until it began its assault on the objective. The column was used to minimize damage to the paddies. The tracks badly rutted the fields as they moved through the mud.

The disadvantage with the column formation was that after two or three vehicles churned the mud; the vehicles following couldn't maintain enough traction to move forward. This situation was countered by forming a daisy chain, made by joining the tracks with tow cables. As new ground was broken, the leading vehicles provided sufficient pull to keep the formation moving.

When the column came to a canal that the lead vehicle couldn't negotiate, the following track commander placed a length of bulk span (varying lengths of eight by twelve inch bridging sections) between the two tracks and pushed the leader through the canal. Once the lead vehicle was through the obstacle, its crew attached a tow cable to the following vehicle and pulled it through. When these two vehicles were through the canal, the other vehicle crews attached cables to the track to their front. The two lead tracks then pulled the others through the canal. Each track added its power to the chain when it cleared the obstacle.

The dikes were small obstacles to maneuver; however, they did impede speed. The column sped across a paddy only to stop before crossing over its dike. Each time a track crossed over a dike and dropped off, the crews insides were jarred. After bounding over ten or twelve dikes, my tailbone became so sore that I could hardly sit on my converted jeep seat. My spine took a horrible beating. I may not have been trudging the muddy paddies but I had my cross to bear.

The paddies, dikes, and canals offered challenges whose solutions stretched the imagination. The sun, however, was my worst enemy.

It sapped my energy and caused headaches that almost incapacitated me. By mid-afternoon I thought that my head would blow apart. Each time we dropped off a dike, my head exploded. I tried several types of headgear to reflect the sun. On the first few operations, I wore my steel helmet, whose weight I thought was the cause of the headaches, so, I put a water-soaked sponge in the webbing of my helmet liner. No relief. I wore only my beret. No relief. I used an Australian bust hat. No relief. I tried an Army baseball cap. No relief. Finally, after a few weeks, my hair grew out from its flattop cut, and the headaches stopped. I may have been going through a period of acclimatization, and once my body adjusted the headaches stopped. Though I didn't pretend to be a Samson, I credited the cure to the length of my hair. It's just that I could rationalize with the best of 'em. I thought my hair formed an insulation that relieved the sun's effects. After the headaches stopped, I adopted the beret as my operational head gear except on a few occasions.

Our missions were to search the various small hamlets located within the thin belts of jungle bordering the canals. These searches were fruitless; we found no arms caches or VC base camps. The terrain and our tactics gave Charlie the advantage he needed to melt away. The terrain afforded Charlie good observation of our approach. There was insufficient concealment to maneuver a large unit, particularly an armored cavalry Troop, through the paddies undetected. The only concealment was the hedgerows. These tree-lined dikes were separated by 200 to 400 meters.

Charlie dug his observation posts into their banks and watched the open paddies. When we broke through an adjacent hedgerow, the observer could exit his bunker, run along the dikes to his hamlet, and give the alarm.

The outposts had enough time to make their run because we moved slowly. We moved at the speed of the infantry who walked the dikes or waded the paddies. The ARVN infantry, laden with forty to fifty pounds of gear, was no match for Charlie who ran with, at most, a rifle in his hand. We were further slowed by the dikes and canals. It wasn't unusual for our infantry to out-distance us when we slowed to cross a dike or ford a deep canal. Surprise was lost. Simply, if Charlie didn't want to fight on a given day, he just moved out of our path. The monotony of these operations was broken only when we fired at pajama-clad figures we thought were withdrawing sentries.

Though we didn't set a time pattern with our operations, once we entered the paddies, our tactics were simple and standard. Generally, we operated within the structure of a combined arms task force of cavalry and one or two infantry units. We broke this organization once, when we hit the mine on my first operation. Regardless of how we were organized, we moved directly to the objective in column formation and then moved into a line formation for the final assault. We neither planned for nor used artillery support. The exception was if we received fire. Then we could request artillery.

Since most hamlets were located on the banks of a wide canal too wide and too deep for the tracks to cross, Charlie could easily escape when the alarm was given. We didn't place blocking positions along the canals to prevent him from sampaning away. Nor did we place a friendly unit across the canal to block him from crossing to the other bank. I'm sure that Charlie watched us many times from across the canal, while we searched his village.

After the troopers searched the objective, we ate, took a siesta, and break a fundamental rule, returned to the road the way we came. We shouldn't have used the same route out as we used going in; we were lucky that we weren't ambushed on our exit. We never were hit, however, returning to the road. Maybe this was because we always seemed to return to the road in a quarter of the time it took us to get to the objective. Though ARVN's sluggishness in getting to an objective frustrated me. I was fascinated by his ability to hit the after-burners returning to the road. Maybe our speed could be attributed to moving over familiar terrain. I think, however, it was that the ARVN wanted to get out of Charlie's domain and to the rice bowl.

During the first few weeks, I gave no advice about how to conduct our raids in the sun because I wasn't asked for advice. And, it took a few operations for me to realize that we weren't getting results because we were operating like amateurs. Also, I was the new kid on the block. I was inexperienced. Vinh had been at this for several years. Who was I to tell him how to fight his war when I hadn't truly been blooded?

In Vinh's defense, there wasn't much he could have done differently. The Troop worked under the direction of an infantry battalion commander whose staff planned and controlled each operation. Vinh had to deploy as directed. If the battalion commander hadn't planned to encircle an objective, there wasn't much Vinh could do.

After the Cai Lay rescue, the Troop began to search out Charlie with more zeal. We roamed the paddies three or four days a week, with better luck in finding small elements of VC. Mostly, we saw only fleeing targets, which the Troop might or might not engage, but that was better than seeing nothing. Occasionally, the attached infantry would catch Charlie in the trees and ask me to request artillery support.

The first time I was asked to call for artillery, I couldn't remember the correct request sequence. I hadn't adjusted artillery in over two years. A surge of frustration and fear swept over me. I couldn't show my lack of professionalism or let ARVN down. After a few moments, I thought to myself, *Screw it, I'll have to try. I think I remember the request elements. I'll let the artillery straighten out the finer points of getting the elements in their correct order.*

"Romeo Bravo Two-one, this is Charlie One-six, fire mission, over," I called.

"Charlie One-six, this is Romeo Bravo Two-one, send it, over," the artillery FDC (fire direction center) answered.

"Roger, Two-one. Coordinates zero one two, ahhh four five niner. Troops dug in at tree line. Azimuth two four zero, estimated. Will adjust," I called.

"Roger, One-six," the FDC answered.

"Troops dug-in. Coordinates zero one two four five niner. Azimuth two four zero estimated. Wait, the FDC called back with the request in its correct order."

I waited.

"Shot out, over." The FDC said after a minute.

"Roger, shot out," I replied.

"Surprisingly, the round fell about 100 meters to the left of the target."

I was pleased with myself. I had correctly supposed that the artillery could compensate for my ignorance. I called in the necessary adjustment. After two more adjusted rounds, I told the FDC to fire for effect, and five rounds came screaming in, landing with a muffled thud in the trees.

"Target, cease fire," I called. "Thanks for the support. If I get a damage report, I'll give you a call." The artillery liked to know if they hit what they shot at and if there were any casualties. They got a morale boost from knowing that they had contributed to the result of an engagement.

"Roger One-six, glad to be of help. Give us a call any time, Two-one, out."

In mid-November we began to be supported by an L-19 Bird Dog, a high-winged, single engine, fixed-landing gear, two-passenger aircraft used by artillery observers to direct artillery fire, or an OH-6, a helicopter that looked like a flying tadpole, used as a scout helicopter in support. These aircraft weren't continuously overhead. They provided convoy cover and supported several operations on the same day. If we gained contact with Charlie, we contacted the aircraft that was on call for support.

The infantry advisors carried PRC-25 (Prick-25) radios, a backpacked radio with a small whip antenna. This radio had a short transmitting distance. If our assigned observer wasn't in the immediate area, the infantry advisor had to call me and ask that I request the needed support. I had a VRC-53 radio in the track. The VRC-53, a souped up, vehicular-mounted version of the Prick-25, had more transmitting power because it used the vehicle's power and a larger antenna. My job was to relay the infantry's request for support and to guide the aircraft into the area. Once the aircraft was in the area of operation, I turned it over to the infantry for direct coordination. If for some reason the infantry couldn't establish contact with the aircraft, I continued to relay between the two. A prerequisite for aerial support was to establish where the friendly units were. We identified our positions by using colored smoke grenades. When the aircraft was overhead, the pilot would ask us to pop smoke. We threw any color we had and asked the pilot to identify the color. We didn't announce the smoke's color. Charlie monitored our radio frequencies and might overhear the color. If he did, he'd pop the same color smoke, causing confusion. After the pilot identified the proper colored smoke, he'd assist within his capabilities. We used this procedure to establish our lines and to identify pick-up points for medevacs, also referred to as "dust-offs."

In late November, our supporting infantry was fired on by Charlie several times, but the only casualties were heat-related. The infantry advisory teams had several replacements. Each new advisor lasted, at most, a half day in the paddies on his first two or three operations before being evacuated from exhaustion. A man had to be in excellent physical condition to walk the paddies all day. The mud created a suction that pulled against every step the infantryman took. After four hours of battling the heat and mud, a new man was finished. I felt sorry for them. It must have been embarrassing for a two hundred pound, six foot tall American to be walked into the ground, or the mud in this case, by a one hundred pound, five foot tall Vietnamese carrying fifty pounds or more of equipment. Each medevac supported my belief that the Army had failed its men by not properly conditioning them before sending them into combat. Luckily, I had been farsighted enough to become an armor officer. I didn't have to suffer the experience of walking the paddies.

I was frustrated with our inability to find Charlie. I was still innocent and didn't consider what would happen when we caught him: someone might be killed. It could be me. I didn't think in terms of casualties, but rather about mission accomplishment. While in Germany, I had practiced various combat missions so often that they had become a game. Whoever was on the hill when the game ended was the winner. No one got hurt. My thoughts could be likened to those of a football coach. It was my job to teach my team to move the ball down the field and score. The team must be aggressive and hit hard, but it needn't intentionally hurt anyone, merely move the opposition out of the way and win the game. I was frustrated because I wasn't coaching the team and, in my opinion, the team wasn't aggressively playing the game. I came to believe that the Troop was being sent where higher echelons knew it wouldn't find Charlie. I discussed my suspicions with Captain Woods and he shared them.

"We've been beating the paddies for days and haven't had a single contact," I told Captain Woods during one of his visits. "What do you think the problem is? Aren't we getting any intelligence about Charlie?"

"I'll tell you Cole, ARVN has an excellent intelligence system. They know where Charlie is," Woods said.

"Then why don't they go after him?" I asked.

"I think they have an understanding with each other not to fight. ARVN sees no need to fight when the 9th Division is doing it for them. They think they can wait and we'll win the whole thing for them. And Charlie has his hands full with the 9th. So, why fight ARVN if he doesn't have to?" Woods explained.

"You know, something else that bothers me . . ."

"What?"

"Even if we caught up with Charlie, all he has to do is swim a canal to get away. We need to establish blocking positions to trap him," I continued.

"You'll find that ARVN will never do that. He always leaves Charlie an out," Woods told me.

"What? Why?" I asked in amazement and disgust.

"Because it's too costly. If ARVN traps Charlie, Charlie will fight harder, which will cost ARVN too many casualties. So ARVN leaves Charlie an out," Woods replied.

"In other words, ARVN is only putting on a show."

"Right," Woods affirmed. "They want to do just enough to keep us happy, so that we'll continue our support."

My frustration wasn't so much from the way Vinh conducted operations or the simple things the Troops didn't do. I had graded enough Army training tests to know that it was easy to catch mistakes when there was no pressure on you and that all you had to do was watch. It was another thing to be in charge and responsible. It was difficult, if not impossible, to remember to do everything when there were a dozen things on your mind and you were reacting to the wishes of a commander and his staff who wanted more information and assigned new missions without consideration of your problems. I knew I'd make many of the same mistakes or omissions that Vinh made. Rather, I was frustrated because I had no input in solving the Troop's problems. I couldn't discuss the situation with Vinh for fear of insulting him. I didn't know what, if anything, Major Evans was doing about my reports. I felt useless!

While we sat on the road fighting the dust and flies, I thought more about how we could trap our elusive little friends. I had no point of reference. I didn't know what had been tried or what had failed. I may have been reinventing the wheel, but I had nothing better to do. It was clear to me that we had to establish blocking positions along escape routes from an objective and to capitalize on speed and surprise if we were to trap Charlie.

I toyed with ways to accomplish our mission. First, since even the infantry couldn't move during the day without being detected, we had to set the trap at night. Even at night a large unit—platoon or company—could be easily detected in the Delta. What we needed to do was move squads into blocking positions at night. The next day these squads could ambush the VC as they moved out of the Troop's path. But this solution was out of the question. The ARVN, to my knowledge, didn't move at night. And it'd have taken well trained, courageous troops to have pulled it off. It was scary to move at night in Charlie's country.

Another solution might have been to rappel squads or platoons from helicopters into the jungles along the canals as we approached an objective. Timing would be critical in this type operation. The problem with this solution was that rappelling wasn't in vogue at the time. I had heard of it being used only a few times and I didn't know the problems involved. For one thing, a hovering Huey is an easy target to hit. So much for that solution. A final possibly was to conduct an airmobile assault in conjunction with our advance. Timing and coordination were the key factors that would determine the success of this type operation.

During our rides through the paddies, we often stopped for siesta in one of the small hamlets sitting in the middle of the fields. As the days wore on, Vinh eventually invited me to join him in the local chief's hut for rice and siesta. The various huts were quite similar. They were one-room thatched structures with packed mud floors with little or no furnishings. In most homes, the only furniture was a large highly polished, mahogany bed. These beds were nothing more than eighteen inch high tables. There were no mattresses or cover on them. The other furnishings consisted of shelves to store food, pots and pans, and rolled bed pallets. The meals were prepared outside in the open, using a homemade mud oven, or over an open fire.

Our visits to the chiefs were short, and more political than friendly, I'm sure. We'd have a bowl of rice and a cup or two of unsweetened green tea. Vinh would chat with the old chief and I'd listen, not understanding a word. Occasionally, Vinh would bring me into the conversation by translating. But mostly, my part was to smile, to thank the old gentleman for the invitation to dine, to comment on the excellent rice and tea, to wish him good health, and a good harvest.

During one of our far-flung forays, the Troop stopped near a subsector team that I hadn't met. During siesta, I visited with the team. It was situated comfortably in a small team house, much like other team houses in the Delta. The senior officer present was Captain Smith, a slender, tall, blond, officer. His glasses accentuated his cool, penetrating eyes and gave him an intellectual demeanor. His appearance exuded self confidence.

After a short visit, I rejoined the Troop, which was to support a Ruff Puff operation that afternoon. After an uneventful ride in the paddies, the Troop headed back toward Cai Be. We again stopped by the team I had visited earlier. Captain Smith was stretched out on a couch reading *Street Without Joy*. Several other books, some half-open, lay on the coffee table and the floor. The titles I could make out dealt mostly with military and political issues concerning Indochina., with a few fiction books included.

"Catching up on the war?" I asked.

"Yeah, I find it interesting to gain other points of view," Smith answered.

"Why so many books at one time," I asked.

"When I get bored with one book, I quit and go to a new one. When I get tired of it, I go back to the first book or to a new one. I may be reading three or four books at any one time."

I thought that system strange. How could he keep the dialogue straight and remember what had been presented by skipping around so much?

"I can't read like that. I have to read a book straight through, so that I can keep the plot or points in order," I said. "I'd get all mixed up if I tried to read three books at once."

"I've gotten used to it. I don't like to get tied to any one subject for long."

"I see that you're reading quite a bit about the political issues of the war, I said, gesturing to his copy of *Street Without Joy*. "What do you think?"

"That we've no business being over here. This isn't our war; it's a civil war," Smith shot back.

I was taken aback. I had never heard a soldier, much less an officer, express any objection to our being in Vietnam. I wasn't well read on the issues. I had accepted our involvement out of faith and through confidence in our national leadership. I sensed that an argument in support of the domino theory wouldn't score any points with this fella. And certainly, the shallow attitude of "my country, right or wrong," wouldn't hold water and only supported my lack of an intellectual understanding of the issues. I kept my own counsel. I thought, if you don't believe in what we're doing over here, why are you here? But I knew the answer to that question. He was an officer; he had sworn and been trained to obey the orders and directives of those appointed over him; he'd do his duty. I had to respect him for that, Nuremberg notwithstanding, we were here to save a people, not to commit genocide.

I don't know when Captain Smith came to the conclusion that the United States shouldn't support the South Vietnam government; it may have been after he arrived in country, when he had time to study the war's background and the policies we were following. Who knows? Whatever his reasons, he was overlooking one important fact in so far as I was concerned: The VC were trying to overthrow a legitimate government whose creation had been agreed to by their supporters in North Vietnam. Now Charlie was using every means of terrorism to systemically murder every legal representative of the South Vietnamese. I thought of the many news stories I had read or heard about Viet Cong mutilations of officials and members of their families. One particular story swept into my mind of a pregnant woman who had been killed in front of her husband and the unborn fetus cut out of her to die on the floor. Another was the story of an official who was disemboweled in front of his family and left to die. How quickly we forget when the going gets rough. I broke off the conversation, uncomfortable in Smith's presence. I returned to the Troop, shaken by the fact that not everyone supported our policies, particularly an Army officer.

After each operation, I made a few notes about my observations for inclusion in my weekly report to Maj. Evans. My comments, for the most part, covered basic items. Mostly, we sat on the road. I wanted to put the infantry on the highway and let the Troop conduct continuous patrolling. Of course, one or two tracks in the paddies would have been easy prey for Charlie. I didn't think of that. I was concentrating on how to find him. That's what the Cav and scouts get paid for—to get shot at and to find the enemy.

I recommended we use Chinooks with sling-loaded AVLBs to support our operations. The idea was for the Chinooks to move ahead and drop the AVLBs over canals so we could cross faster. That wouldn't work. A Chinook was too valuable and too large a target to be out front. I reported on how operations were conducted. We'd sit at the LD) for an hour or more before moving. We'd sit in front of the objective for up to an hour before moving onto or into it. I didn't like the way we approached villages or the way we searched them. I thought we should approach on two axis and surround a village before we searched it. I wanted the troopers to dismount more. They were tied to the tracks. I recommended we use Rangers to set blocking positions in an area of operations for us to push Charlie into. I didn't know what Evans did with the reports, but writing them helped pass the time.

CHAPTER EIGHT

RANGING OUT: NOVEMBER 1967

As time passed, I became less apprehensive when the Troop was back on the road; so I began to range out. My first adventure from the daily monotony came a few days after the Lay Cai chase when the headquarters section stopped at Papa Two-zero. Sergeant Maia suggested that since it was only three klicks into Cai Be that we go in to town to a cafe he knew of for lunch. I hadn't eaten anything other than rice for days, so Maia's recommendation sounded great. I asked Vinh if the Troop was going to do anything other than road security for the remainder of the day. When he said no, we left the searchlight crewmen sacked out and headed for town.

"This place doesn't look like much, but the food is good," Maia said as we drove into town.

"What do they serve?" I asked.

"A variety of Vietnamese food, but I'd stay with the pork or shrimp." Maia advised.

"I always have fried pork and French fries," chimed in Sergeant Lockett.

The cafe was located on the bank of the Mekong River. It was located in a small thatched hut with a dirt floor. The dining room was large enough to hold four tables. We had an excellent view of the river traffic and the market place's public latrine which hung over the river. I noted we were downstream from the latrine.

"The last time we were in Cai Be, the Squadron decided to try to swim one of the tracks across the river. We put it in next to the latrine," said Sergeant Maia.

"What happened?" I asked.

"It went straight to the bottom," Maia replied.

"What did y'all do during the recovery?"

"Stayed out of the way and watched. There were too many chiefs giving advice as it was," said Maia.

"You mean you didn't take the opportunity to go swimming?" I asked facetiously.

"Uh uh! I wasn't getting in that cesspool," said Maia.

We enjoyed a good meal of fried pork and fried potatoes, then we went to the marketplace to look around. The market plaza, actually a street, was filled from one side to the other with people moving about, shoulder to shoulder. We had to push our way through the crowd to visit the various shops. The shops (to the side of the street) and the stands (located randomly in the street) were well stocked with produce, fish, live and dressed chickens and geese, and fly-covered sides of butchered beef. There was also a good supply of consumer goods. My only purchases were an Australian bush hat I wanted to try to get some relief from the sun, and a pillow. On our way out of town, we stopped by to say hello to Sergeant Rodriguez and his team. We were back with the Troop by the end of siesta.

This was the first of many enjoyable visits to the little cafe in Cai Be. Before we left the area some sixty-five days later, the team would have lunch there at least once a week. Our visits became so relaxed that by the time we moved on to Long Dinh, I didn't even carry a weapon when we went to lunch.

Major Evans had a policy that allowed each advisor in the field to return to My Tho for three days of each month for a shower, hair cut, and to have our laundry done. In early November, I sent in a request by the Squadron's courier asking for my three days. I needed a good meal. Most of all I needed a break from the boredom of the road.

The next Squadron courier returned my approved request. The next day, I caught an early morning helicopter flight out of Cai Be. Sergeant Rodriguez called My Tho by radio relay to arrange my pick-up at the airstrip. Major Evans was waiting as the Huey settled gently onto the helipad. He drove me to the new Armor House where I dropped off my laundry with Chin, our house boy. Then we drove to the 6th Squadron's Compound where Evans was dropped off. He let his driver take me on to the Seminary for a shower, as the water wasn't on at Armor House.

Though it was late morning, there were several men in the shower. The shower's continuous use, I learned, wasn't uncommon because of the different schedules of the advisors. A conversation among my fellow bathers centered on the death of a sergeant the day before. He had been an advisor with one of the infantry battalions on operation near Go Cong, east of My Tho. The advisor had been trudging through the paddies when his unit had received mortar fire. The sergeant dove to a prone position when the mortar rounds began to fall. He must have buried his face in the mud, causing his steel helmet to move forward on his head. The helmet's forward movement left the back of his neck unprotected. He was hit by a small piece of shrapnel from an exploding round that fell near him. The wound at the base of his skull was no larger than a fingernail. The missile, however, had entered at an angle that took it into the brain. The advisor was killed instantly. A feeling of deep depression swept over me while I listened to the story. The sergeant's death had been so sudden. I could imagine him sloshing through the paddies, wiping the sweat from his eyes and fighting the mud and his wet fatigues to keep up with the ARVN. He was probably thinking more about his sweating, aching back; his aching leg muscles; and his throbbing, water-soaked feet than the possibility of a mortar attack.

He had done all he could to protect himself. He wore his helmet and probably his flak jacket; yet he had been killed by a small piece of metal that would have caused no more than a scratch had it hit any other part on his body. He had been killed by an unseen enemy without the opportunity to defend himself. What a tragedy. But what was more depressing or frightening was the realization that death could result from small, lightning-quick encounters without warning. Large set piece battles were unnecessary. I shook off the feeling quickly. I couldn't allow myself to become depressed or to think about being killed. If I allowed myself to do so, I would not be able to do my job when the bullets began to fly.

That afternoon I stopped by the PX to pick-up a Seiko watch and another tape recorder. I needed a watch and decided I might as well buy a Seiko to join the chic soldiers wearing the latest Japanese fad. I wanted a second tape recorder to mail home. My wife couldn't find one that would play the tapes I was sending home.

The remainder of the day was spent visiting with Mark Arthur. I told him about our shortage of C-rations and my diet. He told me that I could get condemned C-rations from the ration break-down point at Dong Tam.

"I pick up C's for my team over there just before we go to Cai Be. The vet condemns anything in a bent can or that is outdated," Arthur told me.

"If you go by the vet's office and ask, he'll even condemn a few steaks for you. They feel sorry for us", Arthur added.

The vet was the Army veterinarian. In the Army, the vet is responsible for inspecting food products to insure that they are safe to eat. Sometimes the vets are overly cautious and condemn food just to be on the safe side. I learned in Germany that the expiration dates on C-ration cases allowed for a wide safety margin. My family and I had toured Austria and Italy eating out-dated C's without any ill effects. Therefore, I had no qualms about using condemned rations, so long as the seals on the cans weren't broken.

"The next time I'm in town with my jeep and trailer I'll go over and check it out," I told Arthur.

That evening Major Evans invited me to join him at the Seminary's Officer's Club for an evening of social activity. While we mixing with various officers, Major Evans introduced me to Captains Watts, one of Team 75's L-19 aerial observers. During our talk, I learned that Captain Watts would fly cover the next day for a Saigon-bound convoy. I didn't have anything special planned for the next day, and I enjoyed flying. So, I asked if I could hitch a ride. Both Major Evans and Watts agreed that I could tag along.

"Meet me at breakfast around seven and we'll drive out to the airstrip together," Watts instructed.

"What's the rest of the schedule?" I asked.

"We'll take off around 8:30 and pick-up the convoy around 9:00.

We should be in Saigon by 11:00, he answered. "We can hit the steam bath, so you might bring a change of uniform, and head back around 1:30 or 2:00. We could be back by 5:00."

"Great, I'll see you at breakfast," I said as Major Evans and I stood to leave.

The next morning I met Captain Watts as agreed. After breakfast, a duty driver drove us to the airfield. Watts pre-flighted the L-19 and we were airborne by 8:30. Watts flew lazy circles (boring holes) over the highway waiting for the convoy to begin its roll toward Saigon.

"What's the procedure?" I asked after we had gained altitude.

"We just sit up here and look for anything suspicious. Keep an eye on the tree lines. If the convoy gets hit, we try to locate the ambush or mortars; and we look for sections of the road that might be mined. I'm going to make a quick run up to Saigon first and double back to check for mines and road blocks." Watts answered.

This was my first clear, panoramic view of the Delta from the air. I was awestruck by its calm beauty. Its rice paddies interfaced with serpentine, tree-lined canals stretched from horizon to horizon. To the far northwest, I could make out the edge of the vast Plain of Reeds. A few farmers worked the reflective paddies with their wooden blades and buffaloes, such a peaceful scene to be so deadly. The only evidence of war was the blown bridge at Tan An over the Vam Co Tay River.

The flight was uneventful. I passed the time listening to the never-ending banter between Watts and the convoy's advisor and watching the traffic and tree lines. Captain Watts fed the convoy a continuous stream of information about traffic, road conditions, and danger points. Occasionally, he let me take the controls to try my hand at keeping the plane straight and level or to make a slow, wide turn. It was an enjoyable morning.

A duty driver met us on the parking ramp after landing at Tan Son Nhut. The driver drove us by a snack bar where we had a quick lunch and then to the base steam bath.

What is it about the Air Force and pilots in general, I wondered, as I viewed the large complex of revetments, hangers, and buildings. They have the best of everything. They never get dirty, yet they have a steam bath. They have the best quarters and the best facilities. They don't have assigned vehicles but they never walk. Boy, I got in the wrong business.

What a delight! The steam bath opened every pore in my body. The steam was so thick that I could hardly see the other officers in the room. It was difficult to breathe. The air was hot and heavy with moisture. While I lay on the middle tier of benches lining the walls, I could feel the frustrations of the past weeks gradually disappear. How easy it was to forget the boredom of the road and let my mind drift to thoughts of home, the wife, the kids, and the future. I had been separated from the world for just over a month; Hawaii and a reunion with my wife filled my mind. After thirty minutes in the steam, a cold shower brought me back to earth.

The afternoon flight back was direct. We didn't have a convoy to cover.

"Do you receive much ground fire on these missions'?" I asked as we winged back toward My Tho.

"Yeah, quite a bit."

"Have you ever been hit?" I asked.

"Yeah, three times," Watts answered.

"Where did you get hit?"

"Through the bottom of the fuselage. Actually, the last guy to ride back there got a round in the butt," Watts said.

"Gee, thanks!"

"Yeah, don't worry. We've put steel plates on the bottom of the seats. They'll stop anything Charlie has." Watts said chuckling into the mic.

"That's all well and good, but what about my legs and feet?" I asked jokingly.

"You can't have everything. War is hell isn't it?" He laughed.

I shifted in the seat and watched the ground more closely. I don't know why I looked so hard. I couldn't get out of the way if Charlie shot at us. I was strapped in and would have to take what came. I felt like the biggest target in creation.

Near My Tho, Captain Watts asked: "Are you in a hurry in get back to the Seminary?"

"No, not particularly."

"Good, Oscar-one (one of the other L-19s) needs to be relieved to refuel. He's down near Cai Be boring holes in the sky, but he doesn't want to leave the area uncovered. We've got a battalion in the paddles. I thought we could relieve him." Watts said.

"Fine with me, I don't have anything better to do."

Watts switched the radio to a channel that allowed him to talk with Oscar-one without my hearing what was said. He coordinated the relief and hit the throttle. Shortly, we slowed and began to bore lazy holes in the sky. It wasn't long before Captain

Watts spotted a sampan creeping down a small canal toward the Mekong.

"It looks like we've got something," Watts said. "Did you see that sampan?"

"No, I missed it."

"There shouldn't be anyone out here," Watts said. "It's probably Charlie."

Watts circled the plane back over the canal. On this pass, I saw the long gray sampan clearly in the canal's brown water. There was one man poling it along. In its rear was a covered bundle.

"Yeah, I bet that's a Cong. I'm going to ask Division for permission to fire on him." Watts said as he switched the radio from intercom to a transmitting channel.

I had forgotten that the L-19s carried 2.5 rockets to use as spotter rounds for the fast movers (Air Force jets). I hadn't noticed the rockets under the wings until now. I looked out to see what Watts was going to throw at the helpless transient. Two long slender brown tubes with black fins hung under each wing.

"Division said it was okay to fire away, so here goes," Watts said over the intercom.

Without further warning, the wing I was looking at suddenly rose skyward. All I could see was the wing tip and blue sky. My left shoulder fell against the side of the plane's fuselage, while my stomach continued to travel up and to the right. When I jerked my head to the left, I saw the plane's left wing tip pointing to the ground, trees and water. Then I fell forward against the seat's shoulder harness as Watts nosed the plane down. The outside rockets on each wing blasted away followed by thin white lines of smoke. They were headed directly for the sampan that was visible over Watts' shoulder. My head was pushed back against the bulkhead as Watts brought the plane's nose up. The view through the propeller changed from paddies, trees, and water to blue sky as the nose came up. Watts eased the L-19 over to the right and leveled off. What an exciting feeling and I didn't throw-up! Let's go again!

"Damn, I missed," he said as we circled over the canal. "Well, that's to be expected. This thing wasn't designed to hit point targets. Let's spend the other two rounds. If we miss, we'll go home."

"Fine," I replied.

This time Watts didn't roll in. Rather, he made a shallow run down the canal toward the sampan. Again, the rockets roared earthward. It was the Cong's day. We missed.

On the way back to My Tho, my heart was jumping out of my chest. I had never experienced anything so exciting. I was sure that the roll in hadn't been as exaggerated as it felt. The L-19 wasn't designed for aerobatics, but it had been all I could have wanted. I was especially pleased that I hadn't gotten sick. Gosh, I wished I had tried to go to flight school. But, alas, it was my function to be and remain a "tread-head"(Tanker/Armor Officer).

Back on the road, the frequency of operations and our operating radius increased. Shortly after my return from Saigon, the Troop was ordered into Kien Hoa Province to support a one day operation near Ben Tri. This operation gave the Troop an opportunity to fulfill the true role of armor, that of mobility. Ben Tri was south of My Tho and over thirty kilometers from Cai Be. We would have to disengage, move a long distance, and go into action; the type of operation that brings joy to the heart of any tanker or cavalryman.

We left the Cai Be area during the early morning, drove to My Tho where we dropped off the searchlight crews, and crossed the Mekong River by ferry. From the ferry's loading site, we could see a beautiful temple sitting on the tip of an inland in the center of the river. The temple was silently imposing with its white columns and red tile roof. As we passed the island's tip the monks rang the temple's gong. It had a deep muffled tone. The gentle sway of the ferry, the smell of the fresh water, and the gong's deep sound imposed a feeling of serenity in an environment of turmoil.

We were in Ben Tri by mid-morning. It was exciting to move rapidly to another AO and to see a new part of the country. At Ben Tri, we stopped for a short time to coordinate with the district chief before joining the ARVN Battalion we were to support. We stopped next to a small lake or reservoir near the center of the city. A picturesque open-air, red column, white roof gazebo connected to the shore by a footbridge, set in the lake near the far shore. It was a graceful, harmonious scene that I enjoyed to the fullest while Vinh was with the district chief.

The operation turned out to be nothing more than another ride in the sun. It was unusually hot. We stayed on the move, jumping from one location to the next throughout the day. We even took our siesta in the middle of the paddies rather than dismounted in a tree line. The ARVN infantry received some scattered sniper fire but nothing serious. Charlie didn't want to fight. We stayed in the paddies later than usual. It was almost dark when we headed back into Ben Tri. It had been a tiring day; the sun had sucked nearly all my energy.

Vinh was ordered to remain in Ben Tri over night. The Troop parked next to the small lake that I had admired that morning. After the Troop was settled in, Maia, Lockett, and I decide to go for a swim in the lake. We were covered with sweat and dirt from the long day's ride and search. We went into the water fully dressed. Unfortunately, I didn't get to enjoy the cool water for long. My head was still under water from my initial jump when I realized that I had not removed my new watch. The inscription on the back said that the watch was waterproof but I didn't believe it. I had had too many waterproof watches go bad after wearing them in the shower. So, I came out of the water almost as fast as I went in. I lost my desire for a swim after drying the watch. It had cost over fifty dollars, which was a lot of money to me. I was worried that I had ruined the watch after only a few weeks' use. Fortunately, it never missed a tick for the next seven years.

The next morning Vinh told me that we were returning to My Tho. We would spend the rest of the day there and remain over night before going back to Cai Be. I was overjoyed. I would have an opportunity to go to Dong Tam and scrounge some C-rations.

The Troop arrived in My Tho at mid-morning and went directly to the Troop compound to perform after-operations maintenance and to stand-down. Some of the troopers hadn't seen their family in over a month. A break was needed. Sergeant Maia, Sergeant Lockett, and I stayed with the Troop until siesta; then we went to Armor House to meet the other advisors for lunch. At lunch Major Evans told me that he was going to keep Sergeant Maia in My Tho. Maia was scheduled to rotate in mid November, so he needed to begin his out-processing. Also, Major Evans introduced Staff Sergeant Long, who would be Sergeant Maia's replacement. Long needed to complete his in-processing. He'd join us on the road in a few days. The disappointing news was that the Troop was going to stay in Cai Be for another month rather than moving to Long Dinh (P-16) as scheduled. After lunch, Sergeant Lockett and I took the jeep and headed for Dong Tam.

We had no problem finding the ration breakdown point. It was located in a large warehouse on the north side of the base camp. When we stopped the jeep I noticed a tall, gaunt, red headed E-6 (staff sergeant) walking out of the warehouse.

I greed him with my most friendly, "Howdy Sarge."

"Yes, sir, can I help you?"

"I hope so," I replied, "I've been told that there is a possibility that I can get some condemned Cs here.

"Ah, yes sir," he replied with a big smile. "I see by your berets that y'all are advisors. On my last tour I was with Special Forces up in the Highlands. We were with the Montagnards. I know what it is like to try to live off their food."

"Yeah, it's rough. I've darn near starved the past few months," I said with my most haggard, hound dog look.

"Just help yourself," he said motioning over his shoulder toward the warehouse. You can have anything in a bent can. The B's (Class B rations in large cans that are issued to mess hall) are in the warehouse. The condemned Cs are out back."

The sergeant walked away, leaving Lockett and me to our own devices. Talk about letting the fox in the hen house, we were in hog heaven as we explored the warehouse. Fortunately for the Army and the 9th Division, we didn't have a trailer to carry more rations. We walked through the warehouse to get an idea of what was available. We were amazed at the number of bent cans.

"Boy, I wish we had brought the trailer, we could make out like fat cats," I told Lockett.

"Yeah, the next time we're in My Tho we'll have to get back over here and stock up, " Lockett replied.

We didn't take any B-rations. We went out back and filled the back of the jeep with C's and headed back to My Tho by way of a tailor shop and the MARS station. MARS stations were short wave radio stations manned by Army communications personnel. A MARS operator in Nam would contact a MARS operator in the States who would in turn patch the call into the long distance telephone system. This system allowed soldiers to call home for the cost of a long distance telephone call within the States—a great morale program.

I wanted to price a set of TWs, a khaki-colored tropical worsted uniform, at the tailor shop. I would need a new uniform to wear on R & R in Hawaii. It would cost $32. I ordered the uniform and paid the tailor half his price. When the tailor measured my waist, he told me it was thirty-two inches. I had lost four inches in just over a month.

At the MARS station, Lockett and I checked on the procedure for placing a call to the States. We were told there was a two-hour waiting list and that the best time to call was early in the morning. We couldn't wait two hours. It was getting late and we wanted to get to My Tho before dark, so we headed for Armor House with our bounty of canned food.

That evening Major Evans and Captain Arthur introduced my team to the My Ngoc Bar, located a block from the Armor House on Pasteur Street. Major Evans had christened it, "The Armor Bar." It was a small lounge with two booths and two tables. There was no bar; beverages were kept in a back room. The customary ladies of the evening served our drinks and sat quietly at our side while we discussed issues of common interest. Strangely, the ladies did not follow the common custom of encouraging us to order drinks; probably because they could not speak English and because they were inexperienced. The My Ngoc was off the beaten path and didn't attract the more experienced "daughters of joy."

The sergeants sat at tables next to the front window and discussed "sergeant's business." The officers set at booths along the back wall. Major Evans was more relaxed and less businesslike than during our earlier social gatherings. Therefore, the evening gave me an opportunity to get to know him on a personal basis. He didn't fit my image of the typical cavalry officer. His intellectual manner of speaking and his round face set atop a slightly overweight six foot frame placed him more in the mold of a college professor than a hard-riding, hard-fighting cavalryman. His only outward signs of a true professional were his neatly pressed uniform and highly shined tanker boots (high topped boots fastened by leather strips rather than boot-laces). It didn't take long, however, to realize that he possessed all the attributes of a competitive cavalryman. He had a boyish pride in being a cavalryman, and an intense desire for his team to be the best and to have the best.

During our conversation, Evans mentioned that he had served two years as an exchange officer with a Scottish cavalry unit in England.

"What was it like serving with the Brits?" I asked Evans.

"Great, it was the best assignment I've had."

"I understand the Brits are more relaxed about things than we are," interrupted Arthur.

"Oh yeah, they are. Their sergeants run the daily routine. The officers don't even come in until 9:00 or 10:00 in the morning," Evans answered.

"What do the officers do?" I asked.

"They're the planners and decision makers. They tell the sergeants what they want and the sergeants get it done."

"That must be nice. How do they supervise?" Arthur said.

"They spot check, but they don't look over the sergeant's shoulder like we do," replied Evans.

"I recommended that approach once when I was in Germany." I said. "You would've thought I had committed heresy."

"How is that?" asked Evans.

"It was when I was a second lieutenant, tank platoon leader, my first platoon. I was in a conversation with the battalion commander and a couple of other officers at a battalion party. We were discussing the problems lieutenants had in getting everything done. "You know, the hassle of doin' our admin work plus havin' to be in the motor pool with the troops when they were there. I suggested that we let the sergeants run the motor pool and let the lieutenants do their admin work in the company area. The CO looked at me like I was some kinda fool," I said.

"I'm not surprised, Evans said. "We're hung up on Bruce C. Clark's idea that a unit does well only those things the commander checks."

"I agree with that," I replied. "But we need a division of responsibility."

"Yeah, but the officer is responsible for everything his unit does or fails to do," Arthur said.

"I know, I know," I replied. "I didn't mean to suggest that we be relieved of overall responsibility. What I'm saying is that we should be able to hold our sergeants' feet to the fire for jobs we give them and they fail to do."

"Yeah, I know what you mean," Arthur said. "If my platoon's maintenance was bad, I caught hell. I was in constant fear that a sergeant's poor performance would reflect on my efficiency report. I couldn't say I assigned that job to the platoon sergeant."

"Yeah," I interrupted. "And you can't give him a bad report."

"Why not?" asked Major Evans.

"Because you catch hell from the sergeant that you were ruinin' his career and that you didn't let him do his job the way he knows best. When the CO sees the report, he raises cain. The Sarge is experienced and knows his job. He says. 'If you had demonstrated good leadership, you wouldn't have had a problem.' It is easier to write the sergeant a decent report and hope that the CO won't be too hard on you when he writes yours."

"Agreed," said Arthur.

"Now come on," said Evans. "All you have to do is keep the man at a given job until it is done to your satisfaction."

"I would like to think so, but that isn't as easy as it sounds," Arthur replied.

"Yeah, when it is time to quit, it's time to quit. You have to go through a lotta explaining if you want to work the troops overtime," I said. "You might pull their passes, but they know how to get out of the area without getting caught."

"Look, I don't mean to say that all NCOs are bad; they're not. Most are real good. My second platoon sergeant and my second senior drill sergeant at Fort Polk were great NCOs. I'm just saying that when they don't perform, we should have some recourse," I continued.

"All you have to do is write a counseling statement when someone doesn't perform to your satisfaction. After a couple of those, you can prefer charges and have him reduced for inefficiency," Evans said.

"That sound simple and easy," I answered. "But that takes a lot a time."

"If you don't know the system and work it the way it is designed, you have no complaint," said Evans.

"Yeah, I guess you're right," I said. "Anyway that second platoon sergeant I talked about looked after me."

"How was that?" asked Arthur.

"About the second or third time I went to the track park," I replied, "He met me at the entrance and said, 'Lieutenant, why don't you go back to the company area and find something to do. I'll take care of the platoon while we are in garrison. You can run it in the field.' I said, 'that is fine with me but you know I'm expected to be with the platoon".

"Yes, sir," he replied. But this is my job; you're in the way. I'll cover for you, if I need help getting parts or somethin', I'll come get you.' I said, fine and did an about face and left. I never went back to the track park while he was with me and we never had a deadlined track until after he left."

"What was your relationship in the field?" Evans asked.

"I was the boss. He never questioned any order I gave, and he supported me to the max," I answered.

"Sounds like a good man," Evans said.

"He was. His only problem was that he refused to give a class (formal instruction)," I answered.

"Anyway, what was a day like with the British?" Arthur asked Major Evans.

"Well, we arrived at the regiment during mid-morning after the house keeping details were completed. We had a regimental officer's call to coordinate activities over tea. After the meeting we coordinated with the NCOs to see how things were going and, if needed, to supplement their instructions. After lunch, we went horseback riding or studied military history or other military subjects," Evans answered.

"Sounds like a good system," I said.

"It was. I enjoyed myself, and I learned a lot," Evans agreed.

"You know, I met an English major once. I was ready impressed with him," I said.

"When was that?" asked Arthur.

"In Germany, on my first field problem. My platoon was going down one of those small backcountry roads that were nothing more than two ruts. My tank threw a track and was holding up the column. My platoon sergeant, a drunk, and my crew were trying to jump the track back on. I was standing back watching; I didn't know squat about getting the track back on. I looked down the line of tanks and saw this officer in a brown, turtleneck sweater, and beret walking slowly toward me. He was cordial to everyone as he passed them, smiling and having a friendly greeting at each tank. It was a cold day and we were all in parkas and gloves and still freezing but not this fella. He was dressed as if he were out for his morning stroll in early spring. When he got to my track, he stopped and looked closely at the track and then down the road. He then looked up at me with a sympathetic look and a smile then said, 'Embarrassing, wot?' Without waiting for a reply, he walked back down the line.

"He was right, I was embarrassed. I hated being caught short by one of our allies. I was impressed with how calm he was. If that had been an American major or colonel, I would have been asked a thousand questions about how the track was thrown, what I was doing about getting it back on, and how long I would be. I was glad he didn't ask any of those questions because I didn't know the answers."

We left the club last and walked back the short distance to Armor House. We were a happy relaxed group and the war seemed not to exist. The next morning the Troop headed back to Cai Be.

That evening we broke out a case of the newly scrounged C-rations and borrowed Sergeant Maia's stove from Tom, one of the Troop mechanics and mixed up a "Tanker's stew." We selected several different cans of meats from the C-rations and mixed them together in one of our steel helmets. We heated the concoction over the stove and by dark we dished up the best meal I had had in Vietnam, including mess hall meals at the Seminary. I had broken the code. I wasn't going to be hungry again during this tour.

CHAPTER NINE

THANKSGIVING: NOVEMBER 1967

Sergeant Maia's departure added further to my comfort. I had arranged comfortable sleeping accommodations in the jeep and was eating well. Now I gained a batsman. As I mentioned, Tom had turned up with Sergeant Maia's one-burner gasoline-burning stove. Now every morning, I awoke to the smiling face of Tom sitting on his haunches next to the jeep with his stove heating water so that I'd have hot water to shave with and to brew my instant coffee, I gave him the remains of my C-ration accessory packet in payment for his efforts. The packet contained cigarettes, coffee, cream substitute, sugar, salt, chewing gum, matches, and toilet paper. I never asked what Tom did with the accessories. I assumed that he sold them to the villagers. If that were the case, it served to illustrate how deprived the locals were of what we considered the necessities of life.

The routine returned to normal. We alternated our days on the road and in the paddies. When near Cai Be, the team's visits to the city became more frequent. The advisors went in to visit with Sergeant Rodriguez's team and to eat at our favorite cafe on one day and the searchlight crewmen would go in the next day.

During one of Lockett's and my visits, before Sergeant Long joined us, we decided to walk into town from the Cai Be team house. As we strolled along talking about nothing particular, we passed a partly destroyed building that had once been a school.

"Now that's a shame," I said nodding toward the school.

"How is that?" asked Lockett.

"The future of this country depends on the kids. It will never progress if they don't educate their kids," I replied.

"Yeah, I wonder how many kids were killed when the VC hit the place," Lockett added.

"Who knows, but why fight school kids? They can't defend themselves and you're only taking from the future. I guess the VC want to show that the government can't maintain schools and provide protection," I said.

"I guess so," Lockett answered.

"You know this is where we have to start, though," I continued. "We are trying to move too fast and we expect too much from the Vietnamese. We want to win their hearts and minds overnight. We can't do that. It takes time to teach people how to operate a democracy. We have to start with the kids and educate them. It will take several generations to change their way of doing things."

"You may be right," Lockett said. "But I see the problem as being too much corruption in the government. It steals too much from the people. Look at all the aid we give them, particularly in food. You never see any signs of that aid getting down to the people who need it."

"You're right," I said." The government has to show the people that it is interested in their welfare and can provide benefits. But don't be so naïve or critical of the government's corruption. We have corruption in the States, too. We just cover it up better than most countries."

"Maybe so, but we still have a chance to get ahead," Lockett answered. "These people will never get out of the paddies."

"Right. We have the best system going. And I wouldn't want to change it even with its faults. But our newspapers and politicians shouldn't point fingers and look down their noses when we have the same problems."

"Yeah," answered Lockett, "but we have laws."

"True, but they're broken every day and we look the other way because we are satisfied with the quality of life we get from the system. The Vietnamese aren't improving their quality of life."

It was a simplistic discussion. We didn't have detailed knowledge of the problems that beset the Vietnamese. We based our thoughts on what we had read in the newspapers before coming to Vietnam and what we heard from second-hand sources in country. We knew nothing of land reform, the election system, or nepotism in government. We didn't know the desires of the people. If we had, we wouldn't have known how to fulfill them. Of course we could see how the people lived, but we were sheltered from the political activities in the country. Our world revolved around seventeen tracks. Operationally, we continued to conduct one-day operations, but we ranged farther from Cai Be. During one operation north of the highway, on the edge of the Plain of Reeds, the Troop came under a mortar attack. Only four or five rounds were fired, but one of them hit the front slope of a track. The round must have been from a small sixty-millimeter mortar or a dud, because it only broke open the track's front armor plate. The round's impact caused a four-foot crack in the armor and gave the driver a headache. The incident increased my confidence in the M-113 and demonstrated its toughness. The driver drove the track back to Cai Be under its own power.

The M-113 was an extremely durable vehicle. It had to be to survive the constant beating it took in the paddies and the lack of maintenance performed by the South Vietnamese it received. Though the vehicles were constantly cleaned, before and after operations checks were seldom made. Also, repair parts were in short supply, which added to the maintenance problem. Notwithstanding poor maintenance procedures, the Troop's combat effectiveness was never adversely affected.

I was finally beginning to break the ice with Vinh. I had accidentally found a way to get him to talk. I had become so frustrated with not being able to understand what the Vietnamese were saying that I asked Vinh to teach me Vietnamese. He gave the lessons during siesta. After a few days we got past the "Hello, how are you; good morning; good evening" stage to a few military terms. Soon, we were discussing training and tactics in very simple terms.

During the third week of November, the Troop moved to the southern limit of its assigned area, Papa Two-four, for the afternoon. Papa Two-four was the Pha My Thuan ferry, which crossed the Mekong. We had been steadily on the move for the past several days and hadn't had an opportunity to do our laundry or to send it to My Tho; none of us had any clean clothes. We were to the point that we could smell ourselves. We had all been wearing our last change of underwear and jungle fatigues for three or four days. When the Troop arrived at Papa Two-four, our first order of business was to do our laundry. We had to balance on a small planked pier which lay just above water level to hand wash our things. We used the plank as a scrub board.

We finished our laundry just before noon. Walking back to the command track I met Vinh, who offered me some boiled fish. It was cut into thick round slices. My first reaction was to refuse Vinh's offer. I could see that the fish was the type bred in the hatcheries under the local latrines, a black fish without scales, much like a mud cat. On second thought, I decided to try a bite to see if I could get it down. I couldn't. One bite and I gagged. I couldn't swallow. I had to spit out the bite to keep from throwing-up. I decided that would be my last attempt to eat native food, other than rice, in the field.

After siesta, Vinh moved the Troop to a mud fort used by the ARVN infantry at Papa Two-three for the night. The headquarters section took up a position outside the fort late in the afternoon.

There was enough daylight left, however, for me to survey the mud mounds, which served as both fighting positions and sleeping quarters.

Two loosely strung strands of concertina wire formed the fort's boundary next to the road. The mud bunkers, large enough to house four men, presented a high, four to five feet, profile. There was no discernible pattern to their positioning. They didn't appear to ensure that the defenders had interlocking fires. The horizontal firing ports were near the top of the structures, which required the occupants to stand and fire down or over the heads of an attacker.

The firing ports should have been at or near ground level so that a defender could fire grazing fires (firing only a few inches above ground level). This placement would have required the ARVN infantrymen to dig the bunker's floor down a foot or so to enable them to fire through the aperture. A low, dug-in position would have offered ARVN more protection from direct fires than the high silhouette configuration.

The ARVN individual or squad position differed greatly from those employed by the VC. Charlie dug his positions into the paddy dikes. The tops of the positions were generally level with the tops of the dikes. Occasionally, a position's top would rise a foot above a dike, but these were the exception. Charlie placed his bunker's firing apertures just above water level, providing excellent camouflage and enabling him to place grazing fire against an advancing enemy. It was clear how Charlie could easily overrun the fort. Fortunately, he wouldn't try during our short stay.

The next morning, the Troop awoke to a heavy fog. When I climbed from my jeep, I saw a long line of civilian traffic that had stopped behind us during the night. The day got off to a slow start. Soon the road was covered with people preparing breakfast or purchasing it from farmers who had brought in produce to sell. Our little section of road took on the atmosphere of a marketplace as civilians, infantry, and cavalrymen intermingled to barter for

Chinese soap, fish, and a variety of pastries. I was reminded of a flea market I had seen in Pisa, Italy, during my tour in Germany. Only this market was sitting out in the middle of nowhere. Traffic didn't begin to move until after nine-o-clock.

On Thanksgiving Day, the Troop was given an opportunity to work with the 9th Infantry Division on a joint operation south of Cai Lay. The Troop, reinforced with a Ruff Puff company, would move south from Cai Lay to attack a suspected VC base camp along the Ba Bai River from the east. The 9th Division would conduct an airmobile assault into the paddies on the east side of the river and attack to the west. We'd be supported by American artillery and close air support, directed by an Air Force FAC from an 0-2. Finally, we were going to try to trap Charlie by hitting the objective on both sides of a canal.

We arrived in Cai Lay before the Ruff Puff troops were assembled for the operation. Vinh positioned the Troop near the city's major north-south, east-west intersection and waited. While we waited, some of the troopers began visiting the various food stands to buy their breakfast. Sergeants Long and Lockett joined me at the command track and we decided to walk through the marketplace to pass the time. After a short walk, we stopped at a stand offering a delicacy that looked like a fried pie in raw dough. The pies were selling well and they looked good. We each decided to try one.

Walking away from the stand, I was the first to bite into my pie. I expected the taste of fruit or pork. The substance in my month offered little resistance to my bite. The taste was indescribably terrible. I looked at the hole in the pie where I had taken the bite. The dough was filled with the intestines of either a chicken or a pig. I immediately became faint and felt as though I'd vomit. I couldn't vomit nor could I spit out the concoction without embarrassing myself. I swallowed, went weak and handed the pie to Long. He looked at the pie's ingredients and turned white. Neither he nor Lockett tried their purchases. We offered the pies to the first trooper we passed and returned to the Troop. That was the first and last time I bought food in a marketplace.

It was mid-morning before the Ruff Puffs were assembled and ready to mount the tracks. Vinh and the Regional Forces' commander distributed the Ruff Puffs among the tracks and headed south along Provincial Road 20.

"Falcon One, this is Charlie One-six, commo check. How do you hear me, over?" I called to the FAC as the Troop cleared Cai Lay.

"Charlie One-six this is Falcon One, I hear you loud and clear, how me, over."

"Roger, Falcon. I have you the same. We're leaving Papa One-eight now. How do things look in the paddies, over?"

"This is Falcon. I have you in sight. Things are quiet. Not a soul is moving."

"Great. Maybe we'll have a quiet Thanksgiving, over," I replied. "Let's hope so, out."

Three thousand meters south of Cai Lay, the Troop turned west into dry paddies.

"Falcon One, this is Charlie One-six, what does it look like now, over?"

"One-six, this is Falcon, still quiet. I'll let you know if I see anything," the pilot answered in an annoyed tone.

Guess he doesn't want to be disturbed, while he bores holes in the sky, I thought.

The Troop moved steadily toward the Ba Bai Canal for two thousand meters before the lead tracks began to encounter scattered trees south of Xom Chua (2) hamlet. So far, the operation offered nothing more than another life-jarring ride in the sun.

The objective area was one of the few places where the trees allowed the tracks to maneuver almost to the canal. Vinh halted the command track in a horseshoe shaped paddy, while the platoons continued into the more dense trees. The morning silence was broken occasionally by the high pitched whine of an M-113's engine as a driver increased power to maneuver over an obstacle. There was, however, the always-present squelch of the radio in my left ear.

"One-six this is Falcon, over."

"This is One-six, over."

"This is, Falcon. The 9th is going to fire preparatory fires in one minute, over."

"Roger, Falcon."

Suddenly, the terrifying whistle of an incoming artillery round disrupted the serenity of the morning. One minute, huh.

Before I could react, two rounds fell forward of the command track in the tree line. A third round exploded a few meters behind us. As I turned to see how close the round had fallen, mud clods showered me. I dropped into the track through the top hatch. Placing my elbows on the folded back hatch cover, I went to work on stopping the artillery.

The 9th was firing its preparatory fires east of the Ba Bai instead of to the west, as it should have. Falcon had probably called in the fires from a registration point (a successfully engaged target or point from which additional fires can be adjusted with reasonable assurance that the new target will be hit.) Someone had made a mistake. The rounds had fallen short or the artillery had been misinformed about which side of the river the 9th would land. The reason for the mistake was unimportant. I had to get the firing stopped.

"Falcon, this is One-six, those rounds hit us, over," I screamed into the mic.

"Say again, over," Falcon asked.

I guess I was more excited than I thought. I took a deep breath and as calmly as I could answered, "Your fires are falling on our position."

"Roger One-six, pop smoke so that I can identify your positions, over."

"Roger. Wait."

Sergeant Long was with the lead platoon. "One-six-alpha, this is one-six, over," I called to Long.

"This is alpha, over."

"Roger, Alpha. Pop smoke for Falcon, over."

"Roger, I heard, smoke is out.

"Roger," I answered, as I pulled the pin on a green smoke grenade.

As I keyed the mic, I could see another faint trail of green smoke rising through the trees. "Falcon, this is One-six, smoke is out."

"Roger, One-six, identify two green smokes."

"Roger, Falcon. That's us."

"Alpha, this is One-six, what's your situation?" I called.

"This is Alpha, two rounds landed near us, but no one was hit," Long replied.

Three more rounds came whistling in and explored in the trees and paddy. I was again showered with mud.

"Alpha, this is One-six, did those rounds cause any damage?" I asked.

"Negative, One-six. "

"Falcon, this is One-six, we're still receiving fire, over" I called into the mic without waiting for an acknowledgment.

"Roger One-six, I'm working on it. Has anyone been hit?"

"Not yet, but it's only a matter of time unless your get them to stop."

"Roger One-six, I'll try again, out."

A few moments later, Falcon came back on the air as three more rounds came in. "One-six, this is Falcon, I've advised the artillery to cease fire."

"Roger," I replied as three more rounds landed.

I moved forward in the crew hatch and tapped Vinh on the shoulder. "The FAC says he has the artillery stopped," I said pointing toward the sky.

Vinh only nodded. He had sat quietly throughout the shelling. I admired his disposition.

"Alpha, this is One-six, has anyone been hit?"

"Negative, One-six."

An uneasy stillness fell over the paddy for a few minutes. Then the silence was broken by the scream of a high-performance aircraft. Looking up between the trees, I saw a sleek F-4 Phantom pass over with its nose cannon firing.

"Falcon, Falcon, this is One-six, now we're under an air attack. Call off your birds."

"Roger, One-six."

Before I could complete this call, a second Phantom screamed in, releasing a bomb from each wing.

"Alpha, this is One-six, where did the bombs hit? Over."

"Across the canal, over."

"Roger, how about the cannon fire? Over."

"Some rounds hit on this side, but no one is hurt, over."

"One-six this is Falcon, I called the bird off. Was anyone hurt?"

"Negative, Falcon," I replied.

"Roger, One-six, sorry about that, out."

Shortly, I heard the whump-whump of the Hueys as they approached to insert (an Army term for landing) the 9th's troops. As the copters passed from view, Vinh had his driver backed the track in a slow turn until it was headed east and then moved forward. Vinh was calling it quits. I can't say that I blamed him. The timing and coordination for the operation had been poorly handled. We were lucky that we hadn't had someone killed by our own fires. The way things were going, if we stayed in the area, we'd be fighting the 9th Division before the day was over.

When the Troop cleared the trees and was well into the paddles, Vinh turned the Troop north toward Ap Hoa Hu'ng (2). It was only a thousand-meter drive to the village, so the distance was covered in short order. At the edge of the village, the troopers began their standard procedures for searching a village.

While the troopers searched the thatched huts, I fished out two turkey loaf C-ration meals. I opened one with my P-38 can opener and offered it to Vinh. I had hoarded the meals for the past two weeks so that I could celebrate Thanksgiving with a traditional turkey dinner. Thanksgiving was my family's second most important holiday. Since I wouldn't be able to celebrate with them, I'd do the next best thing. I'd treat Vinh to dinner.

"Vinh, today is Thanksgiving in America. Would you join me in celebration?" I asked as I offered him the meal.

"Yeah, no thank you, Dia uy, " Vinh said with a smile. "The food is too rich for me."

I was disappointed, but I didn't push the issue. Actually, his refusal made me feel a little better. He couldn't stomach American food, even if it were C-rations, any better than I could Vietnamese food.

While I opened my can containing the main entree, two mortar rounds landed in the trees to the west of the command track. The rounds didn't land close enough to cause us any concern, but they did get our attention. Vinh and I looked at each other and then continued with what we were doing. At first, the rounds fell some distance from us with long time intervals between rounds. Before I had finished my meat, however, the sound of the rounds were slipping closer to us and falling with greater frequency. I was beginning to get concerned when Vinh ordered the Troop to mount up and move out.

What a Thanksgiving! We almost get killed by our own people and now no siesta!

CHAPTER TEN

LONG DINH: DECEMBER 1967

A few days after Thanksgiving, the Troop received orders to relieve 2nd Troop at Papa One-six. First Troop had been in the Cai Be area for two months and the troopers were ready for a change of atmosphere. A morale boost was afforded many of the troopers because their families had remained in My Tho, rather than accompanying them on the highway. Being at Papa One-six would allow these troopers an opportunity to visit their families more often. It was a good move for me also. I was ready for something different. I was hopeful that a change of location would bring a change in the Troop's missions. I didn't know what that might be, but I was tired of bouncing through the paddles without finding Charlie. At least, I'd get a change of scenery—though one rice paddy looked pretty much like another.

Papa One-six was at the highway bridge that crossed the Kinh Xang Canal a man-made canal that ran from the My Tho River north into the Plain of Reeds.

The bridge sat in the middle of the small village of Long Dinh. To the east of the canal and south of the highway was the Province Office in an old two-story French colonial house. On the west bank of the canal and south of the road was a small hospital and an abandoned cable tower. An American flag flew from atop the sixty-foot tower. No one knew who put the flag there. To the north of the highway were scattered thatched huts in open rice paddies.

The village was hardly discernible.

Long Dinh Tower photo by Larry Cole

Long Dinh photo by Larry Cole

Our living conditions at Papa One-six were much better than those to which we had become accustomed. The headquarters section positioned itself next to a shed on the south side of the highway and the west bank of the Kinh Xang. The shed was about ten feet by twenty feet with a concrete floor and a metal roof supported by wooden poles. It had no walls, but it did provide us with some protection from the nightly rains. Most importantly, we could use our mosquito nets on our cots. Compared to the way we had been living, P-16 was like moving into a Hilton.

Long Dinh Hilton photo by Larry Cole

US Artillery at Long Dinh

After the headquarters section settled in, I went to inspect the hospital. I was accompanied by Sergeant Lockett and Private First

Class Laney. We went only so far as the hospital's porch. Looking through the screenless windows we could see a few empty old, white steel-framed beds. There was no staff or patients in the few rooms we looked into. Not finding anything of interest, we decided to take advantage of the shade offered by the porch and sat down with our backs against the hospital's front wall.

"This reminds me of the time I got my head bashed in," Laney said.

I looked at Laney in surprise. He was the most likable fella in the searchlight team.

I couldn't imagine his getting into a situation where he'd be beaten up.

"How was that?" asked Lockett.

"I think I've told you I'm from Chicago. To be more specific, I'm from south Chicago. One night, when I was going home from work, some guy took a lead pipe to me, while I was standing on a corner waiting for the bus," Laney answered.

"South Chicago. Isn't that the rough side of town?" I asked.

"Yeah, I guess so, but when you grow up there it doesn't seem too bad."

"Where did you work?" asked Lockett.

"I was a shipping and receiving clerk for Sears."

"What did you do to cause him to hit you?" I asked.

"Nothing, I was working late. I came up from the basement and walked to the bus stop. While I was waiting for the bus, I lit up a cigarette. Just as I put my lighter back in my pocket, some guy walks up and asked for a light. When I reached into my pocket, he hits me. I never saw it coming. He hit me several times on the head with a small pipe and ran off," Laney answered.

"Did you have to go to the hospital?" Lockett asked.

"Yeah, they put seventeen stitches in my head and I stayed in the hospital three days."

"You were lucky the fella didn't kill you. Did you ever see him again?" I asked.

"No, never did, and I don't want to either."

"Did you ever run into any gangsters?" I asked.

"Oh yeah, all the time."

I was surprised and asked, "Didn't that bother you? Weren't you afraid?"

"No, not at all. They didn't bother you if you didn't bother them or try to cut in on them," Laney answered.

"Where did you meet them?" Lockett asked.

"At a small bar I sometimes stopped at after work or on weekends. I knew several what they call street soldiers."

"And they never bothered you?" I asked.

"Nah, they knew I didn't have anything and wasn't trying to cut in on them. They were just regular guys to me," Laney answered.

While we talked, we could hear the sound of tracks moving toward us from the east.

"That must be 3rd Troop moving out to Cai Be, said Lockett.

We sat on the hospital's porch and watched as the Troop approached. When the command track was in front of the hospital, it stopped and the Troop commander, Captain Chau, jumped from his track. With a stick in hand, the commander raced back along the line of vehicles pulling up behind him. Each track commander carried a stick that he used to direct his driver. Our tracks weren't equipped with intercoms like US tracks were. Therefore, our TCs carried sticks to tap their drivers on the head or shoulders in a code that told the driver which direction to go or when to start and stop.

Four or five tracks back the Troop commander jumped up, grabbed the TC, and pulled him to the ground. The TC rolled into a ball. The Troop commander began to kick the TC and to beat him with his stick that was the size of a small club. The punishment lasted less than a minute. The ARVN soldiers who witnessed the beating watched passively as it was administered. Captain Arthur watched in shock from his seat on the command track. He made no attempt to interfere. The only activity in the immediate area was the wild, windmill arm swings and kicks of the enraged Troop commander and his shouts directed at the offender. The trooper, a sergeant, didn't try to protect himself, other than to roll into the fetal position, or to fight back. Neither did he voice any complaint or sound of pain.

Lockett, Laney, and I, like Captain Arthur, watched in wide-eyed amazement. I had heard that the ARVN used corporal punishment extensively. When first assigned to the Cav, I had expected to see enlisted men summarily punished by sergeants and officers daily. This hadn't been the case in 1st Troop. Vinh was a good leader. It was clear that he had better control of himself and his troops than did the Commander of 3rd Troop. When the inevitable happened, it caught me by surprise. I couldn't believe what I was witnessing. My first reaction was to stop the beating, but something told me not to interfere. I had no authority. I was in their Army and country. Whatever the problem, it was an ARVN affair. It was between them and it had to be handled in their way. "When in Rome, do as the Romans" or at least don't interfere with them.

In the ARVN's defense, they had customs and traditions, which were based on their environment, education, and experience. These were vastly different from those of Americans. Therefore, the South Vietnamese couldn't be expected to have the same principles as Americans—they did what worked for them. If a trooper fouled up or disobeyed an order, he was dealt with immediately. There was no waiting for the preparation of non-judicial punishment or court-martial charges, while similar offenses were often committed. The ARVN system was quick and visible. There was no question that the offender had sinned in the eyes of the commander and that he had paid the price. This wasn't always the case with our American system.

Notwithstanding the pros and cons of the two systems, leaders cannot be allowed, in a fit of anger, to punish soldiers. In the heat of passion, one tends to overreact. There's always the possibility of an over-zealous commander, like George Armstrong Custer, using excessive force or an unusual punishment. This was the case in this incident. The sergeant was beaten unconscious and had to be carried into the hospital for treatment. I don't know how long he was lost to the Troop or how his loss affected the Troop. But surely the loss of a track commander for any length of time in a combat situation would have an adverse effect on the Troop's efficiency. I question that the sergeant could have done anything so serious as to justify the treatment he received.

"What was that all about?" I asked Captain Arthur as we met midway between the road and the hospital.

"I don't know. About the time we started across the bridge, I noticed Ho yelling into the mic, but I didn't think anything about it. He does that all the time," Arthur replied.

"Well, whatever he did, he won't likely do it again for awhile," I said. "Do you see much of that type of thing?"

"No, not really, that's the first time. Ho gets excited a lot, but I've never seen him loose complete control before."

"Looks like you got a problem . . ." I began.

"Not me, there's nothing I can do. Discipline and the way it's administered is their problem. If they want to beat up on people to maintain discipline, I can't change it during my watch," Arthur answered.

"Changing the subject, what can you tell me about this area?" I asked.

"Not much. It's pretty much like duty at Cai Be. The only real change in what we do is when we're in My Tho."

"What's the difference in My Tho?" I said.

"We don't go on operations as often and the Troop performs more maintenance…"

"How about the advisors?" I interrupted.

"We don't do much. We get a lot a time to scrounge at Dong Tam and to visit the Seminary," Arthur replied.

"Who's the subsector advisor here?" I asked.

"There's no subsector advisor here. Lay Cai subsector is responsible for this area. Maj. Cox is the regimental advisor."

"Where do I find him?"

"He stays at the provincial headquarters over there," Captain Arthur said pointing to the old two-story house on the other side of the canal.

Later, after the 3rd Troop moved on to Cai Be, Sergeants Long and Lockett and I drove across the canal to introduce ourselves to Major Cox and his team. We found the team in their quarters on the second floor of the house. They lived and worked in the most crowded conditions of any team we had visited.

The three-man team lived in one room that stretched across the front of the building's second floor. The room was filled with beds, a few chairs, and a table with a radio mounted on it. There was scarcely room to turn around without hitting a bed, chair, or table.

Major Cox was a short, heavy officer. His stocky appearance wasn't that of the normal lean figure of an infantry officer who was accustomed to hiking several miles a day with a pack on his back. Major Cox's appearance, however, was more than offset by his affable personality and his professionalism. Out of the paddies, he was a continuous source of jokes and comical stories about his experiences in the Army's Recruiting Command. In the paddies, he was a no-nonsense professional who coordinated activities as well as any officer I met while in-country.

During our first visit with Major Cox, I mentioned my diet.

"Heck, there's no reason for you to live on rice and C's. You can get anything you want except vegetables at the Seminary's commissary," Cox told me.

"What do you mean? I thought that all they had were canned goods."

"They do have a good selection of canned goods but you can get steaks and pork chops too."

"What!?"

"Yeah, they have a freezer in the back. You can get almost any type of meat you want."

"That may be, but that doesn't do us much good out here," I said.

"No problem. It's only fourteen klicks to the Seminary. You can be in there before you're missed. I drive in a couple of times a week. There's no problem so long as you go during the middle of the day," Cox replied.

"Well I'll be damned! I didn't know we were that close. I'll have to try it someday," I answered. I had been dropped at Cai Be in the darkness with only two map sheets that did not show My Tho. Thus, I had no idea where I was in relation to My Tho or Dong Tam.

Unfortunately, I wasn't able to get well acquainted with Major Cox during the Troop's stay at Papa One-six. We visited only a few times. After a long day in the paddies, I didn't feel like visiting with anyone. However, our paths would cross on several operations later in the year.

The day after we arrived at Long Dinh, Vinh took a day's leave to visit his wife in My Tho. Of my days with the Cav, this would be the most frustrating. I lost my temper and self-control and struck Tran for not moving to an ambushed convoy's rescue. The incident cost me a bit of self-respect and caused me to doubt my ability to lead. Was the use of force and fear the only way I could influence another soldier? I hoped not. Luckily, the incident wasn't reported to Major Evans. So, the only trouble the incident caused was my own self-doubts.

A few days after Vinh's return, on 4 December, the Troop was again called to the aid of an ambushed convoy. At about 2000 hours, we heard the now familiar sound of an explosion to the west followed by a crescendo of rifle fire. Vinh immediately moved the Troop toward the action, while I raised Major Cox on the radio to report our move.

As we approached the ambush site, we saw trucks and jeeps strung out along the road in disarray. The explosion we had heard was caused by a control-detonated mine placed near the side of the road. The sapper had misjudged when to twist his detonator. He activated the charge too soon, missing the lead truck. On reflex, the convoy had stopped and fired into the paddies with all weapons, like the Troop had done on my first operation. The excited reaction of the drivers had caused more damage than the Cong. By the time we arrived at the ambush site, the action had settled into a long-range firefight between the convoy and Charlie. South Vietnamese fired from behind truck tires and while lying in the middle of the road or along either shoulder. On the south side of the road, some soldiers lay with their feet in the paddy and their bodies prone on the road's embankment. The trucks with ring mounts for .50 caliber machine guns were manned and the gunners were firing the slow, rhythmic weapons at their attackers. Some soldiers fired M-16s or carbines from the trucks' beds. The air was filled with the acid odor of gun smoke as the sun set behind the nipa palm trees.

Vinh reacted well and quickly. He had the tracks take the ambusher's position under fire and dismounted a squad to go after Charlie. He called the Troop's mortars forward to try to cut off Charlie's withdrawal and I requested artillery illumination to increase visibility. Though our mad rush to the convoy's rescue had saved it from large losses, our reaction wasn't quick enough and well enough coordinated to catch Charlie. When the firing died down Vinh had the Troop assist the recovery. A couple of trucks had to be pulled from the paddies. A few flat tires had to be changed. While the Troop assisted the convoy, Charlie tried to keep our heads down with sniper fire. We returned to our original position at 2400 hours.

The next few days were fairly normal. On 5 December, we drove the paddies and then moved to Papa One-eight for road security. The next day we mounted an operation at 0600 hours. Vinh tried an envelopment of the objective, but the assault was too slow. At least, he was trying something new. On Pearl Harbor Day, we pulled road security between Papa One-five and Papa One-seven. At 2000 hours, there was another ambush. I didn't note who was involved or the results—must not have been a biggie. The next day was spent performing maintenance at Papa One-six.

On 9 December, while the team cleaned weapons, one of the platoons positioned near our shed began to receive sporadic sniper fire. When the first round broke through the stillness, our heads jerked up from our weapons and we scanned the tree lines from where the round had been fired. The sniper's aim was so poor that we couldn't identify where his rounds were striking. When the troopers saw that the sniper's fire was inaccurate, they relaxed and continued their normal duties of watching traffic and cleaning their vehicles and weapons.

The sniper was persistent. He continued to squeeze off a round every two or three minutes. We tried to ignore the shots when they rang out across the paddies; but, as time passed, we became concerned that the sniper's marksmanship might improve with the practice we were allowing him. Finally, I recommended that we go after him. We weren't doing anything productive. We could use a break in the routine. Lockett was ready to go. Long, however, was hesitant. We gathered our rifles and webbing with extra ammunition and headed for the paddies. Ba and two other troopers who were cleaning weapons joined the adventure.

I led the patrol across the highway in the direction of the last shot we had heard. We slid down a shallow embankment and headed for the protection of a hedgerow. We moved in a half crouch at a slow jog. When we reached the hedgerow, another shot rang out. We went to ground and surveyed the distant tree line. We could see no movement or smoke from the weapon's discharge.

Lockett was directly behind me. I turned to check how close the other members of the patrol were. Lockett and I looked into each other's eyes. His eyes were questioning. Like me, he must have been asking himself why we were playing infantry. It wasn't our job to be out here chasing snipers.

We slowly crept along the hedgerow toward the far tree line. The sniper continued to fire at random. We couldn't tell if the rounds were directed at us or toward the platoon's position on the highway. I began to wonder if I had done the right thing. The sniper wasn't causing much of a problem. He was more distracting than anything else. I wiped the sweat from my forehead and eyes. Again, I turned to check the patrol's positioning. I was pleasantly surprised to see that Vinh had dispatched a squad into the paddy to join us. My confidence returned. I couldn't turn back now. The die was cast. Vinh had supported my decision if for no other reason than to insure my safety. To turn back would be to lose face; we continued on.

We crawled along the hedgerow until we were into the paddy about halfway between the highway and the trees. We stopped again and listened. In a few minutes, the sniper fired again. This time the shot sounded as if it came from our front at a left oblique. I looked back down the line and then turned to point in the direction where I thought the round had been fired. I sighted my rifle into the treetops and fired several rounds. The other members of the patrol followed my lead, firing into the trees for several seconds. I waved for a cease-fire and waited. In a few minutes, I fired again and the patrol followed suit. Again, we waited. There was no return fire. We lay against the hedgerow for what seemed an eternity. The stillness was unnerving. I looked back down the line. No one stirred. Each soldier stared at me without emotion. Sweat ran down each face. Our clothes were saturated with perspiration. Flies, mosquitoes, and other insects buzzed around my head. I made no effort to shoo them away. My breathing was heavy with excitement and my heart pounded in my chest. My thoughts and attention were on the tree line. Would the sniper fire on us? Though we were against the hedgerow, we offered a clear target from the direction of the last sound of sniper fire. There was no movement. I raised my rifle and fired again. The others also fired. We waited. Again, there was no response from the trees. We waited. After what I considered a reasonable time, I stood and walked back along the hedgerow toward the highway. The others followed.

When we got back to the highway and were with the Troop, I felt like a thousand pounds had been lifted from my chest. I didn't know if we had hit the sniper or not. As far as I was concerned, we had accomplished what we had set out to do. The sniping had been stopped. The greatest accomplishment was that I had broken the code on how to get Vinh to react. I had to set the example. If I were aggressive, he'd be aggressive. He didn't want to explain the death of a "Co Van" (Advisor), especially, if he hadn't supported him.

After the sniper incident, the Troop sat on the road for the next several days. Our only activity was short moves to various small clusters of thatched huts along the highway. Activity was so minimal that the advisors and searchlight team spent most of our time reading. I managed to read three volumes of Bruce Catton's histories of the Civil War and *I Rode with Stonewall* written by one of "Stonewall" Jackson's aide de camps.

One day during this lull, I received a letter from Jim Mosley, the officer I had told Captain Arthur about earlier. Jim had served with me in the 1st Battalion, 37th Armor in Germany. He had been assigned as the battalion's mortar platoon leader during the time I had been in the battalion's armored cavalry platoon leader. Our families had become close friends and our wives had stayed in touch. He had gotten my address from my wife, Nelwyn, and was writing to tell me that he was on orders to Nam. He wanted to know about the war in the Delta and any tips I might have for him. Also, he extended an invitation to Nelwyn and me to spend my R&R in Hawaii at the same time he and his wife Rose Ann would be there. The R&R trip sounded good to me, but I couldn't give any tips to prepare him for his assignment. He had received a branch transfer from Armor to Military Intelligence and would be assigned to a detachment at Long Binh, working as a staff officer on a large military installation. His assignment would be completely different from mine.

He closed by giving me the most depressing news I had received while in country. Joe Hitt, one of our good friends, had been killed a month earlier. He had been shot in the head by a sniper while standing in the commander's hatch of his tank. I was shaken and saddened by the news. Joe had been a tank platoon leader with me during my initial assignment with the 37th Armor. He had been a good friend and a good officer.

After finishing the letter, my mind sadly drifted back four years. I thought about a few experiences I had shared with Joe in Germany. He had been commissioned through the ROTC program. He had received a regular army commission as a result of being a distinguished military graduate from a California college. I recalled a picnic with our wives at a German roadside park. While we lay on blankets and watched the forest, Hitt outlined his plans for professional development and his career. He planned to be a general. I remembered our first field training at Hohenfels, when Joe complained that the Army didn't afford its officers an opportunity to develop intellectually—one of our minor differences. Most of all, I remembered his accidents. He was the most accident-prone individual I had known. He seldom participated in a field exercise without being involved in an accident. His tank would run into a hidden, snow-covered hole, causing him to fall to the turret's floor, busting his nose and mouth on the main gun's breech-block. Once, when he led a convoy at night under blackout conditions, his driver drove into a crater and rolled his jeep. Fortunately, Joe had been standing up, looking over the windshield, so that he could see better, when the jeep went over the crater's edge. He was thrown clear of the jeep but had broken his glasses and blacked both eyes as well as wrenched his back. I wasn't surprised that Joe hadn't survived.

Duty in the Papa One-six area was much better than at Cai Be. Not only did we have the shed, which provided protection from the elements and a living area, we had a variety of visitors. The Kinh Xang Canal was one of the major arteries for the 9th Division's Riverine Force to move north to patrol the numerous tributary canals within Dinh Tuonh Province and the Plain of Reeds. Frequently, the long, low gunboats and landing craft of the flotilla passed our shed on their patrols and on occasion they stopped near the bridge to allow the villagers to view their might.

The gunboats were impressive. They were painted dark gray, almost black. They were an awesome sight as they slowly cruised up the canal with low superstructures and steel-encased .50 cal gun turrets forward. The gunboat's superstructures were steel with a few steel hatches for ventilation. Steel rods, spaced a few inches apart, encircled their hulls, gun turrets, and the superstructures. The rods provided a standoff of air space of two to three inches against anti-armor heat rounds, B-40 rockets. An incoming rocket striking a rod would explode prematurely, losing its penetrating power before hitting the boat's main armor. The landing craft had low steel roofs over their crew compartments.

Another set of visitors were two Japanese reporters and their escort, a Sergeant First Class Jamerson, from the IV Crops Public Information Office (PIO). The reporters were doing a story on Vietnamese cavalry operations in the Delta. The group stayed three days and went on one operation. There wasn't much interaction with the reporters because they couldn't speak English. I did strike up a friendship with Sergeant Jamerson, who later sent the team several photographs of gals from a USO show he had escorted. We'd have preferred that he had brought the girls with him when he visited, but that's the breaks. The support people and aviators get all the good things in life.

The one thing that Cai Be offered over Papa One-six was a cafe where the team could get a decent meal. The longer the Troop worked the Papa One-six area the greater the team's appetites grew for a good high-protein meal. Our conversations centered on the availability of steaks that Major Cox had mentioned at the Seminary's commissary. Finally, one day when Vinh didn't have anything planned, I mustered up my courage and announced that I'd risk the dangers of an ambush to make a dash into the Seminary for T-bones.

I invited Sergeant Long to accompany me.

"No, sir, I don't want to go in, I'd rather stay with the Troop," Long replied to my invitation.

"Ah, come on, Sarge. The break will do you good," I said.

"No thanks, sir. I don't want to get out on the road."

"I understand, but I don't think there's much danger. Charlie has been quiet for the past few days. Traffic is moving fine and it'll only take us a few minutes to make it to the Seminary, I said.

"I know, sir. But I don't want to take the chance."

"I don't think there's much of a chance of getting hit or I wouldn't go."

"I know, sir. But I'm not going to make it through this tour. I don't want to take unnecessary chances," Long said seriously.

A lump came to my throat. I couldn't say anything for a few moments. I had heard of people having a premonition of death but no one had ever told me that they thought they were going to die. My first thought was one of pity which was followed by disbelief.

"Come on, Sarge. You don't believe in that stuff . . ."

"Yes, sir, I do. I'm not going to make it," Long interrupted.

I had to find a way to encourage him. "Look, we have it good here with the Cav. Look at all the firepower we have. Charlie can't touch us. We have the best assignment in Nam," I said.

"I know, sir, but I don't want to take any extra chances. I'll do my job, but I'm not going to take any unnecessary chances or volunteer for anything."

I gave up. I could see that Long believed what he was saying. I wasn't about to order him to go on a pogie bait (food) run. The trip wasn't that important.

Sergeant Lockett volunteered to drive me when I told him I was going. We left the Troop rear noon and arrived at the Seminary without incident in time for lunch. After lunch, there was another order of business I needed to attend to at the PX before picking up the steaks. I had suggested that the three advisors share the cost of purchasing a portable radio. I thought that a radio would provide a good morale boost. We had all commented on how much we missed listening to music and the news. I think we each wanted to hear a different voice once in a while. So long as we played it only while we were on the highway and during daylight hours, I could see no harm in having one.

Long and Lockett had agreed to the purchase and appointed me to handle the transaction at the first opportunity. The plan was that when one of us left the team, the others would buy his share of the radio. The last man to leave could keep the radio or sell it.

I finished my shopping quickly and returned to the Troop without being ambushed. When I got back, Long had already brought charcoal, but we didn't have a barbecue pit. One of the searchlight fellas scrounged up a piece of wire matting for a grill, and Sergeant Lockett dug a hole in the ground for the pit. By suppertime, we were in business. The meal was excellent, even if I did cook it myself.

Throughout the month, Major Cox relayed intelligence reports almost daily that Long Dinh or some other village in the area would be mortared or attacked on a given night. These reports, with the exception of one, proved to be false alarms. By the latter part of December, I had gone through so many false alerts that I quit taking the reports seriously.

The one legitimate report provided my first opportunity to see helicopter gun-ships in action. One evening, around 2300 hours,

I was awakened by two almost simultaneous explosions. Before I could crawl from under my mosquito net and off my cot, I heard two more explosions in the distance. I was awake enough to identify the second explosion as mortar rounds. Fortunately, they were directed at a target across the canal to the northeast. I ran to the command track and found Vinh talking on the radio. I raised Major Cox on my radio to find out the situation. He told me that the village was being mortared and that he had requested gun-ships. He asked me to stay off the air, so that he could direct them when they came on station.

I gave him a "roger, out" as the next set of rounds hit directly across the road from my track. The rounds continued to fall at random for what seemed an eternity before we heard the whump whump of the choppers. They approached from our rear. The first chopper began to fire his machineguns well behind the shed. All of us on the track pulled our heads into our shoulders and watched from the corners of our eyes as red tracers passed overhead. When the lead ship passed over us, it was engulfed in white smoke as it fired a salvo of rockets. The door gunners worked over the target area as the chopper made a sharp climbing turn to the east and circled for a second run. We were still watching the first chopper when a second one cut loose with his machineguns and then rocketed the target which Major Cox had had an ARVN mortar section mark with flares. I was awestruck by the brilliant display of friendly machine gun and rocket fire. The night was turned into a Fourth of July celebration in December.

The arrival of the chopper gave me a feeling of complete safety and raised my morale a hundredfold. I felt so secure that I jumped from the track and walked into the middle of the highway, so I could get a clear view of the choppers during their firing runs. They made four passes before they broke off their attack. It had been a one-sided affair once the choppers came on station. Charlie hadn't fired a round after he heard the choppers.

I was impressed with the firepower of the gun-ships. As the sound of the chopper's whump whumps faded to the southwest, I thought, *We can't lose so long as we were supported by such awesome machines of death. How can Charlie withstand such power?* I went back to my cot and fell asleep in ignorant bliss. My confidence in helicopter gun-ships, however, would be short-lived.

During one of our shipments of the *Stars and Stripes*, we received a copy that head lined the Pentagon Riot in Washington DC. After Lockett read the article, he was enraged.

"Don't those fools know that all they are doing is encouraging the Cong? All they are doing is getting more of us killed," he raged.

"Yeah, I think you're right," I answered.

"Man, I wish I was one of those MPs. I would've loved to have busted some of those idiots' heads," Lockett continued.

"I agree, but they have a right to voice their opinion," I answered. I was being the devil's advocate. I wanted to keep him going. I was in full agreement with his sentiments.

"Not when it's getting me shot at and is aiding the enemy. If they wanted to fight for the Cong, let them go to North Vietnam and join the Army. Then we'll get a crack at them," Lockett raged on. "If they can't support us and they don't like the good old U S of A, and what it represents, let them leave! I'd buy them a one way ticket if I had the money."

Another subject that got both of us started was the exodus of young cowards to Canada. Succinctly, we thought that if a man couldn't fight for his county or democracy, he shouldn't be afforded the rights of citizenship of the United States. He shouldn't be allowed to vote or to draw social security or whatever. We had no doubt that we supported a just cause and had no patience with those who disagreed with our sense of duty. We believed the deserters weren't so much in disagreement with the government's policies as they were afraid of being shot at by Charlie.

The rest of December was quiet. Part of this was that we and Charlie declared a truce over the holidays. The only activities of interest were the arrival of an Army care package for the Americans, Vietnamese type C-rations for the ARVN, and an American artillery unit.

An Army care package was something to behold for troops that had learned to live on a bare minimum. The package was delivered by truck convoy. It was encased in a four by four foot cardboard waterproof box on a wooden pallet. There was so much in it that I can't remember all the items. As best I can remember, it contained cigarettes, paperbacks, toilet articles, and canned drinks. There was more than we'd ever use. We stored what we could in the trailer and the jeep. The rest we gave to the artillery battery which had set up behind our shed a few days before.

The artillery unit was a 155, self-propelled battery. The battery consisted of five firing sections and an FDC. Each section was mounted in a vehicle that looked like a large tank. Their tubes, that were larger than a tank's main gun was mounted in a box-like steel turret which sat on a full-tracked chassis. Atop the turret was a .50 cal machinegun.

Not only was it reassuring to have the extra firepower with us, it gave us the opportunity to bum a nightly hot meal from the artillery mess. Since it was near Christmas, some crews and the FDC had made up small Christmas trees and decorated them with cigarette packages and other small items the crews could find that glittered. The trees attested to the crew's ingenuity and created an atmosphere of good cheer, though they caused a mild case of homesickness.

At first, I thought it was great to have an American unit co-located with us. After the first night, I changed my mind. Each time the guns fired, I was almost thrown from my cot by the concussion and I thought my ears would burst. After the second night, I was ready for them to move on. They were disrupting my harmony more than Charlie.

The days dragged on. The rides in the sun continued with no results. I came to realize during my long rides how much I had learned in Germany as a tank platoon leader and then as an armored cavalry platoon leader. In Germany, we participated in numerous field training exercises (FTXs) and jeepster exercisers.

On the FTXs, we weren't allowed to get off the macadam and I thought they were a waste of time. The idea was for us to ride along and imagine how we'd employ our units if we were really at war and could maneuver. We played the game as near as possible. We had stand-to (a set time when everyone in the unit was up and started their vehicle engines simultaneously). We met start point (SP), release point: (RP), and LD times. We issued orders. We played the artillery and resupply game. We played the security game. During breaks, the company commander or battalion commander would quiz the platoon leaders on courses of action.

Where possible, we walked the terrain to identify positions. On the jeepster exercises, an exercise where we substituted jeeps for tanks, we fought mini battles over Bavarian mountain trails the way we'd fight our tanks. The more I watched the Vietnamese the more I realized that I had received some mighty good training in the 1st of the 37th Armor. As a result of my experience, a short, pointed report to Major Evans might resemble one I submitted on an operation in mid December:

"19 Dec 67, Troop moved out on operation at 0700 hours. No operations order issued, though time was available. Crossed the LD late because site not checked for mines prior to the move. Troop wasted forty-five minutes sitting at LD, while canal swept for mines. Alternate crossing site selected. Commander could have made reconnaissance of route to LD and of the crossing site. Personnel not alert during minesweeping.

"Assault was on two axes. Assault was poorly coordinated with platoons arriving on the objective at different times. No artillery planned. Objective not cordoned before search. Search poorly done, too fast. Lack of bridging a drawback. Assault route used during withdrawal. Negative results." (Note: Two actual reports are in the Appendix.)

In fairness to Vinh, some of his problems were caused by the political situation. He couldn't use artillery without approval by local civilian officials. There had to be an overwhelming amount of evidence that a village or area was VC-controlled before approval was given. The same was true about the use of reconnaissance by fire, a technique whereby' gunners fired into suspected enemy positions to draw fire, while the crew was in a favorable position to react. Also, crossing the dikes and canals made it almost impossible to time coordinated movements with vehicles. As I said, it was easy to find fault. It wasn't so easy to set everything right.

In late December, I again witnessed the destructive power of the American military. In the late afternoon, Major Cox sent word that an Arc-Lite (a code name for a B-52 bombing mission) was going in just north of the My Tho River to the west of Dong Tam. He didn't have a time for the strike. No one in the team had seen a B-52 strike, so we decided to stay up to watch the show.

The first part of the night was spent with the searchlight crews watching the tree lines with the searchlights in their infrared mode. By 2300 hours, Sergeants Long and Lockett and I tired of searchlight duty. We walked to my jeep and sat down on the road with our backs against the jeep and waited. We had talked ourselves out. We sat staring at the silhouetted trees against the horizon. There wasn't a sound; nothing moved except the mosquitoes. The minutes passed at a snail's pace. We were about to give up the vigil when the horizon suddenly became aglow with a faint white flash to the west which grew in brilliance and size as it spread to the east. There was no warning, no roar of engines, no jet whine, nothing until the sky lit up. Before we could stand, the dull mutter of the exploding bombs came rolling across the paddies like a West Texas sandstorm. The earth beneath us shook weakly in sympathy for the maimed jungle along the river. My teammates and I looked at each other without speaking. Words were inappropriate to describe how we felt about what we had witnessed. It wasn't soldierly to express sorrow for an enemy that had received such a deadly blow. There was no need to say how thankful we were that everything that flew was ours.

The next morning, a Ruff Puff company married up with the Troop for a ride to the Arc-Lite strike area. The Troop was to transport the Ruff Puffs to the edge of the previous evening's target. When we arrived in the area of the strike, Vinh discharged the infantry and we waited, while they searched the grove of mutilated trees and deep craters. I was curious to see the total effect of the strike. But Vinh wasn't interested, choosing to stay on the track. As always, I stayed with him. From our position, however, I could see enough shattered trees and gouged earth to know that the Ruff Puff wouldn't find anything living during their search. I said a silent prayer of thanks that we wouldn't be subjected to such a pulverizing. I wondered how we'd stand up if we were.

I never learned about the results of the strike. When the Ruff Puff returned to the Troop from their search, they climbed on board the tracks without comment. If they made a report to Vinh, they did so over the radio and he never told me what they found. I gave a negative report through my channels. We had wasted several million dollars in bombs to kill a bunch of trees and to plow up several acres of Vietnamese jungle.

In early January, the Troop was spent back to Cai Be for some reason. We spent our time touring the countryside for the most part. The purpose, I guess, was to visit as many villages as possible as a show of force. One day we stopped in a town about the size of Cai Be. We arrived just before siesta, and Vinh decided to let the Troop have the run of the town. Vinh, Long, Lockett, and I visited a local coffee shop for Vietnamese coffee. After coffee, Vinh excused himself, leaving Lockett and me to discuss things in general and to watch the troopers walk hand-in-hand through the town. I had noticed this custom before but hadn't discussed it with the other Americans.

"Now that's strange . . ." I started.

"What's that? Lockett asked.

"Those fellas walking around holding hands. If we were in the States I'd say they were gay."

"Nah, that's just the custom over here. You see it all the time," Lockett said.

"Maybe so, but it's still strange to me," I replied.

"That's nothing. Wait till one of them takes your hand and starts stroking your arm. They like to feel the hair on your arm," Lockett said.

"What?" I said in surprise.

"Yeah, that's right. You'll know you've arrived when one of them starts stroking your arm."

After a while, we decided to walk around town too. We hadn't gone far when two of our troopers walked up beside us. One of them took my hand and started stroking my arm. I looked down at him in shock. He looked up with a big smile. A shiver went up my spine. Well all right. I may not agree with this sign of friendship, but if that's the custom, go ahead. We continued to walk together for a few minutes and then the trooper and his buddy left.

"See, what did I tell you, laughed Lockett.

On another occasion, while we waited to enter a village, one of the troopers offered me some chicken. We were sitting on the track's back deck.

The trooper was munching on a chicken claw when he offered me the contents of his pot. I looked into the pot to see parts of a chicken in a red soup. The chicken's head floated in the soup with its eye staring up at me. I thanked the trooper kindly, but chicken claws and heads weren't my idea of a good meal.

At night, we began occasionally to place ambushes a few hundred meters from the Troop. To provide the ambush with early warning, we placed the searchlights at the end of the column nearest the ambush to watch the approaches into the kill zone. Because of the thick trees and distance, the lights were no help and we never caught Charlie moving through the area.

On 19 January, the troop stopped for the night along the highway where it cut through a small unnamed village a few hundred meters west of Papa-20. The advisors stayed up later than usual for some reason—maybe just to talk, I don't remember. I had just crawled into my bedroll. I was sleeping in the jeep on this particular night, when the frightening whistling sound of incoming high explosive rounds came screaming through the night. Two rounds impacted immediately. Before I could get out of the jeep, men were racing past me toward their tracks. As my feet hit the ground, Sergeant Long and Specialist Young ran up to the jeep.

"Get in the nearest track," I yelled to them. "I've got to get with Vinh.

We have to get out of this."

More rounds fell on the village and the Troop as we ran. The first vehicle we came to was the maintenance track. We hesitated a moment while Sergeant Long stopped to let one of the mechanics climb through the door of the back ramp. I patted Long on the back, turned to wave good luck to Young, then turned and raced for the command track. There was another loud explosion and a flash of light as I passed the left rear corner of the maintenance track. I paid no attention to the explosion. I had no idea how close to me the round had landed. If I had, I might have been transfixed into immobility. I didn't realize I had cheated death by less than two feet.

I ran toward the command track and jumped onto its back left fender the moment Vinh gave the order to move out. The driver accelerated and the track lunged forward, racing out of the impacting rounds. I climbed onto the top of the track and dropped through the top hatch, while we moved to safety. Once inside the track, I felt around in the darkness for my radio's power-on switch. The movement of the track caused my body to sway back and forth, hitting other crewmen, the forward bulkhead, and the radio mounts. When I had the radio operational, I raised Cai Be and reported our situation.

The Troop slowed its pace on the edge of the next group of huts to the east. Vinh had the Troop pull onto the first large open plot of dry ground that the driver came to. When the track rocked to a stop, Vinh turned to me and asked that I call in a medevac.

"How many casualties do we have?" I asked.

"Twelve, maybe fourteen" Vinh answered.

I raised Cai Be on the radio and gave them the dust-off request.

After passing the request to Dong Tam, the RTO advised me that the dust-off would be on station in fifteen minutes. I looked out to see the maintenance track and one of the searchlight jeeps roll up beside the command track and stopped.

Vinh caught my attention and pointed toward the maintenance track. "The dead are in that track, he said without emotion. "Sergeant Long was killed."

What? I thought. That can't be right! Long was okay when I last saw him. I refused to believe the reality of the attack and war. Friends don't get killed. That's the other guy. I jumped from the track and walked to the maintenance track to confirm that Vinh had been misinformed.

Approaching the maintenance track, I saw troopers carrying bodies from the back of the track and laying them side by side on the ground behind the lowered ramp. I didn't see Sergeant Long at first. He lay to one side.

Specialist Young knelt beside his body. I looked down at Sergeant Long's body. There wasn't a mark on him or any blood on his uniform.

"How did it happen?" I asked Young without expecting an answer.

"He was getting in the track when a round hit the top," Young answered.

"Only his head and shoulders were in the track when the round exploded."

"That must have been the explosion and flash that I had hardly noticed when I left them," I thought.

Young continued, "He fell back onto me when he was hit."

"Where was he hit?"

"At the base of the skull," Young answered.

I knelt down and turned Long's head. There was a small round, red mark at the base of his skull.

"It must have been Spaulding from the track," I said. Spaulding was small pieces of metal or aluminum armor that flaked off from inside the vehicle and flew around the crew compartment when a track was hit by a high explosive round.

"How did you get him here?" I continued.

"Sergeant Watts came by right after the round hit. I flagged him down and we got Sarge into the back of the jeep and followed the maintenance track to here."

A cold chill moved up my back. My shoulders, neck, and head shook in disbelief. *Long had been right,* I thought sadly. *He didn't make it.*

I walked to the back of the maintenance track and looked into the crew compartment. The track's light green walls were covered so badly with blood that they were now dark red. A sickening sweet odor permeated the air. The odor was so strong that the troopers removing parts of bodies from the crew compartment had to wear handkerchiefs over their noses and mouths to cut the odor. I became nauseous and moved away to keep from vomiting.

I walked to where the bodies were laid out for the dust-off. There wasn't a complete body in the row of cadavers. I could hardly identify seven torsos. Most of the mechanics had been literally torn to pieces by the concussion and Spaulding. The vehicle's driver and three others were alive but were wounded. Three of the searchlight crewmen were wounded also.

I was thankful that it was dark, so that I shouldn't clearly see the carnage, while I waited for the dust-off. My thoughts were soon interrupted by the whump whump of an approaching chopper. *Praise the Lord! Now I've an honorable excuse to get away from this sickening scene,* I thought. I returned to the command track to direct the chopper into our position. The dust-off's aid men with the help of the Troop's aid men methodically went about the gruesome task of placing the partial remains into body bags. While they worked, I wondered how they could stomach such a glory task. I reasoned in their job that they must have become hardened to all degrees of butchery. It took three trips to fly out the remains. The rest of the night was spent at Papa-20.

The next morning, I inspected the maintenance track to see where the round had hit and to see how much damage it had caused. I found that the projectile had landed on the track's cargo hatch. The hatch, as customary, had been folded back over the back deck. The round's impact caused a small crack and a shallow dent. If I hadn't known, I wouldn't have thought anyone had been injured because of the damage. Unfortunately, the round had landed directly over the rear ramp's door and Sergeant Long's head, killing him and Tom, the mechanic who heated my shaving and coffee water each morning, and six others. The only reason that I hadn't been injured was that the effect of the blast went up in a V over my head.

After inspecting the track, I took my cot and found a shady spot to stretch out and recount the events of the previous night. I wasn't as depressed as I thought I'd be after experiencing my first casualties. I did, however, feel bad about Sergeant Long's death. Lying on my cot, I thought about Long's premonition and Tom sitting on his heels each morning warming my coffee water. I hadn't been alone long when Vinh came over to talk. He expressed his sorrow about Sergeant Long and then dropped a bomb shell.

"Dai uy, we had an ordinance team in this morning to identify the rounds used last night in the attack," Vinh said.

"Did they come up with anything?" I asked.

"They didn't make a definite identification, but they said one part of a timing ring looked like it was from a 105 millimeter."

I was dumbstruck. I looked at Vinh for a long while before I answered.

"Maybe not," was all I said. I couldn't bring myself to believe that our own artillery had shelled us. To keep my sanity and to keep from becoming completely disgusted with the Army, the war, and Vietnam, I couldn't allow myself to think seriously about that possibility.

Finally, on January 25th, the Troop received orders to move into My Tho for a month. Little did I know what awaited me. I'd see a completely different side of duty with an advisory team; a side that would have made war almost enjoyable. Because Tet and its aftermath awaited me, I wouldn't return to the spartan life of the highway.

CHAPTER ELEVEN

PRE TET: JANUARY 1968

The first thing I did when the Troop returned to My Tho was to meet and get acquainted with Sergeant First Class Neal. An enthusiastic and well-qualified non-commissioned officer, Sergeant Neal was on his second tour with the 6th Cavalry. He was well received by the Vietnamese, who remembered his service with the Squadron during 1965–66, when he was awarded the Silver Star for valor.

Sergeant Neal and I spent a short time getting acquainted and then head for the Troop compound to see how the Troop was getting settled in. When we arrived at the compound, only the First Sergeant and two soldiers were in the Orderly Room. Captain Vinh and the other troopers had parked the vehicles and headed for town or parts unknown. I was curious about whether the men had performed their after-operation maintenance before taking off. A quick check of the vehicles set my mind at ease. The Vietnamese were like American soldiers, and probably soldiers of many other nationalities, when time off to hit town was the reward, they did their work in record time and performed to a high standard. The vehicles were topped off, cleared and neatly arranged; even the weapons had been cleaned.

After checking the vehicles, I told Neal that I wanted to look around the compound. I wanted to see how the troopers lived in garrison. I was in for an eye-opener. I was shocked and disheartened to find the barren, Spartan conditions under which the ARVN soldier lived.

The Troop compound was small and austere by American standards. The compound was divided into two areas: The cantonment area and the family living area. An office building, which housed the various troops' orderly rooms, and the enlisted billets, made up the cantonment area. The buildings were painted in light blue and trimmed in dark blue. This color scheme conformed to the Cav's colors, blue and white. Behind the cantonment was the family housing area. The compound didn't have paving or grass to hold down the dust during the dry season or to keep the vehicles out of the mud during the rainy season. Its landscaping consisted of a circular planter along the building's front and around the garrison's flag pole located in front of the orderly rooms. A small tree sat in each planter.

The orderly room building was a one-story cinder block building covered with stucco. The large two-piece windows swung to the inside of the rooms. There were no screens covering them. The building was large enough to furnish each Troop two offices, one for the commander and one for the orderly room or first sergeant's office. Each office was furnished with a single desk and two or three straight back wooden chairs. A telephone sat on each desk. There were no wall decorations.

The Troop billets were another single-story cinder block, stucco veneer building. It was a rectangular building that sat to the east and rear of the orderly rooms. The building was large enough to provide twelve or so two-room cubicles. A single door led into each set of rooms. The rooms were arranged one behind the other. Each room was furnished with eight wooden beds without mattresses. The occupants, if any, had to live out of duffel bags or furnish their own wall lockers or foot lockers. Again, nothing was on the walls. The accommodations were so sparse that they didn't appear to be in use. The single troopers must have lived on the economy in My Tho.

Troop Headquarters' Row photo by Larry Cole

Family Housing Area photo by Larry Cole

The married soldiers didn't live in much better conditions. The senior noncommissioned officers lived in a tile block building on the west side of the compound. The married enlisted men's homes, better described as hovels, were located behind the cantonment to the south. The shacks, which looked as though they'd fall at any

Motor Pool photo by Larry Cole

Troopers' Billets photo by Larry Cole

moment, were separated from the cantonment by a three strand barbed wire fence that ran along an open drainage ditch. The ditch was covered with green slime. The dwellings were a combination of thatch, tin, or plank shacks. They were pushed in side by side, providing no privacy. There was no street. Only a thin, winding crack like ally ran through the area without a discernible pattern. There were no sanitation facilities or running water. We saw several children going for water at a community water point. The water was carried by pogie stick, with a five-gallon tin can on each end of the stick. Some children didn't look to be as large as the cans they were carrying, but they quickly shuffled along, taking short steps, barely putting one foot in front of the other, without spilling a drop of water.

Though the living conditions were what I'd consider horrid, the soldiers and their families seemed to be content. They were friendly, smiling, and uncomplaining. Considering the closeness of the shacks, the neighbors seemed friendly toward each other. The children appeared to be well fed and happy. They played, laughed, and smiled like other children. The games were different but the happiness was the same.

After touring the compound, Neal and I returned to the Armor house to begin our My Tho daily routine.

Duty in My Tho was leisurely. The mornings consisted of breakfast at the Seminary and a visit to the Troop compound. The afternoons, after siesta, were spent at the Squadron compound and taking care of personal matters. The evenings were spent at the Seminary's Officers' Club or at the My Ngoc, our armor bar. All in all the duty was great, after almost four months on the highway.

The greatest contrast in the duty was in the living conditions. The Armor House provided some of the best, if not the best quarters, within Team 75's area. The house was a converted two-story duplex with a small front yard. The west side of the duplex was a three-bedroom apartment. The east side was a two bedroom apartment. The front yard was partitioned by a T-shaped wall, which evenly divided the yard. There were double gates at each end of the front wall. The front yard was used as a parking lot for our jeeps and to house an emergency generator in a small sand-bagged shed which sat against the front wall in the western portion of the yard.

There was a carport on each side of the house. Small covered porches were at the entrances at each corner of the first floor. There was an open balcony across the second floor. In front of the porches were small walls, which provided more privacy from the street traffic. The bottom half of these walls were solid. Their top half consisted of vertical concrete rails that formed a venetian blind effect.

The team used the entrance at the west side of the house for the main entrance, which opened into a sitting room furnished with wicker chairs, a couch, and a desk. The walls were decorated with framed Playboy centerfolds. Behind the sitting room was the team's operations room. This room contained a desk on which an AN/VRC 49 radio was mounted. A map of the My Tho area and several status charts were tacked to the wall. The stairs to the second floor were in this room. Behind the operations room was an unfurnished kitchen.

At the head of the stairs was a hall that provided the entrances to three bedrooms. Evans's and my room was over the carport. The other officers shared two interior rooms. The back inner bedroom opened onto a balcony, where a toilet and shower were located. The front bedroom ran across the front half of the house and had the door that allowed team members entry into the west side (NCO side) of the house. This door led into a bar that was furnished with a wicker bar and two wicker chairs. A Rebel flag hung from the front of the bar. Behind the bar was a large room, which housed the NCOs and the stairs. The eastern ground floor contained another kitchen at the rear of the house. The front room housed the team's theater.

Armor House offered all the amenities. We had comfortable sleeping arrangements with three-quarter size beds and mosquito netting. The two showers had hot water that was heated in a storage tank on the roof. The sun heated the water. The house had only one shortcoming. The kitchens didn't have either a stove or refrigerator. Each team was authorized a convenience package which contained these two items. For some reason, Major Evans's request for them hadn't been honored or he hadn't taken time to go to Saigon to unravel the red tape and get the request moving. That task would fall to me.

Our main social activity was a nightly visit to the officer's club at the Seminary. We spent an hour or two each night at the club visiting with officers from various organizations that used the Seminary as a base or were in and out for a variety of reasons. A large number of officers from Advisory Team 63 Headquarters patronized the club nightly. I became good friends with several of them. Two officers in particular come to mind, Lieutenant Colonel Walters and Captain Hill.

LTC Walters was the Executive Officer of Team 63 and a Medal of Honor winner during the Korean War. A tall, slender redhead with a pale, freckled complexion, Colonel Walters presented an unpretentious and affable personality. He was one of the guys.

Captain Hill had served his time in the field with a subsector and had recently been transferred to Team 63's operations section. A well-educated officer, Captain Hill spent most of his time at the club teaching me the correct after-dinner liqueur to order. I shouldn't say the correct liqueur. It'd be more accurate to say he had me sample a different drink each night to keep me from embarrassing myself in polite company by ordering a rum and Coke after dinner instead of say a BJ. I must say that the effort, though enjoyable, was short lived. About all that I retained was that I liked Black Russians. The other drinks have been forgotten.

Other officers I came to know and respect were the Air Force FAC, Major Gay and the liaison officer from the 9th Infantry Division, Captain Johnson. Major Gay didn't fit the normal stereotype of an Air Force officer in appearance. He was a large man, possibly a little overweight, and a plain dresser. He dressed in fatigues instead of a flight suit and didn't wear a scarf around his neck, but he did fit the happy-go-lucky characterization of an aviator. He was quick with a joke, a flying story, and a laugh. But one wasn't to mistake his happy-go-lucky attitude for non-professionalism. I'd learn later that when he was covering an operation he was a true professional.

Captain Johnson was a steady source of information about the 9th Division and the problems its various units had with Charlie. Though we, the cavalry, had really never become engaged with Charlie in what I'd consider a knock-down, drag-out, shoot-out during my time with them, Johnson always had a new story about deadly 9th Division firefights. Unfortunately, the 9th seemed always to come out on the short end. One particularly gruesome action was when the river Riverine boats assaulted the banks of a VC base camp. They lowered their ramps directly in front of two 12.5 cal machine gun bunkers. The infantrymen were cut down like cord wood when they charged off the boats. So much for the glamour of being a Marine. I like to maneuver. Why charge the enemy head-on when you can go around or sneak up on him through the woods or up a draw? In this case, however, I don't think the 9th knew it was landing in the middle of a base camp. So much for bad intelligence or no intelligence.

While we drank, never to excess, gossiped about the liaisons of fellow officers with the local ladies, which were few, and swapped war stories, which were generally exaggerated and presented in a humorous light; we played horses, ship captain and crew, or liars dice for drinks. These games were played with five dice rolled from a small leather cup. Horses was the easiest and quickest game to play. It was played when the participants wanted a quick win and a quick drink. The game could be played with any number of players. With more than two playing, it was played in rounds. The player with the best roll during a round dropped out. The rounds were continued until only two players were left. The loser of the final round bought drinks for all participants.

Ship, captain, and crew was the most popular game. It took more time to play than horses but it was more exciting. Again, the game was played in one to three rolls. The first player could stop, whenever he thought he had an unbeatable hand. The difference was that sixes were called ships and fives were called captains. You could use only one six as a ship and one five as a captain. You had to roll a six for a ship before you could count a five as a captain. After a player rolled a six and a five, he counted whatever came up on the other dice as crewmen. The player obtaining the largest crew during a set of three rolls was the winner. The last loser bought.

The most time-consuming game and the one that provided the most laughs and the most anticipation was liars dice. A variation for this game was that a roller could keep all or part of the dice under the cup. He rolled the dice, slammed the cup onto the table with the top down, peeked under the cup's top lip, and called his hand. He then carefully slid the cup, so as not to disturb the lay of the dice, to the next player. If that player believed the call, he'd accept the cup, sneaked a peek and then upped the call. As the cup progressed about the table, a player might take out a dice or two to make his call more unbelievable or he might reshake the cup. Whatever a player did, he had to up the call if he believed the last call. If a player didn't believe a call that was passed to him, he could pick up the cup. If the dice matched or were better than the call, the player lost. If the dice didn't match the call, the player who made the call lost. As the game went along, players formed allies, for whatever reason, to set up one particular player as a potential loser and the buyer of the next round. Allies were formed by body language, rather by spoken agreement and would change with each game. After a few calls, it became evident to each player who was trying to set up whom. The game then became a battle of wits by the scheming players to set-up the target. The target, on the other hand, had to find a way to dispute the chain of calls to his favor.

As the dice moved around the table, the sharp looks, name-calling, and joking rose to a high pitch. The longer the game went on and the more drinks consumed, the sweeter a victory and the greater the celebration and the greater was the good-natured ribbing directed at the loser.

The disquieting thing about these nightly outings was that we gave little or no thought to the unfortunate fellas out in the paddies being shot at or killed. I don't pretend to know or understand why we didn't feel guilty for enjoying our easy, carefree lifestyle. Maybe it was because we had each accepted the call and had taken our chances. We had been the lucky ones who had drawn the soft assignment through no effort of our own. Or maybe it was that some of us had pulled, in our minds, our share of hazardous duty and felt we had earned a reprieve. Some had been shot at and missed; some had been shot at and hit; some, as in my case, had lived the lonely life of the road, eating only rice and sleeping in the rain. Or maybe it was that we subconsciously feared what awaited us the next day or the next week and wanted to live life to the fullest before an unheard or unseen adversary sent us home to our families in a plastic bag. Whatever the reason, we enjoyed ourselves without concern for those who weren't as fortunate as we.

One evening over dice, Major Evans and I discussed the reporting system. The results we obtained weren't close to the results we read about in *Stars and Stripes* or those reported in the various news magazines. It was obvious that the president and Congress weren't getting the straight story. At least, they weren't given the situation as I saw it.

"I don't understand why MACV doesn't tell the truth," I said. "We report a body count of three and from the reports in the paper the president gets a count of thirty."

"There's a tendency to inflate the count, so that the president will hear what he wants to hear," replied Evans. "Not a good situation, but a fact of life.

"That's no reason to lie. And how about the role ARVN is reported to be taking?" I said.

"What's that?" Evans asked.

"Well, the papers say that ARVN is taking greater responsibility in the war, I started.

"Possibly they are. We see only a small part of the war, replied Evans.

"Yeah, maybe so, but MACV should tell it the way it is," I said.

"You're right, they should and maybe they do. We do,"

"But somewhere in the chain the reports are changed," I interrupted.

"Maybe so, but that's not our concern," Evans said. "We can only report our views to the next higher and hope that they are included in their views. Remember, MACV gets information from all sources and has a better feel for the whole picture. What we see may not be indicative of the whole picture."

"Ah, come on. The ARVN can't be that different in the other corps," I retorted.

"I wouldn't accuse anyone without facts," Evans said. "Impressions won't hold water."

"Maybe not, but we should be able to insure that our reports aren't altered and if we find out they are we should report it."

"Before you do that, you had better be sure that the issue is worth falling on your saber for," Evans said.

His advice hit me right between the eyes. If I went around the chain of command and played ombudsman, I'd better have my facts straight and be willing to sacrifice my career. At my level, regardless of my impressions, I had no way of knowing if reports were in fact changed. If they were changed to present other than a true picture, I had no way of knowing where in the chain the facts were being misrepresented. I could only do my job as best I could and hope that others did the same.

To better our lifestyle and help us to be equal to or above the other teams, the Armor House needed a stove and a refrigerator.

After some persuasion on my part, Major Evans agreed to have me hand-carry a request for these two items to the main supply depot in Saigon. I didn't really care about the stove or the refrigerator. Why cook when it was only a five-minute drive to the Seminary? However, the mission would give me an opportunity to slip up to Long Binh for a visit with my friend Mosley. My plan was simple. I'd make the trip in my jeep, followed by a deuce and a half (a two and a half ton truck). We'd drive to Saigon during the afternoon where I'd spend the night at the Majestic Hotel. Rumor had it that the Majestic was the place to meet the Saigon upper class. I had visions of the conquering hero entering the lounge to be wined and dined by the grateful cosmopolitans. Ba and the truck driver would stay at a local ARVN compound.

After a good night's sleep, we'd head for the docks to wrangle the stove and refrigerator from the supply types. Then the truck would return to My Tho, and I'd head for Long Binh to visit with Mosley and spend the night before returning to the Delta. The plan met with Major Evans's approval with one exception. He wanted me to go by the Property Disposal Yard at Long Binh to see if we could get parts for the Squadron from badly damaged vehicles stored there for salvage.

The drive to Saigon was uneventful. Traffic was heavy with all types of vehicles represented on the highway. The only interesting event was our crossing of the Vam Go Tay River at Tan An. The bridge had been blown by the VC several months earlier and it hadn't been repaired. We had to cross the river on a pontoon bridge.

Ba dropped me at the hotel late in the afternoon. Neither the building nor its deserted lobby was impressive. After checking in, I dropped my bags in a room that was as large and comfortable as any I had stayed in before. Then I headed for the lounge on the hotel's roof. When I entered the lounge, there were two male civilians sitting at the bar. I sat down a couple of stools from them and ordered my customary rum and Coke. The two men continued their conversation without recognizing my presence. Being the shy type, I drank my drink as slowly as I could and waited for one of the patrons to invite me into the conversation. The invitation wasn't forthcoming. After a second drink, I headed for the dining room and a solo dinner. So much for Army rumors about exciting places to wine and dine. After dinner, I went back to my room to enjoy a good night's sleep.

The next morning Ba picked me up and we drove to the docks, where we met the truck. The harbor was filled with ships off-loading supplies. The depot consisted of several large rectangular tin warehouses encircled by a high chain link fence. The yard between the buildings and the fence was filled with cartons of supplies stacked two and three high. After a few requests for assistance, I was directed to the office of the chief warrant officer who was responsible for one of the warehouses.

"What can I do for you cap'n?" the warrant asked, looking up from his desk when I entered his office.

"I need a stove and a refrigerator," I said, handing him the two requests. He took them and studied them without a change of expression. I thought to myself, *I have a hard-nose here.*

I waited a few moments and then added, "I'm with an advisory team in the Delta. We understand that we're authorized these items as part of a morale package for advisory teams. We haven't had any place to keep them until . . ."

"Ah, I know," the chief interrupted. "Let me check."

He turned and opened one of the file cabinet drawers behind his desk. He looked through the files for a few seconds and then turned back to me. "I don't show that your team has been issued a stove and refrigerator. But I'm not sure that we have what you want in stock. I'll have to check."

He got up from behind his desk and headed for the door. *Here we go with the old warehouse shuffle,* I thought, as we walked down a long aisle bound by stacked cartons. He'll show an effort of looking and then will tell me how sorry he is that he can't help me.

At the end of the aisle, the chief stopped and checked the stock numbers on my requests against the stock numbers on some cartons.

"That's what I thought, we don't have what you've requested," the chief said. "But I can substitute a smaller stove and a larger refrigerator for you."

My heart jumped into my throat. I had to repress a smile and my relief when I answered, "Fine." This was too easy.

The chief had a fork-lift move the two crates from the warehouse and load them on the truck.

Back in his office the chief changed the stock numbers on the request and filled in the block on the requests showing that the items had been issued.

"Good luck cap'n. I hope these make life a little better for you guys. I understand it's pretty rough out there with ARVN," he said as he handed me the receipt

"Yeah, it's pretty bad," I replied taking the receipts. *If he only knew how good the job really was,* I thought. *I have the best job going and the best-kept secret in the Army.* "Thanks a lot, Chief. These will be greatly appreciated by the team and they'll get lotsa good use."

After a short drive, we arrived at Long Binh just before lunch. Though Long Binh was a large supply base, with acres and acres of crates and equipment stored in the open, the cantonment area was small. As I remember, it only consisted of a few square blocks. While looking for Mosley's office, we passed the PX, Officers Club, BOQ (bachelor officer's quarters), and an above-ground swimming pool. After asking for directions a few times, I found the G-2 Section where Mosley worked. He wasn't able to take off for the afternoon, so we had a quick lunch at a nearby snack bar. After lunch, I walked Mosley back to his office, then went in search of the Property Disposal Yard.

At the yard, I talked with a master sergeant about the procedures for drawing salvage parts. He told me there was no problem with the Vietnamese taking parts from the damaged vehicles so long as they had the proper paper work. He invited me to look around the yard but I declined. I couldn't get excited about walking around under a hot sun looking at junked tanks, APCs, artillery pieces, and trucks.

From the Property Disposal Yard, Ba took me by the billeting office and then to the BOQ, where I dropped my gear. Then we headed for the PX. I didn't have anything to do for the rest of the afternoon, so I decided to take advantage of the swimming pool. I needed a swimsuit. When Ba dropped me at the PX, I released him for the rest of the day with instructions to pick me up the next morning at the officers' club.

The PX was crowded. I was surprised at the large number of Australian and Thai troops shopping. I knew that both Australia and Thailand had sent troops to Vietnam, but I didn't realize that they were operating so near Saigon and American bases. I thought they were operating further north in I Corps or II Corps. They were an orderly group, but they appeared to be trying to buy out the place. Each man had his arms full of clothing, radios, cameras, and pogie bait (junk food).

I picked up a swimsuit and went back to the BOQ to change. Shortly, I was laid out on the raised wooden deck surrounding the pool. I spent the afternoon alternating between taking short dips in the pool and long sun baths. About 1630 hours, I headed back to the BOQ to change back into my jungle fatigues before meeting Mosley at his office at 1700 hours. From the office, Mosley and I went to his BOQ so he could clean up. Then we headed for the club where we had a leisurely meal. During the meal, we planned our R&R contingent on the wives' approval.

We'd recommend a July date for our meeting in Hawaii. The rest of the evening was spent reminiscing about our experiences in Germany and about old friends. Mosley told me about what had happened in the battalion after I left. When I left, he was the battalion's adjutant with about six months left on his tour. As Arthur had told me, shortly after my departure for Fort Polk, the battalion had moved from Crailshiem to Ansbach, about thirty kilometers north of Crailshiem. He had a few stories about the confusion and problems connected with the move. He also told me a little about his schooling at the Army Intelligence School at Fort Holabird. What's new or what's interesting can be said about an Army school? Particularly, an intelligence school. That stuff is all hush-hush you know. Quickly, the conversation passed to me. I told him about the Army's latest policies concerning basic training.

All basic companies were to be commanded by captains. Drill instructors were to attend Drill Sergeants School before working independently with recruits. The Army's new psychology was to ease recruits into the Army and its discipline instead of abruptly tearing them down and then rebuilding them in the image it wanted. I was expected to be with the recruits during all training. The open door policy allowed a recruit to call on the commander without his sergeant's permission or knowledge during a specified time each week. The AWOL (absent without leave) policy required us to track down our runaways and get them back to the company without reporting them absent. The idea was to get them through basic and to Nam. The party line was that recruits don't go AWOL if they are properly led. If a company had an AWOL, the problem was one of poor leadership or the lack of leadership. So, we didn't have AWOLs that anyone above brigade knew about. Mosley listened in wide-eyed amazement and disbelief. What I told him was a complete departure from his West Point training and three years' experience in Germany. Also, I related a few stories about my favorite recruits.

There was the rancher's son from West Texas, a sturdy fella about five feet six inches tall with a big burly chest, the type fella you'd think could whip the world. From the day he entered basic training, he begged for a discharge under any circumstances. He approached me several times crying and asking for help in getting out of the Army or at least out of going to Vietnam. He had just gotten married before being drafted and his wife needed him. She couldn't make it without him. On family day, his folks and wife came to see him and I saw what his real problem was. The family arrived in what's believed to be typical Texas-style, driving a new Cadillac and the men wearing big cowboy hats and boots. My recruit's wife was the prettiest little gal you could imagine. She was blonde, hardly five feet tall, and didn't weigh one hundred pounds. Each time I saw him and his wife during the weekend, she was leading him around like a pet bull. I can't say that I blamed him; she was a cute little thing. I had to laugh to myself when I saw them. It wasn't she who couldn't survive without him. It was him who couldn't get along without her. I told Mosley I thought he was more lovesick and afraid of losing her than he was of getting shot at by Charlie. It may have been a little of both.

Then there was the fella from Houston who was the only person who ever made me feel uneasy by just looking at me. He was a little fella, just over five feet, and slender as a rail. He was a high school drop-out from the rough part of Houston. He had been bumming around East Texas and Louisiana with his father for the past couple of years, living off the land, taking what they needed when they needed it. He had no respect for anyone or for authority. His drill sergeant had trouble handling him and asked me to talk with him about his attitude. One day, at a dry fire marksmanship range, I called this little outlaw over for a talk. While I questioned him about his attitude, he looked up at me with ice-cold blue eyes that showed no signs of fear or respect. Nothing I could say would cower him. If anyone was cowered, it was me. I had the feeling that he'd just at soon cut me open and walk around me as look at me. He made it clear that he did what he wanted and took what he wanted and wasn't afraid of anyone or anything. I believed him. Then near the end of his cycle he proved his point. He came in late one night from post privileges and started through his barrack cussing the blacks. Seven of them took exception to his remarks and went after him. From the accounts I heard the next morning, he made a pretty good showing before he broke and ran for the orderly room with the mad seven in hot pursuit. They caught him in the orderly room. During the ensuing fight, he ran a fist through a glass window in the door to my office. Then he ran into my office. That morning when I came in, my office was a wreck and covered with blood. After an investigation, I gave him an Article 15 (non-judicial punishment administered by the commander with the consent of the offender). He may have deserved more; but again, we were interested in putting people into Nam, not jail. He wasn't a complete dummy. He was to be assigned to the artillery after basic, so he had to have scored well on his aptitude test.

Also, I told Mosley about the young Cajun from the South Louisiana bayou who was visited by a mother—not his—and her three lovely daughters. The mother came into my office asking that I discharge our young Cajun on a hardship discharge. It seemed that she and her daughters were pregnant by him and they had no means of support without him. I didn't know if her story was true, but it was imaginative. After I explained the discharge process, I never heard from her again.

Then there was my favorite, one Private Hardin from New Orleans. Hardin was a real string bean. He was about six feet tall, give or take an inch, and weighed no more than a hundred twenty pounds. He was from a large family who were all on welfare. There were five children, of which Hardin was the oldest. Both the mother and father were arthritic and couldn't work. The mother, however, was pregnant. Arthritis doesn't stop everything. Hardin was their only source of income, other than a monthly welfare check. His mother had to have him home.

Every weekend, after the recruits were given post privileges, Hardin went AWOL. He wasn't hard to find, though. We'd ask the Military Police detachment in New Orleans to go by his home to see if he was there. He always was. The MPs had him back in the company by Tuesday.

Hardin couldn't do anything right. He had two left feet. He was sick. He was too weak to do physical training. You name it and he couldn't perform. I received daily letters from his mother, his pastor, concerned relatives, his lawyer—I don't know how the family could afford one—and even his congressman. Each correspondent told how unfit Hardin was for military service and how much his family needed him at home.

I received weekly telephone calls from his mother, who spent a small fortune listening to me explain the process of getting Hardin a hardship discharge, telling her he didn't qualify for a discharge, and that the Army was the best thing that could happen to him. Their first request was rejected. Hardin was counseled by the chaplain, by the psychologist, by me, and by the battalion commander. Still, he wanted out. Hardin insisted on a second submission.

He was to be trained as a heavy equipment operator after basic. I told Hardin that, considering his circumstances, he had a good deal in the Army. My argument was that the Army would train him for a high-paying job in the road construction industry. When he got out of the Army, with his training, he'd be qualified for a good job in that industry. I assured him he could do much better in the job market after his service than he could without the training and experience he received in the Army. In the long run, he could help his family more by completing his service. My rationale didn't go over. He wanted out.

Then during the last week of the cycle, the recruits had to take a PT (physical training) test as part of their final qualification score. These scores were averaged and companies with, I believe, an eighty-nine or higher average received a commander's trophy. All companies were expected to win the trophy. So, high PT scores on each recruit were important to the cadre. As an incentive, I offered any recruit who maxed the test a three-day pass. And who do you think maxed the test? That's right! Good old Hardin, the fella who couldn't do a push-up the day before.

The biggest surprise, however, was that Hardin was back at the company on time after his pass. He had only a few days before receiving his two weeks' leave after basic. I guess he thought it wasn't worth his effort to go AWOL when he'd be home in less than a week.

The topper came on graduation day. The brigade and I were responsible for him until he signed into his new unit. If he went AWOL en route, the AWOL would be credited to my company. Considering Hardin's record, the odds were that he wouldn't show at Fort Leonard Wood, the Army's Engineer Advanced Training Center for enlisted men, in two weeks. The brigade commander didn't want one of his companies to have an AWOL statistic. His solution was to order me to have Lieutenant Hemphill drive Hardin to Fort Leonard Wood and sign him in. I was glad to get rid of Hardin, but I couldn't see going to such lengths to save one statistic. Besides, the brigade commander didn't have the authority to give the order. His saving grace was that we all wanted Hardin out of our hair and Lieutenant Hemphill liked to travel.

Meanwhile, back at the officers' club, there were several attractive Do-nut Dollies (Red Cross girls) in the club. Some were eating in small groups and some were eating with officers. Naturally, the subject of their availability came up. Mosley told me that he understood that fifty dollars could purchase the favors of one for the night. He was quick to tell me that his information was only hearsay. Fifty dollars was too rich for his blood. I believed him. He had a wife and three children. I had the same. He couldn't afford a fifty-dollar night out. Why should he be any different? We were both the same pay grade, and there was the moral issue. Anyway, we went to the BOQ alone. So far as I'm concerned, the myth of loose Red Cross girls went unproven.

The next morning Ba picked me up on schedule and we headed back to My Tho. Just before we got to Highway 6A cutoff to the Seminary, we passed an American engineer unit, working on Highway Four. I wasn't surprised to see the unit. I had heard that an American engineer unit had been sent to the Delta to help the Vietnamese repair the highway. I was in a hurry, so we passed by quickly without paying any attention to the unit.

Back in My Tho, the rest of the week was spent installing our new stove and refrigerator. On Sunday, I went to the Seminary for a late breakfast. After breakfast, as I passed along the waiting line, I noticed a good-looking, well-built young soldier. He looked familiar. I took a second look. To my shock, it was Hardin! Of all the people I never expected to see again, it was Hardin, especially in Vietnam, but there he was standing tall. He must have gained fifty pounds and he was wearing Specialist Fourth Class insignia on his sleeve.

"Hardin, how are you?" I said with a smile.

"Fine," he replied with an embarrassed look. I could tell right away that he didn't want to talk with me.

"It looks like the Army has agreed with you. What are you doing down here?"

"I'm with an engineer unit working on the highway, sir, he replied.

"What do they have you doing?" I asked.

"I'm driving a grader."

"That's great. I told you the Army would train you for a good job. How's the family, by the way?"

"They're fine, sir."

The conversation was strained. Hardin clearly didn't want to reminisce. I cut the conversation short and moved on.

"Well, it was good to have seen you," I said as I walked on. He may not have been glad to see me or have been grateful to the Army for making a man of him, but I was. It gave me a great feeling of pride in having been part of his development. I hoped he made it home, many wouldn't. The end of January was drawing near. Tet was around the corner. This year it'd be a time of terror instead of a time of celebration.

CHAPTER TWELVE

TET—CHARLIE ATTACKS: 31 JANUARY 1968

The last five days of January were a time of anticipation for First Troop's soldiers. The Tet celebration began at the end of the month. Tet is a combination of Christmas and Mardi Gras, a time of merriment and friends visiting friends and family gatherings. Everyone was gearing down from the war and gearing up to a festive mood. Both sides had agreed to a truce, so the ARVN began to relax. The troopers had been on the highway for over three months. Many hadn't visited their families during that time. Though life wasn't particularly hard on the road, it was boring and it didn't offer the amenities of a large town like My Tho—namely girls.

Tet was the celebration of the Lunar New Year, celebrated each year by a week of feast and merriment. The dates fluctuated between the end of January and the middle of February, depending on the moon's cycle. But Tet is more than this; it's also a celebration of national pride, like our 4th of July, that gave the people an opportunity to honor their history and accomplishments.

As was generally the case, rumors and intelligence reports abounded that Charlie wouldn't honor the truce. But no one gave these reports any credence. We had been receiving reports for over a month that Charlie was going to attack. Like the farmer in Chicken Little, we had become numb to the warnings. Tradition had to be upheld. Charlie may come or he may not, but Tet would arrive and it would be celebrated. Why else go on fighting? Tet would be celebrated and the ARVN high command was going to do its part to see that it was. An order went out to allow half of each command to take leave.

With half the troopers on leave, there wasn't much for the advisors to do. We spent most of our time at Armor House catching up on personal matters and awaiting the coming show. I looked forward to Tet. I was interested in seeing the parade of the dragon. I had seen Chinese dragon parades in the movies when I was a kid and I imagined the Tet parade to be much the same. I was excited about witnessing the real thing. I could see the dragon dancing and leaping through the street to the accompaniment of drums and firecrackers. I wondered if the participants would wear costumes and how they'd act. Would it be like Mardi Gras? How would I know? I had never been to Mardi Gras.

By the 30th, the Troop's present-for-duty strength was down to the ordered 50 percent. Rumors of an impending attack continued to circulate, but no one took them seriously. However, before day's end, the rumors became reality! By late afternoon, any ideas of celebrating were shattered by a rash of guerrilla attacks, which broke out in the northern III Corps area.

Though there was no enemy activity in the My Tho area, General Trang, the 7th Division commander, decided to take no chances. He alerted the division and ordered the 6th Cavalry to alert positions in and around My Tho.

Vinh had arranged the use of old Armor House at the Squadron compound for a unit Tet party. The party was just getting under way when the alert order was brought to Vinh by a Squadron runner. The runner advised Vinh that he was to move the Troop to positions along Hung Vuong Street and to report to the Squadron command post for a briefing. Before Vinh could leave the room, Major Evans came in and asked that I accompany him to a briefing at Sector

House, located at the north end of Hung Vuong Street near the 32nd Ranger Company compound.

While Major Evans and I walked to his jeep, he briefed me on what was causing the commotion. His tone was matter-of-fact and showed no emotion. His manner was one of non-concern.

This is probably just another drill, I thought, *no need to worry.* Besides, Charlie had never attacked the large towns and during my brief tour he hadn't shown signs of wanting to fight; neither had ARVN. Why get excited?

When Major Evans and I arrived at sector, it was a boiling caldron. There was a loud hum of voices as various officers coordinated activities and discussed reports from the north. Looking around the room, I recognized nearly all the officers. I had met them either along the highway or at the club. As my eyes moved around the room, they locked on to my old brave and considerate friend Major Ruff of Cai Lay fame.

Lieutenant Colonel Walters, the Sector Executive Officer, called the group to order and introduced the Sector S-2, Intelligence Officer. He briefed us on the attacks in III Corp and gave us MACV's assessment of what was taking place. He didn't present a picture of a major, country-wide offensive nor did he have any information about Charlie's activities near My Tho.

After the S-2's briefing, the S-3, Operations Officer, briefed us on the 7th Division's and the Sector's RF and PF Troop dispositions. It was the normal fire hydrant briefing. About all I retained was that all units were on alert and personnel were being called back from leave. Also, 1st Troop was assigned the mission of securing the division tactical operations center and the central town.

The sector advisor then gave us his assessment and the usual pep talk about staying alert and being ready. Though he tried to appear concerned, he failed to convince me that we were about to face a Communist onslaught that would change the course of the war.

Leaving the room after the briefing, I felt someone at my side. It was good old Major Ruff. He was all smiles.

"What do you think, Cole?" he asked putting an arm around my shoulders

"I don't know. It sounds serious," I replied matter-of-factly. "But we've been alerted so often without anything happening that I can't get excited."

Stepping onto the porch, Major Ruff saw Vinh's command track. "Are those your tracks?" he asked.

"Yeah, we drew town security," I answered.

"Say, look, my hooch is right around the corner. How about asking your counterpart to park a track in front of it tonight?"

A flash of anger swept through me, the nerve of this guy! To hell with him! After the way he treated me in Cai Lay, how dare he ask me for anything? I couldn't care less what happened to him. Charlie could have him with my blessing.

"Sure," I said lying.

"Great, the coffee will be on all night. Come by any time." he said as we walked down the walk to the gate.

My track was parked in front of the gate. As I climbed on top, Ruff headed for home.

"Remember, the coffee will be hot," he called over his shoulder as he walked away.

"*Right. Screw you,*" I thought, re-arranging the pillow under my bedroll which Sergeant Neal had laid out on top of the track.

"What's happening, Sir?" Neal asked as I stretched out on my poncho and maneuvered my hips and spine around the various protrusions that reached skyward from the track's aluminum top.

"Charlie has mounted several attacks up north. They think we might be hit down here tonight, I said rolling over and pulling half the liner over me. I dropped off to sleep without a thought of asking Vinh to move a track to the Major's hooch or a moment's concern about not getting a good night's sleep.

I awoke to the soft puoom, puoom of impacting mortar rounds shortly after 0400. The rounds were falling on the 32nd Ranger's compound to the north of our position. Before I could shake the sleep from my mind and eyes, our driver had the track's engine running and Vinh was on the radio. While he talked, the mortar barrage directed at the Rangers grew heavier. I didn't need Vinh to tell me that Charlie was serious. Vinh was talking a mile a minute without a break. I raised the division TOC on the advisor net to find out the situation.

"The Rangers are under heavy assault," the duty officer replied to my request for information. "Most of the battalion is on leave and they are asking for help." I recognized Captain Craig's voice.

Our driver gunned the track's engine and spun the track around to face the Rangers' compound. Before the track came to a complete stop, we were headed toward the bridge that crossed the Bao Dinh Canal and led to the Ranger Compound. Three tracks of the 1st Platoon sped past us and crossed over the bridge into the compound. Vinh had his driver stop the track short of the bridge. We waited, listening to the falling mortar rounds, machine-guns, M-16 rifles, and AK-47 assault rifles. It was my first time to hear the distinctive sound of an AK-47. My only source of information was Captain Craig. Vinh was too busy receiving and sending reports to talk. Craig told me that the Rangers' situation was serious.

While I listened to the Rangers' battle, the sound of exploding mortar rounds to my left or west caught my attention. I tensed and strained my eyes and ears to identify this new threat. I saw nothing in the darkness.

Within minutes, the tracks that had crossed over into the Rangers' compound raced back across the bridge, passed us, and continued down the street. Vinh was too busy to tell me what was happening, so I sat and waited. I can't recall what was going through my mind, but I don't remember being particularly concerned. There was a steady stream of conversation over the advisor's net as Captain

Craig talked with various advisors and tried to keep us updated. The 1st Troop was the only unit in the Squadron engaged. Even so, I hadn't noticed any enemy rounds directed at us.

After 1st Platoon passed us, Vinh had our track move a few meters back from the bridge and to the east side of the street. Just as we stopped, I received a call from Captain Craig.

"Charlie One-six, this is Delta Tango Three-zero, over."

"This is One-six, over."

"Roger, One-six. We have a report that the Ranger's situation is becoming desperate and that they are short of ammunition. I need you to send someone over to check out the ammunition situation, over."

"Roger Three-zero, out, I replied into the microphone.

I reached over and tapped Vinh on the shoulder. When I had his attention, I told him I had been told to check out the Ranger's ammunition status. He only nodded in acknowledgment.

I grabbed my M-16 and motioned for Neal to follow me. "Come on," I called jumping from the track. He followed without hesitation. We hit the ground running and headed for the south end of the bridge. As I ran for the bridge, I knew Vinh would be waiting when I got back. At the bridge, we fell into a prone position at its northwest abutment and took up firing positions. Breathing hard, I turned to Neal.

"I've been told to check out the ammunition situation in the Ranger compound. Cover me", I said, looking into Neal's calm eyes.

"No, sir. I'll go. You need to stay with the Troop. Cover me." Neal said, raising up on one knee and lunging forward before I could say anything. I must admit that I wasn't too excited about crossing the bridge and wandering around in the dark, trying to find the Ranger Advisor. I didn't call Neal back as he raced across the bridge into the darkness.

I lay in a prone position, aiming my M-16 toward the middle of the bridge. While I waited, looking into the darkness, a coal of fire hit my stomach. For the first time during my tour I had time to realize that I was in a life-and-death-struggle. To make matters worse, I wasn't protected by the armor of my track or the Troop's machine guns. I was on my own in the darkness with weapons firing to my front. Fear hit hard and I wanted to run back to the command track. But I couldn't; Neal was on the other side of the canal and he might need help. Could I move if he called? I lay peering into the darkness and saying over and over to myself, *hurry, hurry, hurry.*

My wait wasn't long. Soon, I saw Neal running toward me. He slid down beside me breathing hard.

"How were they?" I asked.

"Fine," he replied breathlessly.

"Do they need any ammo?" I asked.

"No, they're in good shape."

"Let's get out of here," I said getting to my feet and starting to run.

Neal followed. I didn't think to ask who "they" were. I didn't care. Neal had given me the answer I wanted and I could give Captain Craig a report. I wasn't interested in asking questions.

I climbed over the side of the command track and dropped down inside. On my knees, I grabbed the radio's microphone and pushed the push to talk button. I didn't bother to put on my headset. I could hear by the radio's speaker.

"Tango Three-zero this is Charlie one-six, over."

"This is Three-zero. What did you find out, over?"

"They're in good shape."

The track lunged forward, throwing me backward. I caught myself with my left hand before hitting the floor. Righting myself, I pressed the push to talk button again.

"We're moving. I'll get back to you," I said without the formality of proper radio procedure. I stood in the cargo hatch to look out; the sound of the vehicle's tracks was deafening. The track was moving so fast that I didn't think it was safe to climb onto my seat behind

Vinh. Vinh turned to me and said that the 2nd Platoon was under attack at the traffic circle.

A savage firefight had erupted between the two forces. The VC poured a withering volume of B-40 antitank fire into the 2nd Platoon's position. Fortunately, heavy return fire from the troopers spoiled the enemy's aim and the platoon's tracks were able to withdraw 100 meters east along Nguyen Tri Phuong Street without loss.

When we reached the intersection of Nguyen Tri Phuong and Hung Vuong Streets, the driver spun the track to the west along Nguyen Tri Phuong and came to a stop behind the 2nd Platoon tracks. We had driven into a hornet's nest. The ground seemed to erupt around the tracks. The platoon sat fully exposed in the middle of the street. Its 57 mm recoilless rifle track was forward, firing into the buildings on the north side of the street. The other tracks, one on either side, sat to the 57 mm track's rear, giving covering fire.

To the platoon's right was the walled garden of the Catholic School; to its left was a hospital. Charlie was firing from both the garden wall and the hospital, and from buildings further up the street to the northwest.

Vinh quickly surveyed the situation and saw that the platoon had apparently stopped the VC assault. This had hardly registered when I was thrown forward. Our track was backing into the intersection. We stopped, did a neutral steer (maneuver where the driver locks one track and engages the other causing the track to pivot on one locked tracks) to the left and headed south down Hung Vuong to the next intersection and then turned west up a side street.

Vinh was moving to the 3rd Platoon's position. He had ordered the platoon to counterattack the flank of VC that had pushed the 2nd Platoon from the traffic circle. As the 3rd Platoon neared the traffic circle, it also received heavy automatic weapons-fire from Charlie, who was hidden in the buildings. That platoon stalled as well. Vinh had to get the troopers moving—a stationary track in an urban area at night is a dead track.

Our driver maneuvered the track into position behind the 3rd Platoon about a half block from the traffic circle and to the right side of the street beside a large tree. The darkness was filled with red tracers as they whipped savagely into the buildings. The noise was deafening. I could see the mouths of the troopers moving, but I couldn't hear what they were saying over the high volume of automatic weapons' fire. The situation was total bedlam. The troopers fired in all directions without command or a target. They fired indiscriminately at windows, cars, trucks, or anything that might offer a hiding place for Charlie.

When the track stopped beside a tree, I moved to the right side of the cargo hatch, behind the .30 cal side gunner, to see if I could see anything on that side of the street. I had just moved behind the gunner when I was blinded by a bright white flash followed by a loud explosion. Something heavy hit me in the chest. Within seconds, I regained my sight. I was holding the gunner. His face was a mass of red. The tree, less than a foot from the track, had been hit by a B-40 round at our head level. The gunner's face had taken the brunt of the B-40's fragments and the tree's flying bark. I wasn't scared.

I hardly had time to realize what had happened when the track was on the move, again throwing me and the gunner back into the track. I laid the gunner on the vehicle's floor. He looked up at me calmly without making a sound. His breathing was normal. He'd live but lose an eye.

I struggled to stand in the cargo hatch. The track was moving fast and weaving, so it was hard for me to regain my footing. When I did get my head up, we were at the traffic circle and sliding around the corner onto Nguyen Tri Phuong Street. The driver accelerated and headed back toward Hung Vuong and the 2nd Platoon, which was still holding its position.

The 2nd Platoon's tracks and our track weaved past the 2nd Platoon and dispersed at the intersection. Our track spun around in the intersection and faced back toward the 2nd Platoon and the traffic circle. Just as we stopped, the 2nd Platoon's leader moved his platoon's 57 mm recoilless rifle track forward. For a few minutes, it was seemingly holding the enemy back with a steady stream of recoilless rifle fire. Charlie, however, managed to maneuver a B-40 crew through the buildings on the north side of the street into a position, which would enable it to fire on the 57 mm track.

Just as the 2nd Platoon was about to counterattack, the 57 mm recoilless track received a direct hit from a B-40. Before the B-40's bright red flash could dissipate, the crew was dismounted and running toward us. As the antitank fire increased, the remainder of the platoon withdrew quickly to positions along Hung Vuong. This allowed the VC to move into the Catholic school on the northwest corner and into the hospital on the southwest corner of the intersection of Hung Vuong and Nguyen Tri Phuong Streets.

With this sudden success, Charlie pressed his attack, through the courtyards of the hospital and the school, in an effort to enter the city proper. The fighting was furious. Red tracers crisscrossed in the black night. Loud explosions pierced the night and drowned out the constant pounding of the machineguns. Charlie fired into the fully exposed troopers from concealed positions. We couldn't distinguish their muzzle flashes because they were firing from deep within the buildings. Nonetheless, the troopers held their positions and returned an overwhelming volume of fire from their .50 cal and .30 cal machineguns. Charlie was no match for the massed firepower of the tracks. His attack stalled on the west side of Hung Vuong.

Vinh moved the command track along Hung Vuong Street, stopping near various tracks as they engaged VC positions. Finally, Vinh positioned the command track near the Hung Vuong—Phan Hein Dao intersection. The tracks at the intersection were exchanging automatic weapons fire with several pockets of VC to the northwest of Hung Vuong. The night vibrated with the sound of the weapons. From the volume of fire the Troop was receiving, I decided to call for the big guns from Dong Tam. I dropped into the track and changed my radio's frequency to the 9th Division's artillery frequency.

"Romeo Lima Two-one, this is Charlie One-six, fire mission, over."

"This is Lima Two-one, send it, over."

"This is One-six, roger. Coordinates four six seven, ahh four five five. Troops in buildings. Request spotter round, will adjust, over."

"This is Lima, roger. Coordinates four six seven, four five five. Troops in building. Fire Spotter, Wait . . . Shot out, over."

"Roger, shot out." I replied.

In a few moments, I could hear the round whistling in. A small cloud of smoke popped to the north.

"Lima this is Charlie One-six. Over, drop one hundred, over."

"Roger, drop one hundred, wait . . . Shot out, over."

"Roger, shot out," I replied. The round came singing in. It burst short.

"Lima, this is Charlie One-six. Short, add five zero, over."

"This is Lima, roger, add five zero, wait . . . Shot out, over."

"This is Charlie One-six, roger." The round burst over the building I wanted to flatten.

"This is Charlie One-six, target. Fire for effect, over."

"This is Lima, roger, wait . . . Shot out."

"Roger, shot out, I waited. Three rounds whistled toward the target. Oh no! They passed over.

"Cease fire! Cease Fire!" I yelled into the mic as the round impacted to the north near the Sector House. The artillery hadn't changed its charges or sight settings to allow for the difference in the type rounds fired or something. I didn't know the problem. I wasn't an artilleryman. I only knew that I was directing fire onto a friendly position.

Lima this is Charlie One-six. You were over. Drop one hundred, fire one round, over."

"This is Lima, roger. Drop one hundred, wait . . . Shot out, over," Said the cool, undisturbed artilleryman.

A single round came sailing in on target. Whatever the problem, the artillery had made the correction.

"Lima, this is Charlie One-six. Target, fire for effect, over."

"This is Lime, roger. Fire for effect, wait . . . Shot out."

"This is Charlie One-six, roger."

Momentarily, five rounds came thundering in. The target area disappeared in a cloud of smoke. I sat and watched the rounds fall until the huts behind the school began to burn. While I watched, all I could think was that I had fired on Americans. Oh no, Lord! Please, oh please, don't let it be that I was responsible for killing Americans. I didn't think about the innocent South Vietnamese civilian caught in the bombardment.

"Lima, this is Charlie One-six. Target, cease fire, over."

As dawn broke, the battle slowly developed into a series of man-to-man skirmishes.

Heroic action became commonplace. Troopers continually dismounted their tracks to assault VC positions with hand grenades and to fire into enemy positions from fully exposed positions in the center of the street.

Most of the enemy fire seemed to be coming from behind the school's garden wall. which ran along Nguyen Tri Phuong Street. I watched several troopers charge forward and try to heave a grenade over the wall. I was amazed that they couldn't get a grenade over the wall. Finally, I could stand it no longer. Old Big'un would show them how it was done.

I jumped from the track and ran into the center of the intersection, pulling a grenade's pin as I ran. I stopped, threw my hand straight back with locked elbow and came up and forward with the grenade. When my hand was directly over my head I let fly. I looked up to follow the flight of the grenade as it sailed over the wall.

Uh Oh. It was flying straight up. It'd come down not more than ten feet from me. I turned and raced for the track. It'd be mighty embarrassing to be wounded by my own grenade. I'd never live it down. Luckily, I was out of range before it exploded. I don't think I ever ran that fast in my life.

Breathlessly, I climbed back on the track and fell into my seat behind Vinh. So much for playing infantry. I'd better leave the fighting and dirty work to the troopers. As an infantryman, I made a much better advisor. Fortunately, the Vietnamese are a polite people. They looked away to hide their smiles. Even Neal covered his smile as I hung my head

Attempts throughout the morning were made to recover the damaged 57 mm recoilless rifle track. Finally, near mid-morning, during a lull in the fighting, I noticed a lone soldier run across Hung Vuong. Charlie immediately opened fire on him before he could reach the safety of a large tree on the southwest corner of the intersection.

"Who's that," I asked Vinh.

"Corporal Ut," he answered without taking his eyes off Ut.

The troopers took up Charlie's challenge. They poured on covering fire. Ut crouched behind the tree until he thought it safe to move. Then he sprang forward to the next tree. Charlie continued to direct a heavy volume of fire at Ut in an effort to drive him back. Although bullets kicked up dirt all around him, Ut continued to work his way from tree to tree toward the abandoned track.

Another track moved to the center of the intersection to provide better covering fire. This was all the distraction Corporal Ut needed. Before Charlie could redirect their attention to him, Ut sprang onto and over the back ramp and into the cargo compartment of the disabled track. He removed the .30 cal machinegun from its mount on the right side of the track, spun, laid it across the gun shield on the commander's hatch, and began to fire into enemy positions—just like Audie Murphy, who was awarded the Congressional Metal of Honor for a similar action in Southern France during WW II.

Hung Vuong Street photo by Larry Cole

Approach to traffic circle photo by Larry Cole

Seeing this, the TC supporting Ut's actions moved his track into position behind the disabled vehicle. Two troopers jumped from the rescuing track. They connected tow cables to the 57 mm recoilless track and jumped back onto their track before Charlie could direct accurate fire at the two vehicles. Within minutes, both tracks were back within friendly lines.

Catholic Church photo by Larry Cole

57 mm Recoilless Rifle track's position photo by Larry Cole

While 1st Troop and the Rangers held Charlie back, Major Evans and the other 6th Cavalry advisers were trying to get to their units. Major Evan's first indication of the battle had been around 0900 hours when he heard distant rifle fire. He contacted the division with the radio in Armor House's operations room to learn of the attack. He organized patrols from the advisors and a few military policemen who were staying at the Armor House for a few days, ordering them to investigate the neighborhood and to find a way to the Squadron compound. The first patrols ran into Charlie within a few blocks. After an exchange of fire, the patrol withdrew to Armor House. Charlie must have thought that he had engaged the US 9th Division when he saw Americans moving along the street, because he went to ground.

Strangely, this exchange may have saved the day. Evidently, Charlie was trying to envelop the 1st Troop's southern flank. When he ran into unexpected opposition he dug in to investigate. This provided the ARVN an opportunity to reinforce with the rest of the 6th Cav and the 3rd Battalion, 11th Regiment.

The 3rd Battalion moved into positions along Nguyen Trung Long Street near the 7th Division's TOC and began a slow, house-to-house movement north toward 1st Troop along the west side of Hung Vuong Street at 0900 hours. I don't remember when the Cav units moved. Sometime during the morning or early afternoon the 2nd Troop moved to the southern flank of the 3rd Battalion to guard the 7th Division's Headquarters. The 3rd Troop moved to secure Binh Due Airfield.

While the 3rd Battalion crept up Hung Vuong, the 1st Troop continued to hold Charlie at bay. First Troop's battle settled into one of returning sporadic fire. When Charlie fired at a track, the entire Troop would lay down a fusillade that drove Charlie to ground. The troopers, in most cases, couldn't tell from where the shots were fired. Soon the street became covered with .50 cal and .30 cal brass. The local brass dealers would make a small fortune cleaning up after the fight.

Between eruptions, I monitored radio communications between advisors and requested artillery. Occasionally, I could identify shots fired from houses north of the school. When we did, I called in the big guns. The morning was filled with the continuous thunder of the 155's at Dong Tam.

The normal mayhem of radio communications associated with tactical operations wasn't present. Transmissions were cool and calm. There were no continual requests for SITREPs (Situation Reports). There was no check and recheck of reports for accuracy. There was no demand for quick action and quicker results. Maybe this was because the senior advisors had been caught in their quarters and couldn't get to their C & C (Command and Control) Hueys. Or maybe it was that a group of young captains were running the show and didn't know what questions to ask. Whatever the case, the battle was being fought by company-sized units and their advisors without senior officers looking over their shoulders. Things were going well though, maybe better than if we had all that supervision. I could overhear a steady flow of reports from Captain Woods, the 3rd Battalion's advisor. Everyone on the net knew when each house and block was cleared. The Rangers to the north continued to be pressured and received intermittent mortar barrages. Some infantry advisors were reporting a shortage of ammunition and grenades. The cavalry didn't experience these shortages. We carried three layers of filled ammunition boxes on the floor of each track.

During one of the lulls, I noticed several civilians who lived in the area controlled by Charlie begin to evacuate their homes. At first, there were only a confused, reluctant few. They couldn't seem to decide whether they could look for help from the VC or from the ARVN soldiers. They made their decision only after seeing the government soldiers moving forward to assist the civilian wounded. Once they had made their choice, they poured into 1st Troop's positions, dragging their dead children by their heels or carrying their wounded grandparents. One old man, half dragged between two women, had his hip half shot away, with raw bone and torn, dangling flesh clearly visible. It was a disgusting, sickening scene. I felt sorrow for the people, but no responsibility for their plight. It never entered my mind that I was partly to blame for the destruction. I had requested and directed much of the artillery that caused their wounds and deaths. But it wasn't me, it was Charlie who was to blame. I was the defender. Charlie started the shooting. I was only reacting, doing what I was trained to do without hesitation: trying to save my unit. Such was the justification for one's actions and lack of feeling.

Charlie took advantage of this mass exodus to escape the advance of the 3rd Battalion and the murderous fire of the Cav. As refugees moved along the streets toward troopers' positions, guerrillas in green uniforms could be seen withdrawing toward the traffic circle and the rear of the school. Seeing this, our troopers immediately occupied the hospital and front rooms of the school.

The movement of the civilians created a potential threat to the South. They moved freely between the opposing forces as they shifted their small belongings to more peaceful areas of the city or moved large pieces of furniture from burning dwellings into the street. The lack of attempts to identify infiltrators caused the South Vietnamese problems for the next two days. Charlie took advantage of the situation to infiltrate individual snipers and small units into the central city. From time to time, I could hear small fire fights to our rear. The sounds of the engagements weren't sufficient to concern me. They, however, were annoying. Nor do I recall who eliminated these small incursions. I mention them to illustrate a small problem that could have become a major one.

During late morning, Major Evans tried to break out of the Armor House again. His small group had moved only a few meters when it was taken under fire at the Pasteur Street intersection. In the heated exchange one of the MPs was killed before the group again withdrew to the Armor House.

Major Evans would tell me later that he was giving up hope of seeing another day.

By noon, the troopers, without infantry aid, had completely stopped Charlie's advance, cleared the hospital, and the front rooms of the school's south wing. I visited the hospital to see the extent of its damage. A few nuns were helping the last of the patients from the courtyard when I entered the grounds. Walking through the various rooms, I was appalled at the unsanitary conditions and the austere atmosphere. The rooms were furnished with old steel frame beds with uncovered mattresses and porcelain wash basins on rickety wooden nightstands. There were no screens on the windows or mosquito nets over the beds. Several of the rooms had bullet holes in the walls and bloodstains on the floors. I don't know who fired the shots, but I could tell from the shape of the holes, which showed little flecking or jagged edges, that they had been fired from inside the room.

At 1300 hours, the 3rd Battalion arrived at the intersection and crowded behind a three-foot wall in front of the school waiting to assault. When the signal came, the infantry rose up, climbed over the wall with remarkable ease, and entered the school's south wing. The initial assault, however, was the only quick, unopposed move they'd make for the next four hours. Once they moved past the rooms the 1st Troop had cleared, a deadly battle erupted in the building's corridors.

While the infantry battled for the school, 1st Troop supported them from positions along Hung Vuong. I sat and listened to the muffled sounds of M-116s, AK-47s and grenades. Every few minutes an infantryman was carried from the building. "Why didn't they work their way to the roof and then work down? That's US doctrine, I thought. They probably couldn't use a chopper to put a squad on the roof. It'd be shot down. But maybe by using grappling hooks and ropes, they could get a squad up one corner and onto the roof. They could then blow a hole in the roof and start down. I didn't say anything, however. It wasn't my place to advise the infantry. And I wasn't sure of the tactic.

Throughout the battle, 1st Troop supported the infantry with automatic weapons fire. The troopers occasionally fired into the school's upper floors and the Troop's mortar platoon fired into the area behind the school. I continued to monitor the radio. Around mid-afternoon, I heard the vibrating voice of a chopper pilot come on the net.

"Delta Tango Three-zero, Delta Tango three-zero, this is Freighter Three-three, inbound your location, over," the pilot called.

"Roger, Freighter Three-three, this is Delta Tango, over."

"This is Three-three, need your pad's location and approach instructions, over."

"This is three-zero, roger. The pad is at four niner seven, ah four four niner. It's in an old soccer field next to the Tango Oscar Charlie, approach from the southeast. Charlie is to the west. You may draw fire if you come from that direction. What are you flying? Over."

"We're a Chinook carrying ammunition. Is the LZ cold? Over."

Hallelujah, just what we need, ammunition. Now the Rangers should be able to hold out, I thought.

"Three-three this is three-zero. We're drawing some sniper fire now and then. You shouldn't have any problem though, over."

"This is Three-three, roger. I can't come in unless you assure me I won't draw fire, over."

Now who does he think he is, I thought, someone special? *We're all getting shot at down here.*

"This is Three-zero, I can't guarantee that. But the sniping isn't too heavy now. You should be able to get in and out without any problem, over."

"This is Three-three, I say again, I won't come in if I'll draw fire," the pilot said in an irritated voice.

What?! I thought. *You been drawing all that extra pay to drive that sky truck around and now that we ask you to earn your money, you chicken out.*

"Three-three this is Three-zero. We need that ammo. You can make it," the duty officer replied in a pleading tone.

"Negative, Three-zero. I'm pulling off. I Won't land if the LZ is hot, over."

"Three-three this is Three-zero. We need that ammo. You can pull up if you receive fire. Come on in," called the pleading duty officer.

"Negative," replied the pilot. I'm not coming in if I'll draw fire." His tone was one of disdain and superiority.

"This is Three-zero, we need the help, over."

"Negative, I'm going home," I heard the pilot say as the sound of his rotors faded away into the distance.

Now ain't that the pits! Man! At the bar, you'd think those guys are the bravest and greatest America has to offer. I don't want to hear any of that again! How could he leave us hung out to be drawn and quartered? I was furious and disgusted. Aviators! High-priced taxi drivers who won't perform when you really need them! Go on back home to your hot shower and clean sheets. Tell everyone at the bar what a hot mission you had today. And have a good laugh at the overly excited grunts. Sleep well!!

While time crawled for me, Major Evans was still trying to break out of Armor House. Fortunately, Charlie hadn't tried an assault. By 1500 hours, Evans had found that the southern route along the My Tho River was still open. He assembled his group of MPs and military intelligence types for another escape try. Evans assembled what vehicles he could with the men available to drive. While he was disabling the other jeeps, one of the MPs came up to him.

"Sir, I've got a problem."

"What's that?" Evans asked.

"I don't have a quarter-ton license," the MP announced.

Evans, ever cool, replied with a slight smile, "I think the situation warrants driving a jeep without a license."

Evans walked over to shoot out one of the searchlights with his .45 pistol. When the bulb popped, the MP again approached Evans with a downcast face.

"Sir, I've got another problem."

"What's that?" Evans inquired.

"I can't drive a stick-shift."

"Well dammit, you get about thirty seconds to learn or stay behind," Evans snapped, finally losing his cool.

When the convoy moved out, the MP had learned. The jeep bucked and jerked along the streets during its mad dash around Charlie, but it made it to the 6th Squadron compound.

The afternoon dragged on. Lieutenant Colonel Thoan visited the Troop shortly before 1700 hours to talk with Vinh. He stayed only long enough to tell Vinh that the Troop was to support the infantry in a push down Phan Hien Dao after they cleared Charlie out of the school. He was leaving about the time I noticed him. Still, it was good to see him. He was the only senior officer I saw until the battle was over. I don't think the Squadron commander left his headquarters. This pointed up a basic problem in South Vietnamese leadership. Commanders had a tendency to command by radio instead of in person. Colonel Thoan proved to be the exception. I was taught at the Armor School, you can't push spaghetti, you have to pull it. Meaning, a leader has to get out front and lead by example. This isn't to say that colonels are expected to lead the charge; to the contrary, that's why we have lieutenants and captains. But a Squadron commander can and should visit his troops during lulls in a battle to let them see him and to encourage them. Of course, if his presence is needed to influence the favorable outcome of a battle, he should be up front leading if that's what it takes.

Shortly after 1700 hours, the infantry began its move west along Phan Hien Dao Street with our 1st Platoon in support. The command track followed closely behind.

The platoon had gone only about 100 meters when it received enemy fire from the rear. The infantry hadn't cleared the upper floors of the school or the houses along Phan Hein Dao. The firing took the ARVN completely by surprise. They pulled back to Hung Vuong to reorganize and try again. The second time we tried with supporting artillery. We moved forward about 100 meters and stalled again. The supporting artillery was falling so close that some shrapnel fell on the command track between Neal and me. One piece bounced onto my hand. The skin wasn't broken, but the shrapnel was hot enough to cause a minor burn. While we waited for the infantry to clear a house, a captain from Sector climbed up on the side of the track.

"How are you doing?" he asked with his elbows resting on top of the track and his feet on the right track.

"Fine, we're having problems getting the infantry to clear the upper floors, but other than that, okay. It's just going slow," I replied.

Maybe he could tell me about the long artillery rounds last night. "Say, did y'all receive any artillery fires at sector house last night?" I asked.

"Yeah, we had a round hit in the front yard this morning," he replied.

"Was anyone hurt?" I asked.

Damage Phan Hien Dao Street photo by Larry Cole

Street behind the church photo by Larry Cole

Damage Phan Nguyen Phuong Street photo by Larry Cole

"No, we were all inside," he said jumping from the track. "I was just sent to see how things were going." He was gone.

Thank the Lord. I didn't kill any of our people.

Again, Charlie held and pushed us back. We tried again and were meeting with some success when Squadron ordered us back to Hung Vuong. It was getting dark.

Damage Phan Nguyen Phuong Street photo by Larry Cole

Both the 1st Troop and 3rd Battalion pulled back to the east side of Hung Vuong to regroup. We gave up the ground we had taken, including the school. The 2nd Troop, which hadn't moved all day, remained in position along Nguyen Trung Long. The 3rd Troop was relieved at Binh Due Airfield by a company from the US 9th Division and moved to secure the Seminary. The first day was over; Charlie had been stopped, but he was not giving up. The night and next day would prove even more deadly.

CHAPTER THIRTEEN

COUNTERATTACKS: 1-2 FEBRUARY 1968

The evening was quiet except for sniping, probing of the Rangers' position and the continuous bombardment of Charlie's positions by the 9th Division's artillery. This shelling caused devastating damage to the western third of the city. The conflagration turned the skies a bright crimson.

Just after midnight, Charlie got serious with the Rangers and assaulted in strength.

"Delta Tango Three-three, this is Romeo Six, over," the Ranger advisor called.

"This is Three-three, over."

"This is Romeo Six. We're receiving heavy mortar fire and small arms fire. I think Charlie is going to assault, over."

"Roger, Six. Can you give me a location? I'll try to get you some support."

"Roger, I think they are about two hundred meters to our northeast, at ah ah wait....five zero ah one, ahh four six five. Request gunships or artillery, over."

"Roger, Six. I'll see what I can come up with, wait."

In a few seconds, the TOC duty officer was back on the air. "Romeo Six, this is Tango. Negative on gunships and artillery. They are all committed. I do have a Spooky inbound, over."

"This is Romeo Six. Great! He's even better, over."

"Roger, we need you to mark your position, over," The duty officer said.

"This is Romeo Six. I don't have anything except a flashlight. We used all our flares, over."

"Roger Six. I'll have the Spooky come up on the net. We'll see if that will work. Break, break, Tango, tango," the duty officer called to all stations on the net. "This is Delta Tango Three-three, he was the net control operator as well as the duty officer. Clear the net. We've a Spooky coming in. Priority is to Romeo Six, over." Each station answered in turn with a roger.

I could hear the distant roar of the C-47's engines as I searched the sky.

Shortly a cool voice came over the net, "Romeo Six this Fire-fly Five-zero your net. What you got? Over."

This is Romeo Six. We're under assault from the northeast, over."

"Roger Six, can you mark your position? Over."

"Roger, I'll try. All we've got is a flashlight, over."

"This is Fire-fly, okay give it a try but I don't think we can identify from this altitude, over."

I could clearly hear the slow rumble of the plane's engines as it circled overhead.

"Romeo Six, this is Fire-fly, cannot identify. Have you turned on the lights, over"

"Roger Fire-fly, over"

"Can't identify, over."

"Roger Fire-fly, can you fire into coordinates five zero one, ahh four six five. They're getting close. They'll begin to come over the wire soon," the cool Ranger said.

"Negative Romeo. I have an area weapon. We may hit some of y'all, over."

"Roger, Firefly. Can't you get us something? We have a few Charlies in the wire, over."

"Negative Romeo. I need to identify your position before I can fire. It's too dangerous to friendlies, over."

"Break, break," I said into the mic. "This is Charlie One-six. We have searchlights. Will that help, over?"

"This is Tango, it might. Give it a try, over."

"This is One-six, roger. Break, break. Sierra Six this is One Six, over."

"This is Six. I overheard. Good idea. I'll get a team to you, out." I waited.

"Charlie One-six, this is Romeo Six, hurry. They're in the wire, over."

"Roger, Romeo. We'll do the best we can."

"Break, break. One-six, this is Sierra Six, I have a crew on the way, over."

"This is One-six, roger, out."

The Spooky drummed overhead, circling lazily in the black night, while we waited.

Two searchlight jeeps came speeding up to the command track. When I jumped from the track, Sergeant Williams walked over to me.

"Okay Sarge, what I need is for you to go down to the bridge and illuminate straight up, so that Spooky can identify the Ranger's positions," I said walking passed him to the jeep.

Williams was right behind me. "Hey, I'm not going down there," he declared.

"What do you mean you're not going? That was an order," I said in shocked surprise.

"Just what I said, sir. It's too dangerous."

"We'll go, sir," said Specialist Young from the other jeep. I didn't wait. I had a volunteer. All I needed was one light any way. I'd take care of Williams later. "Okay, park short of the bridge, elevate the light as high as you can, then lower it in that direction. I pointed to the northeast. Now, get going, but don't stay with the jeep after you point it toward Charlie. It's going to draw fire."

PFC Ward, Young's driver, jammed the jeep into gear, popped the clutch, and headed down the street for the bridge. I ran back to the command track.

"Sierra, this is Charlie One-six, over."

"This is Sierra, over."

"This is One-six. I have the lights. They'll illuminate shortly, over."

"Roger, go to Fire-fly and direct him in, over."

"Roger, out." I replied.

"Fire-fly this is Charlie One-six, over."

"This is Fire-fly, I overheard. Just tell me where the gooks are from the light, over."

"Roger, Fire-fly. It'll be on shortly, out."

In a few moments, the searchlight came on throwing a beam of white light straight up into the heavens. "Charlie One-six, this is Fire-Fly. I have your light. Where are the bad guys, over."

"This is One-six. The crew will point toward Charlie in a second. The lines are about two hundred meters to the northeast. Suggest you fire a short burst and then let Easy Six walk you in.

Roger One-six. I'm to the west; it'll be a few minutes before I'm ready. Out."

"Charlie One-six this is Easy six. I overheard. I'll take it from here, thanks, over."

"This is One-six, roger out."

In a few minutes, Spooky was on station and a red cylinder of fire arched into the jungle northeast of the Ranger Company. I listened as Easy directed the Spooky fire. It took three eruptions of the mini-gun to break Charlie's attack. The night returned to the artillery. I recalled the searchlight.

The remainder of the night was quiet except for mounted patrolling through friendly areas. At first, I tried to look into every window as we rumbled through the streets. I could imagine Charlie ambushing us from any of the houses or buildings lining the streets. But soon I relaxed and my stomach told me I was hungry. I dropped down into the track and opened a can of C-rations. I sat on ammo boxes with my back against the forward firewall between the engine compartment and the crew compartment. I fought to maintain my balance, while I ate. I swayed from side to side and occasionally forward with the motion of the track. The track maneuvered through the city like an infantryman moving from covered position to covered position, zig zagging and speeding ahead and then slowing. While I ate, I realized that I was dead tired. When I finished my meal, I lay down on the ammo boxes that covered the floor and tired to sleep. It was an impossible task. The tracks clattered in my ears and the mosquitoes were trying to eat me alive. I had forgotten to use any repellent during the day. I felt around in my rucksack but couldn't feel the repellent bottle. The mosquitoes were buzzing around my head and biting my face, neck, and ears so badly that I gave up and climbed back on the top deck. This was the only time during my tour that I remember being disturbed to the point of discomfort by mosquitoes.

Vinh patrolled for over two hours. When he commanded the driver to park across from the school, Sergeant Neal and I laid out our bed rolls, a poncho with liner, against the low masonry wall behind the track. I quickly fell to sleep and slept soundly.

At first light, the US 9th Infantry Division committed two battalions of its Riverine Force to the battle. The Americans entered the city's western sector and began to drive north, while the ARVN commanders held their positions and planned future actions. The 9th used the city's reservoir for its eastern limit during their move from hut to hut.

While the 9th moved north, the 7th Division needed to maintain contact with the Americans' east flank. The TOC's security would be degraded if the Cav's 2nd Troop was used. The 3rd Troop was on the west flank of the Americans and the ARVN infantry had their hands full. The mission fell to the 1st Troop. Vinh sent the 3rd Platoon. He and the command track weren't far behind.

The 3rd Platoon couldn't maintain contact from their tracks. The platoon had to dismount the crews and move from hut to hut along the reservoir's east bank. Vinh and I watched as the troopers vanished into the mass of hovels.

After several minutes with no sounds of action, I turned to Lockett, who was riding with me now, and said, "Get the radio. Let's go see what's going on."

We dismounted the track and moved along a narrow path between the huts and the reservoir. We crawled close to the walls of the huts as we moved in search of the 3rd Platoon. Just as we reached the platoon, shots rang out from the far side of the reservoir. Bullets zipped over our heads, lodging in the wooden walls. Lockett and I hugged the ground and tried to worm our way lower. I looked across the reservoir and saw men wearing American uniforms moving in the cracks between the huts.

"Give me the mic," I said, turning my upper body and head as best I could toward Lockett.

"Sierra Six, this is Charlie One-six, we're receiving fire from the 9th. They're on the west side of the reservoir. Can you get on the horn and tell those guys they're firing at friendly?" I said excitedly, without waiting to use proper radio, telephone procedure.

"Roger, One-six, I'll try to get them to stop," Major Evans replied.

A few more shots rang out but didn't impact near us. In a few minutes, Major Evans was on the radio, "I got through to the 9th's TOC and passed the word. The firing should stop soon, over."

The 9th's TOC must have gotten the word down because we didn't receive any more fire from the west. Lockett and I tailed along with the 3rd Platoon for a few more minutes without incident. I reported to Major Evans that it appeared that the houses were clear and asked permission to return to the command track. When Lockett and I reached the track, Vinh headed back to the rest of the Troop located on either side of the Hung Vuong, Nguyen Tri Phuong intersection. We were back in the fold by 0830 hours.

Just before 0900 hours, I overheard Captain Arthur tell Major Evans that the 3rd Troop was going to attack down Nguyen Tri Phuong toward the bus station. I sat expectantly with my headset glued to my ears. I heard nothing but squelch. Shortly, my attention was drawn to the intersection. Two tracks came speeding into it from the west and immediately turned back in the direction from which they came. The turn was so rapid and sharp that the crew was thrown around in the hatches. They had to hold on to keep from being thrown from the tracks. They were followed shortly by two more tracks. I was caught completely by surprise. I hadn't heard anything over the radio about a contact nor had I heard the noise of a firefight. I was on the radio immediately to find out what had happened.

"Clear the air, One-six," Major Evans said in reply to my inquiry. "Three has been hit hard."

I listened as Captain Arthur reported the action to Major Evans. The gist of the conversation was that the 3rd Troop had attacked east along Nguyen Tri Phuong. Their mission was to capture Charlie's headquarters believed to be in the city's bus station. The 3rd had moved out without an artillery preparation or infantry support. They moved in a column formation. They had moved only a few hundred meters when the buildings on both sides of the street erupted with B-40 and automatic weapons fire. All four platoons were hit simultaneously. Again, the troopers couldn't see their well-hidden enemy. The initial volley knocked out two tracks. This split the 3rd Troop in half. The lead elements continued to battle their way forward, losing two more tracks in front of the bus station. The four tracks that cascaded into the intersection managed to drive through the hail of B-40s. The remaining 3rd Troop vehicles returned to the Seminary.

While 3rd Troop withdrew, Captain Arthur was on the radio requesting an air strike to destroy the knocked-out tracks so that Charlie couldn't seize their weapons. After the third air strike, the FAC told Arthur that the next flight would make a strafing run on the bus station. Before the flight came in, the FAC was back on the air.

"Charlie Three-six, this is Hawk. The bad guys must have heard that the next strike was for the station. They are clearing out to the north. I can see them swimming the canal, over."

"Roger, Hawk, lay it on them anyway. Maybe they won't all get out, over." Arthur replied.

Damn, I thought. *Charlie must have been monitoring our net. We talk too much. No wonder he knows every move we make. We're worse about talking on the radio than a kid playing with a new toy. All we're doing is getting people killed with our big mouths.* I shook my head in disgust. I knew I was as bad as anyone. When the real action started, I and the others had nothing to do except direct American supporting fires and report. Out of excitement and trying to be of use, we talked too much and gave out too much useful information. Charlie didn't need spies in our compounds. All he had to do was listen to our radio nets.

Throughout the rest of the morning, 1st Troop remained in blocking positions along Hung Vuong and fired its mortars into the bus station area.

At 1300 hours, Vinh received orders to assist the 3rd Battalion in retaking the school at 1500 hours. The Cav and the infantry spent the next two hours preparing for the assault. The infantry was re-supplied with ammunition. The cavalry cleaned their weapons. Both units ate their rice and coordinated the assault. During the preparations, Vinh and I sat atop the command track watching the Troop's mortar platoon fire round after round into the area directly behind the school and listing to the whistling of the 9th Division's artillery impacting further to the west. The western section of the city became a flaming, smoking inferno under the continual bombardment. Occasionally, when Charlie fired from the adjacent buildings he was answered by the chatter of the troopers' machine guns.

When the hour came to jump off, Vinh sent the 1st Platoon racing through a gate into the school's front courtyard with all weapons blasting. A few minutes later, the infantry rose up from behind the walls across from the school and assaulted. The troopers shifted their fire from the ground floor to the upper levels as the infantry approached the school and disappeared into the building's corridors. The 2nd Platoon, followed by the command track and elements of the 3rd Battalion, assaulted down Phan Hien Dao. At first, it appeared that the two units had learned their lessons of the day before well. However, after a quick surge forward, the drive encountered the same problem as that of the day before. The upper floors of the buildings weren't cleared and sniper fire was breaking out to the rear of the lead elements. However, there was no pullback. The units held fast for a few minutes to determine the enemy's positions and then the infantry eliminated them.

Abruptly, the tempo of the battle changed from quick, daring moves to slow, methodical action. For the next three hours, the infantry moved slowly and painfully through each house along the street to insure that they were clear of VC. Meanwhile, the Cav supported them by firing into known or suspected enemy positions and the American artillery pounded unceasingly.

Although the two units were working together better, some problems were still experienced by the soldiers. They had great difficulty in keeping track of the forward progress of the infantry in the houses. Repeatedly the gunners of the lead tracks would start to fire on a suspected position only to find at the last second that friendly infantry occupied it. Luckily, no casualties were inflicted because of this lack of communications.

Another problem was the inability of the tracks to maneuver in the narrow streets. This was compounded by the entire Troop being deployed in a column formation along the street. Often times, the lead or second vehicle would have to wait for the entire Troop to back up before they could maneuver into a better firing position. Fortunately, the infantry had cleared the antitank teams from the buildings before they could fire on the immobile tracks. However, a few times the lead vehicles did back into following vehicles while trying to maneuver into better firing positions.

The assault stalled. I could tell from Vinh's tone as he spoke on the radio that he was trying to get the lead track moving. But his efforts were futile. The more excited he became, the more unwilling the lead track drivers became to move forward. There was only one way to get the Troop moving: go forward and personally encourage the lead vehicle's driver to get going. I became caught up in the excitement of the battle, but felt useless sitting behind Vinh watching. Maybe I could do something to affect the outcome. I'd go forward.

I tapped Vinh on the shoulder and said, "I'll go get them moving." He only nodded his agreement. Without saying anything to Neal, I jumped from the track and ran forward beside the tracks. The .30 cal machineguns fired over my head as I ran. I could smell acid smoke in my nostrils as I went. When I reached the lead track, I climbed its front slope. The driver had dropped down in his compartment but had left the hatch open. I reached into the hatch and hit the driver on his helmet. He looked up at me through the hatch with a vague, blank expression. I motioned for him to rise up and get going. While he adjusted his seat, I motioned the TC forward. He looked at me as though I were crazy and didn't move. The driver looked over his shoulder to see the TC's reaction. When the track didn't move, I climbed a little higher on the track and shouted that he had to get moving. I tried to look as mean as I could. After yelling at him a couple of times and stinging my arms around over my and his head and pointing forward, he nodded his head in agreement. With this agreement, I decided that discretion was the better part of valor. It was time to get out of there. I jumped from the track when it moved forward.

The assault continued to the objective at Phan Hien Dao and Tran Quoc Thanh. The two units paused briefly before they received orders to pull back for the night. The Cav reluctantly obeyed. They didn't want to give up 500 meters of hard-won enemy territory.

When the two units were back on Hung Vuong, the 3rd Battalion was relieved by a battalion from the 12th ARVN Regiment, and 1st Troop took positions along Hung Vuong. A 12th Regiment battalion went into position in the school courtyard. They didn't place outposts in the school, however, to warn of Charlie's return.

The evening was quiet in the city past midnight. The artillery fired only harassing fires, which were hardly noticed. It was so quiet that Neal, Lockett, and I sat on the street curb next to the command track and discussed the battle in general and wondered what was happening in the rest of the country.

At 0400 hours, I was awakened when a small group of VC crept into the school and opened fire on the 12th Regiment, sending infantrymen cascading over the courtyard's wall and to the safety of the Cav. When the last infantryman cleared the school, Charlie opened fire on the Troop across from the school. The troopers quickly returned the fire, silencing the VC position. The remainder of the night was quiet.

When dawn broke, the city was deadly still. Nothing seemed to be moving. Vinh sensed that the enemy had pulled back. He reported the situation and requested permission to send out foot patrols to make contact. While Neal, Vinh, and I stood in front of the command track waiting for the patrols to return, a Mr. Wilson, his wife, and a couple of other American civilians ran up to us. Wilson was a civilian contractor whom I had met at the Seminary's O-Club. He was breathless and excited. Flinging his arms in all directions he yelled at me.

"Cap'n, you got to help us. Bob Winn, another civilian contractor, and his wife are trapped behind the hospital, next to the church. You've gotta get them out," he said with a red face, spittle spraying from his month.

Oh Lord, I don' t want to go back there, I thought. *Charlie may still be hiding in the school and the church.* But I didn't have a choice. I couldn't ignore the request without appearing to be a coward. Besides, Americans were involved. I swallowed to drive the lump in my throat down. A ball of fire hit my stomach.

"Okay, we'll get them. You'll have to guide us, I said, heading for my jeep. Neal was right behind me. "You drive," I said motioning to Neal. Wilson and I, with rifle in hand, jumped on the jeep's hood.

Wilson directed us half a block west up Nguyen Tri Phuong and then south down a crack between the hospital and a church. The crack dead-ended at the rear of the church. I jumped from the jeep's hood and hammered on the wooden door centered in the crack.

"Winn, come out, we're Americans."

The door flew open almost immediately. Winn raced at me in wide-eyed amazement. His wife followed close behind.

"Thank God you've come. We thought we were goners," Winn said as he pushed past me.

"Hurry, let's get out of here," I said, turning back to the jeep.

I didn't have to encourage Winn or his wife. They were climbing into the jeep before I could get back on the hood.

When we were set, Neal crammed the jeep into reverse. With tire squealing, he backed out of the crack onto Nguyen Tri Phuong. He wheeled the jeep around toward our positions and sped forward. We were back with friendly Troops in less than five minutes. The Winns and Wilsons hugged me and thanked me profusely. Then they disappeared into the crowd of Vietnamese that were beginning to move around the tracks.

When the patrols returned from searching the buildings along Nguyen Tri Phuong and Phan Hien Dao Streets without making contact, Captain Vinh ordered the Troop to move cautiously along the street, dispersing crew members from the tracks to clear the buildings.

Vinh, Neal, and I walked behind the lead scouts. We walked down the middle of the street. Neal and I were armed with our rifles. Vinh carried only his pistol. When we reached the traffic circle, we were met by a patrol from the 9th Division. Just as we were congratulating ourselves on having won the battle, a group of three VC, dressed in black pajamas, broke from a building on the east periphery of the bus station and raced west on Nguyen Tri Phuong. The patrol leader, Neal and I instinctively dropped to a kneeling position and fired just as the VC reached a small bridge that spanned a tributary canal of the Bao Dinh. I was excited and reacted on reflex. This was the first bad guys I had seen. The closest I had come before was seeing the muzzle flash of rifles in a few cases.

When my rifle fell back into position, I saw that I had been so excited that I had fired without using my sights. I had looked over the rear sight instead of through the sight. None the less, the Charlie I fired at had fallen face down in the street. The other two VC ran across the bridge and disappeared. I didn't know if I hit him or if one of the others had. If it was my round that brought him down, it was an unlucky shot for him—or the will of God. I had pointed, not aimed.

I rose up and ran to see the damage. If he was alive, maybe we could get some information from him. Reaching the VC, I saw that he was alive. Part of his buttock was shot away. I needed a medic and a guard. I straddled him and rolled him over and with a smile started to try to tell him I'd get a medic. He looked up at me with hate in his eyes. There was no fear or plea for mercy, only hate. He gritted his teeth and kicked up with his left foot into my groin, but he was too weak and missed his target. He's got more ass than balls. His attempt to bite the hand that intended to help him angered me. I rolled him over again and kicked him in his wound.

VC Headquarters My Tho Bus Station before the attack photo by Larry Cole

VC Headquarters My Tho Bus Station after the attack photo by Larry Cole

Looking up, I saw a column of ARVN troops passing headed toward the central city. I motioned to one of the passing infantrymen to come to me. I crossed my wrist and pointed to the VC—to indicate tie and guard him. The infantrymen smiled and nodded. I ran to catch up with Neal.

Just as I caught Neal, we heard a loud explosion. We both dropped to the street. Instinctively, we realized that we weren't in danger and stood up.

A group of American soldiers were running toward a large tree further up the street. Neal looked at me, "Someone must have set off a booby trap."

"Yeah, guess you're right," I said, looking around. I didn't see Vinh or any of our troopers. "I think we've gone far enough. We better get back. All that's left to do is mop-up."

Heading back, I was anxious to see how my VC prisoner was being handled, whether he would have a medic or had been moved. Crossing the bridge, I didn't see the guard; he must have been moved. Then I saw the stretched-out, pajama clad form lying at the side of the street. I walked to him and looked down. The side of his head had been blown away. *Oh no,* I thought, *the infantryman misunderstood. There'll be no information from this fella.* I was both disgusted and nauseated. I didn't want to see the poor guy killed. He had fought a good fight for his cause and had lost. He couldn't harm anyone now. He was out of the war with honor. He shouldn't have been shot in cold blood. There was nothing I could do now. I walked on. What a war! What a war!

When I got back to the building the VC ran from, there were several Vietnamese soldiers and advisors cleaning the place out. I looked through the door and saw some black pajamas lying on the floor. *This must have been the VC headquarters,* I thought. Looking around the room, I saw an open crate of M-3 submachine guns (the American grease-gun, used by tankers). Two soldiers were helping themselves to the weapons. *Boy! Charlie left a lot of goodies,* I thought.

They'll make good trading material. I personally liked the grease-gun. I had fired it often in Germany and liked the way it handled. Also, I could see where it was hitting. I grabbed three sets of pajamas as souvenirs for the kids and all the M-3s I could carry and walked back into the street. I ran right into Major Evans who was walking up the street in front of 1st Troop's command track.

"What are you guys doing?" he asked.

"We're taking a few war trophies," I answered.

Evans was furious. "That's the RF headquarters! Put that stuff back! I'll not stand for any looting!"

"We thought it was VC," I answered.

"Well it isn't. Put it back," he said walking on.

I turned and went back into the headquarters and dropped a few of the subs. *Hell, I want one of these for myself. The others will make good trading material. They'll think Charlie got them,* I thought.

I went out to the command track and tossed seven subs into the crew compartment.

First Troop's lead platoon continued along Nguyen Tri Phuong until it met the 3rd Troop moving toward the bus station from the Seminary.

When the two cavalry units met, the battle for My Tho ended. The South Vietnamese, with the aid of the 9th Division, had won the city. The battle had been costly in lives (101 killed, 110 wounded, and 24 missing), equipment (three tracks with weapons lost and two damaged), and property (over one third of the city was destroyed by artillery). The enemy had sacrificed 716 killed and 82 captured. But most important, the VC hadn't overrun the city.

The Troop pulled back to Hung Vuong Street to re-supply and reorganize. Vinh called the Troop together to congratulate the troopers on their performance and to outline activities for the remainder of the day. We were to re-supply, refit, and move out at 1500 hours to open the road to Saigon. While he spoke, an antique hearse sat at the curb next to the formation. It was an ornately beautiful conveyance, drawn by two small horses. It was black with glass windows on each side to allow for viewing of the casket. There were long black plumes at each corner of the carriage. The irony was that life and death had merged at this moment and continued on toward the fulfillment of destiny.

Back at the command track, I noticed several nicks in the vehicle's aluminum armor. I hadn't realized that the track had taken fire. I had sat relaxed atop the vehicle without helmet or flack vest during the battle it was too hot to wear the heavy vest) and watched the carnage. The exploding report of our weapons had wrapped me in a womb of security that protected me from the knowledge that the track, its crew, and I were the target of a determined enemy. Walking around the track, I saw several AK-47 rounds lodged in the armor. At the right rear of the track, a ruptured water can hung in its mounting straps. It must have been hit by a B-40. The width of the can and its water had provided enough stand-off to prevent the weapon's heat cone from penetrating the track's armor. I was amazed at our good fortune and Charlie's poor aim. We had sat for two days in the open, no more than one hundred meters from the enemy, and had suffered only one casualty, the gunner that fell into my arms during our brief encounter at the traffic circle. We had been fortunate and I was grateful to my Creator.

While Vinh worked with the Troop, Neal, Lockett, and I drove to Armor House. The streets were littered with debris and dead, badly burned cows. The shops were unattended. They lay open for the theft of their products, but no one bothered them. The people and soldiers were too busy putting their lives back together. At Armor House, we found nothing disturbed. We showered, changed uniforms, and headed back to the Troop. At the Troop, the troopers were busy performing after-operations maintenance. They cleaned weapons, checked fluid levels, refueled, and made minor adjustments and repairs. There was nothing for the advisors to do until we moved out, so we took a tour of the battle area.

While we were looking through one of the burned-out buildings, Major Evans found us and called me aside.

"I need you to recommend men for awards. Have you thought about it?" he said when we were alone.

"Not really, sir. Off the top of my head I'd recommend Neal for a Silver Star for his performance at the Ranger Compound on the first night. And I'd recommend the ARVN who was responsible for recovering the knocked-out track for the highest award we can give him, I replied.

"Okay, fine. Write them up when you get time."

"Okay. "

"I've talked with Colonel Jones. He has approved the CIB for us." Evans continued. Also, I'm putting everyone in for a Silver Star for the battle except you. The Vietnamese are putting you in for the Cross of Gallantry with Palm. The Colonel says that's enough. You don't need two awards for the same action."

I immediately went from cloud nine to the pits of depression. It was great that I could now wear the CIB. It'd show at a glance that I had served in combat. But, if I deserved a medal, I wanted it to be an American award. I was pleased that Vinh or someone had recommended the Vietnamese award. It couldn't, however, take the place of an American award. I tried to hide my disappointment. I hadn't done anything to deserve a medal, but if the others were going get one, I should too. After all, I had been in the hottest part of the battle for three days.

"Fine, sir, I understand." What could I say? Captains didn't question the judgment of colonels.

Seeing my disappointment, Evans added, "I'll tell you what. I'll put you in for an award for the action down Phan Hein Dao Street. Maybe I can get it through."

My team and I continued our tour of the city. The western section of the town had almost been leveled. The few masonry buildings had been hard hit. Their roofs were gone. Their walls had been partially destroyed. The wooden huts behind the school were nothing more than a pile of blackened ash covered in some cases with twisted metal roofing. We found a half-dozen charred bodies in the blackened ruins. I hoped that they were Cong. If they hadn't been, they were now, to the body counters anyway.

The streets were littered with the personal effects of the citizens. They had tried frantically to save what they could. On Nguyen Tri Phuong Street, a small Buddhist shrine caught my eye. It was unharmed. Not a scratch. It was the type that sat at the entry to most homes. I had seen many of them in the rice paddies near Cai Be and Cai Lay. The shrine was a small vase filled with incense sticks. It sat on a small wooden platform mounted on a three-foot pole. I stood and looked at the shrine for what seemed like several minutes.

"A Deity, by whatever name, and its possessions seem to survive the worst that man throws at Him," I thought.

We returned to 1st Troop shortly before 1500 hours. We readied ourselves to move out and open the road to Saigon. Little did we know that we would have two more days of hard fighting.

CHAPTER FOURTEEN

THE BRIDGE: 2 FEBRUARY 1968

The column of tracks crept past the Seminary toward Highway Four. I wondered why we had been picked for this mission. We had been in the thick of the present fighting and had only pushed Charlie from My Tho that morning. Now with Sergeant Lockett on the command track with me and Sergeant First Class Neal with the mortars, First Troop was moving to open the road to Saigon.

I wasn't apprehensive as we slowly passed from the city. I was naïve enough to believe that we had given Charlie a good licking. I thought that he had most probably melted away into the jungle as he had after past battles. I was wrong. Within minutes of passing the Seminary, the lead tracks came under fire simultaneously from both sides of the road.

Immediately, the column erupted with a fusillade of automatic weapons' fire. Some track commanders tried to form a herring-bone formation (vehicles stopped and alternately turned at forty-five degree angles) in the road. This was considered the best counter-ambush formation for an armor column. Other TCs, however, merely stopped their vehicles in the middle of the road and began to fire.

"Sierra, Sierra, this is Charlie One-six, we have a contact, over," I shouted into the microphone.

"Roger One-six, whaddaya have, over?"

"This is One-six. I don't know. I can't see anything, over."

"Roger One-six, keep me advised, out."

As usual, Charlie wasn't to be seen. The TCs fired at any building, bush, or tree that could be a possible enemy position as they slowly inched their tracks forward. I dropped from my seat behind Vinh into the track's crew compartment. My head, shoulders, and chest were exposed as I moved from side to side in the track searching for some sign of the enemy. I couldn't see far into the jungle, which grew up to the road's macadam. Though I couldn't see Charlie or discern that we were receiving fire from the jungle, I sensed that he was out there looking through his sights directly at me.

The command track's crew became more and more excited as the firing wore on. Maybe they saw something I couldn't. Maybe they knew something I didn't. Whatever the reason, I became caught up in the excitement. I grabbed my newly acquired submachine gun and began to blast away into the jungle. I smiled to myself as the .45-caliber rounds impacted into the trees and I felt the weapon's recoil. *Hot damn, what a weapon,* I thought. *This is better than an M-16 anytime. I can see where I'm hitting.* I fired into the tree tops. I fired at mounds of earth. I fired into the windows of the one masonry house I could see. Any of those places might shelter Charlie. *Okay, okay, enough of this,* I finally thought. *I'm not here for this. I'm supposed to advise and direct indirect fires. I've shown the crew I'm willing to do my part.* I climbed back up onto my seat and looked up the column.

The apparently one-sided battle raged on. Black smoke billowed from both sides of the road. Troopers stood fully exposed on top of their vehicles to throw grenades into the jungle.

"Sierra, Sierra, this is One-six. We're stalled, over."

"Roger, One-six. We have a flight of F-100s on station. Can you use them, over?"

Silly man, certainly I can use them! I can use anything you give me, I thought.

"Roger, Sierra. Send them in, over."

"Roger, One-six. I'll have the FAC come up on this push, out."

"Charlie One-six, Charlie One-six, this is Thunder Two-one, over," a cool, clear, unemotional voice came through my headset.

"Roger Two-one, I have you loud and clear, over."

"Roger One-six, I have a flight of two. What can we do for you today, over?" the cool voice asked.

"Roger Thunder. We're on the road leading out of My Tho toward Highway Four, over."

"Roger, I have the road, over."

"This is One-six, we have Charlie on both sides of the road. Can you make a run along each side, over?"

"Roger, One-six, both sides of the road. How close do you want it, over?"

"As close as you can get, over."

"Roger, we'll be coming from the south, out."

I leaned forward and told Vinh the air strike was coming in. He nodded his understanding.

Soon the battlefield exploded with the sound of .20 millimeter rounds impacting in the jungle. I looked up in time to see a sleek, silver F-100 streak over head to my right. The roar of its engine sounded like thunder as its nose raised and peeled up to the right. Its cannons and engine had drowned out the other sounds of the battle.

What a beautiful sight! We got gem now, I thought. Immediately, a second F-100 passed to my left. I jerked around in time to see it climbing up to the left.

"One-six, this is Thunder. How was that, over?"

"You're too far out. Can you come in closer? I couldn't see where you were hitting, over," I said over the sound of chattering machineguns.

"Roger One-six, a little closer, out."

Shortly, the second pass came in. This time I could see the .20 millimeter cannon rounds clipping the trees about thirty meters from the road. I didn't notice the effect of the second plane's discharge. Still, this wasn't close enough for me. I could envision Charlie jumping from the shoulders of the road and charging the tracks. I didn't want any part of hand-to-hand combat or looking into Charlie's eyes when I shot him from the track.

"One-six, this is Thunder. How was that, over?"

"This is One-six. A little better, but can you come in closer, over?"

"Roger One-six, but we can't control the strike that well. We might get some of you, over"

"This is One-six. Understand, do the best you can, over."

"Roger, here we come. Get your heads down, out."

I could hear the roar of the Mike .20 cal rounds tearing up the road to my rear. I looked to my right just in time to see a peppering of the jungle not five feet from the asphalt. *Great! Just what I wanted.* I turned to my left in time to see the same effect from the wing man. *That's great, just great! What do you mean you can't control your fire? You fellas could hit a gnat at five hundred meters. Y'all really know what you're doing. Give it to 'em,* I thought with an air of confidence. *Man, no one can beat us with all this firepower,* I thought in the imagined safety of the protective fires that surrounded me. I had become completely caught up in the exhilaration of the moment.

"Thunder, this is One-six. That's just what we need. Pour it on, over."

"Roger, One-six, we have fuel for one more run, over."

"Roger, Thunder. Put it in the same place. Thanks for your help, over."

"Anytime we're in the area just give us a call, out."

The roar of the cannon came up the road again. When the sortie passed our track, I could see the rounds clipping the edge of the asphalt. Now that's close. This had hardly registered, when the second F-100 came in, its 20's rounds marching up the left side of the road. Something told me that these rounds would be even closer than those on the right side. I covered my head and rolled over behind the commander's hatch. Immediately after the roar of the twenty mike-mike passed, I felt something hit me in the left leg just below my buttock. It felt like someone had kicked me. I felt my leg. It was wet and sticky. I looked at my fingers. They were red. I'd been hit! Had Charlie got me or had the Air Force done me in, I wondered? *It doesn't make any difference. I'm not badly hurt,* I thought.

I looked over at Lockett. He was also laying on his side. I pointed to my hip and smiled. Lockett smiled back and pointed to his posterior. We exchanged a thumbs up sign and laughed. I don't know what was so funny or why we were so happy. Maybe it was that we had both earned Purple Hearts with wounds to a much-threatened area of the body or maybe it was that we were alive. Whatever the reason, we weren't in a funny position. Nonetheless, I was excited. My adrenaline was flowing. I was unconcerned about the battle that raged around me. My only thoughts were how I could help open the road.

Suddenly, I realized that the column was no longer moving forward. *I'll show Wolfe and Thomas who can soldier,* I thought as I picked up my radio's mic. *I'll get this column moving and open the road.* Wolfe was the battalion commander I'd had trouble with in Germany. He didn't think much of me or my ability. Thomas was my company commander during that same period. He, also thought I had no future in the Army because I didn't have a college education.

"Sierra, Sierra, this is One-six, over."

"This is Sierra, over."

"This is One-six. We're stopped. I'm going forward to see if I can get them moving." I dropped the mic without waiting for an answer and jumped from the track.

I ran under the chanting machine guns to the head of the column. The acid smell of cordite filled my nostrils. I pounded on the lead track's plain board and motioned to the driver by pumping a clenched fist up and down over my head and alternately waving him forward. The track jumped and inched forward. I jumped out of the way. With clinched fist pumping into the air I shouted, "Great, great, keep moving. You're dead if you stop." The driver couldn't understand me, but I was caught up in the excitement of the moment. I was acting on instinct. I moved back down the column motioning each track forward. When a track couldn't move forward, I'd reverse my direction and moved back up the road to get the leaders moving. I don't know how many times I ran back and forth on the road or how long I ran. It seems that it was all afternoon. I recall thinking I could never run this long when I played basketball at Odessa High School. My old coach would be surprised—but proud. Oddly, I wasn't afraid. I was conscious of only two things: the constant chatter of our machineguns firing over my head and the movement of the tracks. There was no realization of being shot at by Charlie. My consciousness was consumed by only one concern: keep the men moving forward.

After a while, I gave up running the road and climbed on the lead vehicle. I wasn't tired, but I could keep the track moving forward if I stayed with it. Hopefully the others would follow. There was none of the old Armor "high diddle diddle right down the middle" and charging forward here. When being shot at, TCs become more cautious and movement is slow.

By using threatening motions, I kept the track moving. After some time, we worked our way almost to a bridge that spanned a narrow canal. An old French fort sat on the far side of the canal to the west of the road. Sitting next to the TC, I noticed a long black object sailing leisurely through the sky toward the column. It was a B-40 round! I watched it closely, like an outfielder watching a baseball drop toward him. No problem, it'll fall short. Then there were two more rounds in the air. No problem, one will be short, the other will be wide. Then there were three, no four, rounds in the air. Again, the rounds went astray. Well enough of this! Those bastards can't hit an elephant in the ass with a bass fiddle. I need to report to Major Evans anyway. I jumped from the track and ran back down the column under the protection of the booming .50 cals and chattering .30s. Again, I couldn't discern any enemy fire.

Back at the command tract, I reported to Major Evans.

"Sierra, this is One-six, over."

"Roger One-six. What's the situation, over?"

"This is One-six. We're just short of the bridge, over." It was the first bridge north of the Seminary. There was no need to give a coordinates. Evans knew about where the Troop was.

"Roger. Is the bridge intact, over?"

"Roger," I replied.

"Roger, can you tell if it's wired (had demolitions been placed to destroy the bridge), over?"

"This is One-six. I couldn't tell, over."

"Roger, I need you to get back up there and look underneath to see if it's wired, over."

"Oh no, I don't want to go up there. I'll be out front alone. Charlie might have guards under the bridge," I thought.

"Roger, I'll go see. I'll get back to you, out."

I jumped from the track and ran along the right side of the road. As I ran, I prayed that Charlie wouldn't have anyone under the bridge. In my mind's eye, however, I could imagine several black clad figures lying in wait for me.

When I got to the front of the lead track, there was a bright flash and an explosion. The track next to me seemed to rise up from the road a few feet. I was in full stride. I seemed to turn in mid air, reversing my direction. Charlie had finally got his act together. He had scored a hit on the front slope of the lead track. "To hell with the bridge, I'm not pushing my luck," I decided without hesitation.

I ran back to the command track without stopping to see what damage had been inflicted on the lead track. Again, I was reacting on instinct. I wasn't thinking or planning—only reacting.

"Sierra, Sierra, I called breathlessly. "The lead track has been knocked-out, over."

"Roger, One-six. How about the bridge, over?"

"This is one-six. I couldn't get up there. We need artillery on the old fort, over."

No answer.

"Sierra, this is One-six," I say again. "We need artillery on the old fort, over"

No answer.

"Sierra, Sierra. This is One-six, over."

No answer.

"Oh no! What a time to lose the radio," I said aloud to myself. Throwing the mic back into the track, I jumped from the track. *Maybe I can get the second vehicle around the disabled track and continue the attack,* I reasoned. I ran through falling brass and acid smoke to the front of the column. I could hear nothing but the sound of our machineguns. I didn't investigate where the smoke was coming from.

When I got back up front, the crew of the damaged track was still on board firing their weapons into the fort. I motioned the second track around. It didn't move. I motioned again. It didn't move. Before I could climb on the track, Lockett was at my side. I don't know where he came from. I had lost track of him and Neal after the last F-100 strafing run.

"Vinh sent me after you. We're pulling back," he shouted. I didn't question the decision.

"Okay, let's help get a tow cable on this track, I said heading for the front of the vehicle positioned behind the knocked-out track. Each track had at least one tow cable attached to a front tow hook located on the lower portion of the front slope. The other end of the cable was pulled up over the plain board and attached to the track with a variety of quick disconnects. I motioned to one of the track's crewmen to disconnect the upper end of a tow cable and to toss it to me.

Lockett instinctively knew what had to be done. He was at my side.

I grabbed the cable and pulled it from the trooper when he freed the upper end. Lockett and I turned and guided the rescuing vehicle forward. It had only a few feet to move. When the track was close enough to connect its cable, Lockett and I automatically moved to the downed track's rear trailer hitch. The hitch swiveled and the part that needed to be up had rotated down. Lockett and I worked feverishly to right the hitch and to open the catch. It was frozen, or we were all thumbs. We worked elbow to elbow and shoulder to shoulder trying to open the hitch. The sounds of the battle had increased. We sensed that Charlie was getting more serious. We didn't have much time. We had to get out of there. Finally, Lockett managed to open the hitch. I dropped the cable into the opening and Lockett slammed down the hitch. The cable wouldn't come out. Its eye-shaped connector was too large to pass through the hitch.

I couldn't feel Lockett at my side. When I looked around he was gone. I looked down. He lay on the macadam with his arms outstretched. His eyes were closed. He wasn't breathing. There was a small red spot on his upper lip directly under his nose. *He's dead,* I thought. A ricochet off the back ramp must have caught him.

The driver of the rescuing track immediately began to back up, tightening the cable. Instinctively, I jumped onto the left rear fender of the disabled vehicle to keep from being run over. I turned as best I could and yelled at the driver, "Stop, Stop!" It was too late. Because the rescue track pulled with only one cable, the damaged track was pulled at an angle toward Lockett. I watched and shouted "stop" as the disabled track was pulled half way up Lockett's legs. There was nothing I could do. I climbed on top the disabled track and motioned for the driver to continue. As he backed away, the left track of the knocked-out vehicle was pulled over Lockett. I hung my head and closed my eyes in shame. Why hadn't I tried to pick him up? Maybe he had only been unconscious. Maybe I could have saved him. I should have recovered the body at least. I felt terrible. I had failed him and his family. Who would provide for his wife and child? I failed! I failed! "Oh, God forgive me! Watch over his family. Ease their pain," I prayed in Jesus' name.

The Troop backed down the road until the bridge was masked by the jungle. Then the tracks moved to the sides of the road to enable our damaged vehicle to be pulled further into the safety of the Troop. The Troop slacked its fire. Both sides seemed content to call it a day. When the damaged vehicle reached the command track, I switched tracks.

After mounting the command track, I told Vinh that Lockett had been killed. He only nodded his head. What could he say?

The tracks did a neutral steer, and we crept back into My Tho. A continuous vision of Lockett lying in the road pounded upon my mind. The red spot on his lip growing larger and larger. I alternately chewed myself out for my failure and then excused myself by thinking there was nothing else I could have done.

The excitement of the battle began to pass, and my adrenaline level fell with my spirits. I became extremely tired and thirsty. I was beat. I checked myself out. Yeah, I was all in one piece, just a little steel in my butt. I took off my beret to wipe the sweat from my forehead and to scratch my head. I was surprised to see three small shrapnel holes in the beret. I hadn't thought to put on my helmet or my flak vest. I felt around the liner of the beret and found one piece of shrapnel still in the liner. I looked around at the crew. We were fewer in number, but I couldn't tell who was missing. I checked the track. My radio antenna had been shot away an inch or so above head level. It was no wonder that I had lost radio contact. I climbed down into the track and got an extra antenna that we carried for such emergencies. When it was in place, I called Major Evans.

"Sierra-six, Sierra-six, this is Charlie One-six, over."

"One-six this is six, what happened to you, over?"

"This is One-six. My antenna was shot away, and I just found out. We're pulling back. Lockett is KIA (killed in action), over."

"This is Six, roger, understand Lockett, KIA. Do you have him with you, over?"

"Negative, he's still on the road, over."

"Roger, the Troop is to stay on the street tonight. Meet me at Six-three's location [Sector House) when you get in, over."

"This is One-six. Roger, out."

It was dark when the Troop parked along Hung Vuong Street. Vinh again positioned the command track outside Sector House.

At Sector House, I was greeted as the conquering hero. Big deal! Lockett was dead, and we hadn't taken the bridge. Someone asked if there was anything I needed. My throat was so dry I thought I'd die of thirst. "You have a Coke" I asked.

"No, all we've gots is Budweiser."

Man, beer makes me sick, and Bud is supposed to be a strong beer, but I had to have something, I thought. *I can't drink the water.*

"Okay, give me one," I said.

I was handed a beer. I took a little sip. It was the greatest-tasting liquid I had ever put in my month. I took a larger sip. *Yeah, this is great stuff,* I thought. I began to guzzle the beer. In three gulps it was gone. I asked for another. I sipped it while I told Major Evans what had happened. He assured me that I had done all I could.

"Where's the body?" he asked.

"Right in the middle of the road, the last I saw."

"Okay, we're going to try for the bridge again tomorrow. We'll recover the body then. How's the wound?"

"Yeah, it's nothing. Only a scratch. I'll be able to go tomorrow."

"Okay, get a good night's sleep. You've earned it," he said walking from the room. Back at the track, I immediately fell asleep and slept soundly until Sergeant Neal woke me for the day's mission.

At first light, the Troop rolled out of My Tho. Just past the Seminary Vinh moved the Troop west into the paddies. Shortly, we fell in with a unit of ARVN infantry advancing through the paddies toward a jungle tree line. I don't recall the unit nor do I recall what the other troops of the Squadron were doing. The 3rd Troop may have been refitting from its losses during the battle for My Tho. The 2nd Troop may have been in another part of the attack or providing security for My Tho. I don't recall.

First Troop moved on line with the infantry. The platoons' tracks intermingled with the infantry as they advanced on the trees. Vinh had the command track drop back and then stop in the middle of a paddy. I watched the tracks and infantry approach the jungle. Soon, I could tell from the sound of rifle and automatic weapons' fire that the battle was joined. Vinh and I watched from about two hundred meters back. That was okay by me. My butt was beginning to hurt. It was getting hot. I didn't want to get into a fight in the jungle. I was content to watch and to listen to the staccato chant of automatic weapons fire and the reports of the infantry advisors. The battle seemed to be seesawing back and forth. Charlie was both well dug-in and in the trees.

"We have a bunker over here. We can't move," one advisor would say.

"We have a sniper to the right. We're pinned down," I'd hear another say.

"We need some artillery in here," another would report.

I watched the tracks jockey in and out of the trees and around in the paddies. The troopers were doing the best they could but they weren't much help. The jungle was too thick. I continued to listen.

"Get one of those PCs over here to give us some help."

"Yeah, they can't get through the trees."

"Look out, those things will run over you."

"Hell it's bad enough watching for Charlie without staying out of those thing's way!"

"We're getting heavy fire from those huts. We need artillery or air, over."

I watched while Neal and the mortars fired round after round into the trees.

"We've a flight of F-100s coming in. Move your troops. Pull back."

"Roger. I have targets for them."

Vinh pulled the Troop back to the far side of the paddy to await the impending air-strikes. My butt grew sorer by the minute. I dismounted and laid down on a raised path that ran along the tree line. I lay on my side, propped up on my right elbow, head in hand, watching the air-strikes go in, just like a Roman emperor watching a festive orgy in his imperial palace. Only I was hot, sweaty, and thirsty. At least, I wasn't being shot at.

The air-strikes took over the battle. Alternately, I watched F-4s and F-100s swoop in to drop their panels of death. What a show! Boy, Charlie is catching hell now. Little did I know!

The firing lasted until siesta, then died down and faded away. The air strikes continued under the direction of the infantry advisors. "That's fine. Let the Air Force do a little work. It's too hot to fight anyway. Besides, one has to eat. There's no rush. Charlie will be there when we get ready to go at him again," I thought.

After a two-hour break, Vinh moved the command track back into the middle of a paddy. The platoons moved forward to support the infantry. Soon, the battle was raging at a higher pitch than the morning fight.

An infantryman appeared at the edge of the trees and moved back into the paddies. Then another followed, then another, and another, and another. *They're withdrawing! What for? It doesn't sound that bad,* I thought. I looked over at a thatched hut that sat in the paddies. It was connected to the jungle by a narrow causeway. Four infantrymen came running from the hut and ran along the causeway toward the jungle. Now come on, fellows, the fighting is two hundred meters over there. The soldiers were almost to the trees when two of them turned and ran back to the hut. In a few seconds, they returned to the causeway carrying a pot of rice between them. Ah, the power of the stomach. If y'all are brave enough to run back for your rice bowl, why can't you do the same to save your country?

The infantry continued their withdrawal. Soon, only the tracks remained to face Charlie. The troopers jockeyed the tracks in the paddies to fire at various VC positions. There was nothing for me to do except watch and shift my weight off my left buttock.

I calmly sat on the track's back deck with my right hand on my right hip forming a triangle with my arm. I felt my right arm's shirt sleeve move. That's strange. There's no wind. I looked at my sleeve. There was a hole in it. A bullet had passed between my upper arm and chest, catching only my shirt sleeve. I stared toward the jungle from where I thought the round came. I'm not going to let that little rascal know he almost got me. I sat staring into the jungle for what I thought was several minutes, but was more like a few seconds. Then I slipped down into the track and moved up behind the commander's hatch for the protection offered by the gun shields. So much for valor. I had made my point. Besides, I needed to stand up. It hurt too much to sit. Damn, that was close!

We passed away another hour before Vinh received the order to pull back. I was glad. I was burning up and thirsty enough to drink a small lake. It was late afternoon when the Troop got back into My Tho. I ran Major Evans down at Squadron and told him that I had to go on sick call the next morning. The wound in my butt had become so painful that I couldn't sit normally. I had to stand or sit on my right hip and leg. My head was burning with fever.

I passed a restless night, getting up every few hours for a drink of water. That morning, freshly shaven and showered, I told Major

Evans that I'd be back that afternoon and left for Binh Due airfield to catch a chopper to Dong Tam. It'd be over a month before I returned.

CHAPTER FIFTEEN

JAPAN: FEBRUARY 1968

During the short flight to Dong Tam, I kept thinking of the fight for the bridge and Lockett. I thought that had I been in charge and had called in artillery on the old fort, we could have taken the bridge. I'd have hit the fort with two or three artillery barrages then charged when the last round hit, while Charlie still had his head down. Charlie may have been able to get his head up to fire a round or two, costing a couple of tracks, but I'd have taken the fort and the bridge. I could picture running my ACAV through the fort's gate and cutting down Charlie, while the track sat in the center of the stronghold. Ah, alas I wasn't in charge. I'd never know if I could've won.

The Huey pilot was kind enough to touch down at the 9th Evacuation Hospital's pad to drop me off. I was met at the chopper by a medic who led me into a screening room where an attractive nurse in baggy jungle fatigues checked my temperature and blood pressure. She was coolly professional. A young, tired doctor came in and asked me to drop my pants.

"Hmm, he's badly infected. Get him into surgery," the doctor said without so much as a how do you do.

"Get undressed. Put your clothes over there. Put this on," the nurse directed, handing me a green smock with open back. "When you're ready, we'll get you to surgery," she said as she started from the room.

"What about my uniform?"

"Just leave it. We'll turn it in to supply."

"What about when I leave?" I asked.

"Don't worry about it. We'll give you a new one when you're ready to leave."

Now that's a waste of money, I thought. *That's an almost-new uniform.* But there was no use debating with her. She was too busy, and only following orders. The hospital, of course, probably called them "policies." The Medical Corps lived in a world apart from the rest of the Army; long hair and captains aren't captains, they're doctors. Oh well, they're the best. They give us their all and do wonders. I guess we can tolerate them and allow their little excesses.

While I undressed a medic asked me questions about my unit, service number, and so forth. When he had filled out the necessary paper work, he led me out of the sandbagged hut and into a similar hut next door. We entered a brightly lit, crowded operating room.

"Okay, lay down on the table, face down," the taller of the two doctors told me. He must be the surgeon.

"Let's see what we have here," he said opening the back of my smock.

"Hmm. Yep, you have some shrapnel in there and you're badly infected."

There was no hesitation. He knew exactly what he wanted to do. "This is what we're going to do," the surgeon said half to me and half to the others in the room. "We're going to give you a local and then open you up. You've got a lot of infection. We're going to need to go in deep to get the shrapnel and to allow the wound to drain".

"Whatever you say," I said, placing my chin up on my hands to get comfortable. *I don't care what you do so long as I don't feel it and can walk away,* I thought.

I stared across the room at the wall and listened to the doctors casually go about their business.

"There, I have it. Here, give this to him. He may want it for a souvenir," I heard the doctor say.

I looked around to see a nurse handing me a small piece of metal about the size of a fingernail.

"I think we need to pack it pretty heavy with gauze. Leave a pretty good piece hanging out so the wound will drain," the doctor said to someone and walked around to the head of the table. "Okay, you got a lot of infection and we're going to have to let it drain for a few days. What we're going to need to do is scrub the wound and change the dressing three times a day. We can't sew you up until we get rid of the infection. Any questions?"

"No, sir."

"Fine, the nurse will get you over to the ward. Good luck."

Now that's efficiency. I'm out of here in less than an hour. No coffee breaks for these guys. I followed the nurse to another sandbagged hut with walls lined with steel cots covered with OD blankets.

The ward was half full. I looked along the row of beds. One was filled with a soldier in a body cast that ran from his toes to the top of his head. There were only openings for his eyes, nose, and mouth. "What happened to him," I asked.

"He sprung a booby trap in My Tho, I think," replied the nurse.

Must have been the explosion I heard during the mopping up in My Tho two days ago, I thought. The nurse put an IV in my arm and turned to leave.

"What about my unit?"

"Don't worry. We'll notify them," she said as she left the ward, leaving me to my thoughts. Guess I won't get back tonight. A vision of Lockett lying on the asphalt jumped into my mind.

I lay in my thoughts until late afternoon. The nurse returned with a pan of water, soap, brush, and gauze.

"Now this is gonna hurt," she said as she went to work washing the wound. I tensed and drew air through my teeth. I closed my eyes and gritted my teeth. *Damn, the cure is gonna be worse than the wounding,* I thought. As the nurse worked on me, I clung to the bed. I wanted to run. I wanted to climb the wall. I had never had anything hurt so badly.

"Can you be a little easier?" I asked with tears in my eyes.

"Sorry, there's no other way," she replied with a sympathetic tone.

I had just gotten comfortable when the door at the far end of the room opened. Who should walk in but John David Crow, the Texas A&M football All-American and 1957 Heisman Trophy winner. I had seen him many times on the A&M campus in 1956 but had never met him. "Fish" don't just walk up and say "Howdy" to All-American football players. Also, he had entertained me on many Sundays when he played for the Saint Louis Cardinals. Because of him and the other Aggies playing with the Cardinals, they were my team during the late fifties and early sixties, before the Cowboys. *Good of him to drop by,* I thought watching him work his way down the aisle.

"Howdy, Army," I said when he got to my bunk. He looked surprised. "I was at A&M during 1956–57. I used to see you and Pardee (another of A&M's great All-Americans and player for the Washington Redskins) around campus and at the movies, I said.

"Yeah, I see. Good to see you. How you doing," he asked with a hooked smile.

"Oh, fine. I'll be up and around in a few days."

"Where'd you get hit?" he asked.

"In the butt," I said pointing to my posterior.

"I thought you were supposed to keep that down, he said with a chuckle.

"Yeah, like any good Aggie, I forgot. When I got my head down my butt went up."

He smiled. "Well, I hope you get along well. Good luck," he said as he walked toward the door.

I felt better. I deeply appreciated his effort and concern. *It's good of him to come over,* I thought. I bet he never expected to get caught in this when he volunteered.

The next morning when the nurse came to clean my wound, I wanted to run and hide. While she worked, she told me that I was going to be sent to the 3rd Evacuation Hospital in Saigon. It'd take some time for the infection to go down and they needed the beds. Casualties were mounting as the counteroffensive raged in the Delta's jungles.

At mid-morning, a medic led me, dressed only in my smock and white hospital slippers, to a waiting Huey. Its rotor was turning slowly as I approached. Climbing aboard, I saw the soldier in the cast lying on a shelter. The cast was beginning to show spots of pink.

The 3rd Evacuation Hospital was located in the center of Saigon. We were met by medics who took each of us to our assigned wards. It was almost lunch. After I was shown my room, I was directed to the mess hall. Strolling back to the ward, who should run into but Lieutenant Colonel Walters. He had been wounded in the arm.

We greeted each other as old friends and began to exchange war stories. Colonel Walters wanted to know how the battle went and how I was wounded. I was curious about him. I had always been told that the Army didn't put a Medal of Honor winner back in harm's way. So much for old wives' tales.

"When did you get hit?" I asked.

"I got it right at the start," he replied.

"Where were you?" I asked.

"When we got word that the VC were at the traffic circle, Cap'n Stewart and I went down to take a look."

"What in the world were you doing out there?" I asked in surprise.

"Someone had to find out what the VC had and were up to."

"How did it happen?" I asked.

"We were climbing across the roofs when several VC jumped us."

"How about Cap'n Stewart?" I asked.

"He got away clean," the colonel replied.

I thought, *Now that's an old war horse for you. He didn't have any business that far out front.* Being at the point where he could best influence the action and setting a good example is one thing. Conducting a reconnaissance or leading a combat patrol is uncalled for. I had to take my hat off to him, though. He had guts.

We continued our talk for some time. We exchanged what information we had about mutual acquaintances and philosophized about the battle. Neither of us had any question about the Americans and South Vietnamese winning. Charlie had finally come out to fight and we had him right where we wanted him. We'd win.

I spent the rest of the afternoon trying to hide from the nurse. I wasn't successful. The treatment was so painful that it almost made me sick to my stomach.

The doctor came and looked at my wound. All I got out of him was a, "Hmm, I'll look at you tomorrow. All we can do is let you heal."

The next morning, during my roaming, I again saw the soldier in the cast that had come up with me from Dong Tam. His cast was becoming redder. Also, I ran into Colonel Walters again. After we talked for a while, curiosity overcame the cat. I had to know how he won the Medal. It's a question generally not asked.

"Sir, would you mind telling me how you won the Medal," I asked.

"Oh, it was nothing. I was a platoon leader. We were ordered to take a hill. We got pinned down and I lost my weapon. I got up with an entrenching tool in my hand and charged to the top. The others came with me," he replied in all modesty.

"Did you take the hill?"

"Yep."

I could tell he didn't want to talk about the action, so I let the subject drop. Quite a guy. One of America's best.

The next morning, I reported to the doctor at a desk in one of the halls. After examining my wound, the doctor looked up at me with pleading eyes.

"Would you mind if we sent you to Japan?" he asked.

I tried to conceal my elation, "No, Doc, if you think it's necessary."

"Yes, I do," he said, more relaxed. "You'll heal slowly here because of the climate. You need to get to a more sanitary environment."

Why would he be afraid to tell me that? "Whatever is best, Doc." I'd always wanted to visit Japan.

"We'll try to get you off on a flight tomorrow."

The remainder of the day and the next were spent roaming the hospital hall, visiting with various other patients. The evening of the following day I was bused to Tan Son Nhut Airport where I boarded an Air Force C-41 cargo plane converted to an air ambulance.

The aircraft was divided. One side was for litter cases and the other was for ambulatory patients. The litters were stacked three or four high. The walking wounded sat on the right facing the rear. It wasn't Pan Am or TWA. We were seated in rows of four in small canvas covered aluminum tube seats.

Sitting in my window seat, who should I see on my right my friend in the cast from My Tho and Dong Tam. It was getting to be a small world. Was I never going to get rid of this guy? I said a little prayer to the Lord that he would make it. Surely he'll live if they have kept him alive this long. These doctors do a heck of a job. But this is getting depressing. His cast was now totally crimson.

It was near midnight when the pilot announced that we were on our final approach into Tokyo. I looked out of the window for a breathtaking, beautiful view of the city's night lights. The window scene was filled with multi-colored lights glittering from the ground.

As far as I could see, from horizon to horizon, were lights. I had never seen a more impressive view nor have I since.

During our approach, an aircraft crewman told us we'd be quarantined for our first ten days in Japan because of the possibly of our carrying diseases. We'd be separated and assigned to various Air Force hospitals in the Tokyo area. We were to wait in the airport holding area until it was determined to which hospital we'd be assigned.

When we deplaned, my friend in the cast was put in an ambulance and carried away. I wouldn't see him again. I never found out how he was wounded. The doctors had kept him knocked out. Nor would I know that happened to him. We went to different hospitals. I've thought of him often. I hope he made it.

While I waited for my assignment, I weighed myself on a set of scales in the hall. I was a lean 195 pounds. I had lost 40 pounds since arriving in Nam.

I was assigned to the Johnson Air Force Base hospital. After checking into the ward, the nurse asked if I'd like to call my wife. I jumped at the chance. "Can I do that?" I asked in surprise. The Army didn't allow long-distance calls from duty telephones. Most telephones on an Army post were what were referred to as Class C phones, which could be used only for on-post calls. The off-post phones were located at unit's headquarters, but long-distance calls couldn't be placed from them.

"Sure, use that one," she said pointing to a phone on the desk. "You have to dial nine to get off-post. Then dial zero for the operator

I was sure my wife would be worried. I hadn't written in over a week. The call was short. An international long-distance call was expensive for a captain in those days. All I remember of the call was that she was surprised I was calling from Japan and that I had difficulty getting her to believe I wasn't seriously wounded.

Again, I was assigned a private room. The next morning at breakfast, I ran into Captain Hill, my social graces instructor from the Seminary, in the mess hall. Other than for Colonel Walters' reconnaissance, I hadn't realized that Sector had been involved in the battle. They must have been on a different radio net. I hadn't monitored them.

Hill had been shot in the wrist during the second day of the battle. He had arrived at Johnson two days earlier. We spent the next two days dodging nurses, telling war stories, reminiscing, and planning our assaults on the Johnson Officer's Club and Tokyo. I wasn't too lucky with my nurse-dodging exercise. I had to suffer a scrubbing at least twice a day.

During our wanderings through the halls and wards, we fell in with a Captain McDonald, late of the 27th Wolfhounds, 25th Infantry Division. McDonald had been wounded more than two months earlier. He had been hit in the abdomen by a 12.5 Russian machine gun round while charging a VC bunker. The 12.5 machine gun is equivalent to our .50 caliber machine gun. I can't image anyone living to tell the story after being hit by one.

McDonald was the old pro. He knew all the ins and outs of the hospital, the base, and Tokyo. He told us how to get off base before the end of the quarantine period, how to get to Tokyo, where to go in Tokyo, and about the steam baths on post. He was a walking encyclopedia.

I don't recall why he had been at Johnson so long. Generally, if a patient's wounds took over two months to heal, the Army sent him to the States to recuperate. Somehow, McDonald had managed to stay in Japan. Maybe his condition was considered too serious to make the flight. His scar indicated the 12.5 had put a good-sized hole in him. Anyway, he was in no hurry to leave; he had a thing going with the cute little Japanese ward assistant. He might not be able to travel, but according to him, he could still make love. What a constitution!

On the third day, I was climbing the walls. I had to get out. I had managed to evade my scrubbings at least two times a day.

I think the nurse was too busy to run me down—thank God. I borrowed some clothes and shoes from McDonald. They were too small. I looked like the Hollywood version of a Tennessee hillbilly come to town for the first time, shirt sleeves too short, pants legs too short, no belt, shoes so small I could hardly walk, and no socks. All that was missing was a high-peaked, floppy hat. Thus attired, I headed for Finance and then the BX. Both were within walking distance. At Finance I drew a casual pay, a payment that military personnel may draw at any Finance Office when in transit. A soldier, airman, or sailor can draw up to the amount owed him as of the request date. In some cases, they can draw an advance. I didn't want an advance, however. Drawing an advance, I had learned, was the best and surest way to foul up your records for about six months. With cash in hand, I headed for the BX. Within an hour, I was properly dressed and ready to hit the club, but that had to wait until 1700 hours.

Hill and I were at the door when the club opened. A steak dinner was in order. By 1800 hours, the dining room and bar were beginning to fill with other patients, doctors, nurses, and pilots. It was a friendly crowd. It was particularly easy to become acquainted with our follow patients. Surprisingly, the doctors were quite open. The Air Force pilots, on the other hand, were a bit standoffish. I guess they had found a group where they weren't the center of attention and who could match them war story for war story.

Hill and I made the rounds talking with first one and then the other. Finally, I settled in with an old Chief Warrant Officer, Mr. Warner. A W-4, the highest warrant grade, he was all of forty years old. That was old to me. We struck up a friendship that lasted for the next week. Our talks resulted in numerous lively debates over the virtues of our chosen branches of service and continuous card games, Ship, Cap'n, and Crew as our principal game of choice.

Our most lively discussions centered on the command relationship between commissioned officers and warrant officers.

"I had this new cap'n report in and make his first check ride with me. He didn't know from zilch. I had to tell him every move to make," Warner would say.

"What do you mean you told . . ."

"I was the rated aviator."

"That don't make no difference. He was a cap'n. He outranks . . ."

"Oh, no. When I'm in the aircraft, I'm the senior pilot. I make . . ."

"No you don't. Not when I'm around. I have the responsibility. I make the decisions," I'd say.

"Not in an aviation outfit. The warrants are more experienced. When we're in the aircraft, we make the decisions. Most commissioned officers don't have the expertise. . . ."

"That doesn't make any difference. He's the boss."

"Not in aviation. The most qualified officer . . ."

"You're not an officer, you're a warrant . . ."

"I mean the most qualified person, okay? Most officers don't know how to handle certain weather emergencies or how to use instruments," Warner would point out.

"Look, officers plan and direct. They tell us where to fly but not how to fly. What if I were on board and wanted you to land and you thought it unsafe?"

"I won't land."

"I'd court martial . . ."

"No, you wouldn't if I'm the aircraft commander."

"You're not, I am."

"Only if you've been assigned as the aircraft commander. And you wouldn't be if you didn't have the same experience and rating I had."

Neither of us could convince the other. Later, I'd learn to understand the officer/warrant relationship in aviation units and in other units as well. Warrants are the specialists or technicians.

They are the most knowledgeable soldiers in their field. Officers plan, coordinate, provide direction, and supervise. They are the generalists. I had only been in line units, where the command structure was rigid. The only warrant was in the motor pool and in a world of his own. I guess the same could be said of aviators. They most certainly were in their own world—just ask them!

I didn't give Warner too much flack. I had grown to like and respect him. He had been wounded flying in artillery ammunition. He was told that the LZ was cold, but about ten feet from the ground, his Chinook took one round through its chin bubble. He was hit in the foot. The quick reaction of his co-pilot saved the aircraft.

One evening, Warner tried to get me to go to the base Japanese bathhouse.

"Cole, you need to try the bath house. It's quite an experience."

"What? I'm not getting in a tub and let some woman wash me." I didn't want to tell him I was much too modest.

"Why not? It's great to lay in that tub and let her scrub your back and then lay on a table, while she messages you and walks up and down your back with her bare feet."

"Am I naked?" I asked.

"Yea."

"Is she?"

"No, she wears a bathing suit," he answered.

"No fair. If I've gotta be naked, she has to be."

That was that. I hadn't been near a woman in over five months. What if I got excited? How embarrassing! Besides, I hadn't been sewn up yet. I wasn't going to get infected again. It wasn't worth the scrubbings.

Hill and I began to make our plans for a sojourn into Tokyo. We had to know how to get there. We had to find a place to stay. We had to find out where to go. Fortunately, between McDonald and a teenage Japanese orderly, Ichiro, we got all the information we needed.

"You can try to stay at the Sanno Hotel," McDonald told us.

"Why there?" Hill asked.

"It's an Army resort hotel in downtown Tokyo. That's the place to stay. It only costs seven or eight dollars a night. It has everything," Mac informed us.

"So what's the problem?" I asked.

"You have to have reservations and they give them by rank. Generally, only field grades get in," Mac said.

"That's okay. I'll call in and tell them I'm Captain Cole, USN." A Navy Captain is equivalent to an Army Colonel. Both are field grade officers. Army captains are company grade officers.

I made the call and arranged the reservation without exactly lying.

On our second Friday in Japan, Hill and I struck out after being briefed on how to catch a bullet train into Tokyo. I had been in Japan eight days, Hill ten days. We had our schedule set. We had both served in Germany and liked German food. A German restaurant was first on our list. Our Japanese orderly recommended a geisha house and a nightclub. We opted for the nightclub. Neither of us was interested in paying for a night's entertainment; we wanted to see the town. Mac recommended a small bar that stewardesses frequented.

We crowded into the train and found the hotel without any problems. The hotel was as described. It had everything, a gift shop, a barbershop, a public bath, a coffee shop, and a tour guide desk. The room was small but you couldn't have everything for eight dollars and fifty cents a night. After checking in, we caught a cab for a hair-raising drive to a recommended German restaurant next to the American Embassy.

We must have been early because we were the only customers in the house as we took our seats at a table. We both ordered schnapps. I ordered Cordon Bleu, my favorite.

Before our meal came, two staggering, loud men and their ladies came in and took a table across the room from us.

"Watch this," said Hill, always the man of the world.

Hill called the waiter over and told him to serve the couples a drink on him. When the drinks were delivered, the men recognized us by raising their glasses toward us. We nodded in reply.

During the meal, a round of schnapps was delivered to us, compliments of the gentlemen across the room. We finished our meal and relaxed over a cup of hot, black coffee. After cheesecake, the taller of the two men swaggered over to our table. He introduced himself as the sales manager of a major American food distributor. We told him who we were. He asked about Hill's arm, which was still in a cast. Hill told him about his wound. The gentleman looked at me inquiringly. "I'm sitting on mine," I said.

"Well gentlemen, allow me to pay for your dinner," he offered.

"Oh no, we couldn't allow it," Hill said with a smile.

"But I insist. I'll put it on my expense account. It's no big deal," the gentleman retorted.

"Well, if that's the case and you insist, all right," Hill replied.

I was dumbstruck. Things weren't off to a bad start. After finishing our coffee, we decided our next stop would be the airline bar.

We took another frightening taxi ride to the bar. It was a hole in the wall, a smoke-filled rectangular room not much more than ten feet wide. There was an over-stuffed bench along one wall and small booths along the other all. At the far end of the room sat the largest woman I had ever seen, pounding out ragtime, accompanied by a string bean with a banjo. They belted out one oldie after another to the immense delight of the customers. Soon, a joyous, resounding hootenanny filled the room.

We made the acquaintance of several civilian naval inspectors whose job it was to travel the Pacific inspecting ship's hulls. They were a great group but didn't offer to pay for our drinks. It came time for Hill and me to leave and meet Ichiro. The airline place hadn't met expectations. No shapely stewardesses were dispatched our way.

We left the bar near midnight and made our way to the nightclub where we were to meet Ichiro. Our timing was on target; he was standing in front of the club when we arrived. We were ushered into the club, provided a hostess, and began our observation of Japanese culture. I don't know if all clubs provided a hostess or not. Ichiro explained that this club furnished the service. If we were unsatisfied with the management's selection, we could trade companions any time and as often as we liked until we found one we liked. We stayed about two hours without making a swap.

The next morning, the first thing on my agenda was to have a shave. An old home town buddy, a former sailor, W. L. Sibley, told me that a Japanese shave was a delight to experience. "They warm your face with a hot towel and then pinch up small sections of skin which they shave a pinch at a time," Dub had told me. He was right. The shave was a delightfully relaxing experience.

The remainder of the day was spent strolling the streets and shopping for souvenirs. That evening, we found a steakhouse and dined on Kobe beef complete with flying knives and pounding condiment containers. It was an excellent meal. After dinner, we took in a stage performance that had been recommended by the Sanno's concierge. It was my first attendance of a professionally staged play. I couldn't understand a word and don't remember the plot, if I ever knew it. I was most impressed with the setting, movement of scenery, and changing of sets. The curtain was never drawn. It was like watching a movie. The climax or ending was the most impressive segment, complete with a burning and collapsing temple. Almost as entertaining as the play were two elderly lady American tourists. They alternately cried, screamed, and crowed throughout the performance. They left the theater in tearful praise of the play. I guess it was good; at least the production effects and scenery were worth the money.

The next morning we had eggs Benedict for breakfast and continued our tour of the vicinity near the Sanno. That afternoon, before hopping the train back to Johnson, we stopped at a local Howard Johnson's for a late lunch. At one of the back tables was Captain Neuman, one of Hill's ward mates. He was finishing his weekend as well. He, however, had taken a different approach than Hill and I. He had opted to hire one of the ladies from a club for a night's entertainment. For twenty dollars, I think, he had the pleasure of the lady's company for the night, a room in a geisha house, breakfast, a morning bath and massage, and liberties until noon. He was elated over the experience.

The days and evenings back at Johnson dragged by. I spent my days reading magazines and swapping war stories. It's surprising how tiring doing nothing is. Even the scrubbing ceased. Late in the week, the doctors decided to close my wound.

"What we're going to do is put a few stitches down deep and close you with surgical tape, the doctor told me. "Then we're going to send you to Camp Zama for ten days recuperation."

"When do I get the stitches out?" I asked.

"There's no need to remove them. They're self-dissolving."

"How come you're not using stitches on the outside?" I asked.

"The tape is better. It'll hold the wound closed, cause a stronger bond, and leave less of a scar, he replied.

I laid face down on the table and waited for my shot to deaden the pain. The doctor started to work.

"What, no shot?" I asked.

"No, the nerves are close to the surface of the skin. There's nothing that deep. "You won't feel a thing," the doctor told me. He was right. I didn't feel any pain.

The next day Hill, Neuman, and I were transferred to Camp Zama. All in all, I had a good stay at Johnson. The medical care couldn't have been better. The social life at the club was entertaining, and the patients were made to feel a part of the crowd. I had only one embarrassing experience.

Two evenings before leaving for Zama, I had been invited to join a group of doctors and nurses. During the small talk I met a tall, attractive brunette from Lubbock, Texas. Odessa, my home town, was 130 miles south of Lubbock. The two high schools were in the same sports district then and had a big rivalry. When I was a sophomore, Lubbock had won the State Championship for the past two years. We broke Lubbock's twenty-nine game or so winning stretch. Now here was someone I had something in common with. I should be able to have a good conversation with her. I guess she wasn't a football fan. She let me know real quickly through the tone in her voice and short answers that she didn't have time for a lowly captain of Armor. I decided she had her sights on the big money, a doctor. Whatever the case, she made me feel foolish for having tried to strike up a conversation.

At Camp Zama, we didn't have anything to do except report to the doctor every third day or so. We spent our time walking the installation and window shopping in the PX. We did make two more trips into Tokyo.

The later trips into Tokyo weren't as interesting as the first. Our time was spent shopping for souvenirs to send home to wife, kids, and mothers, and buying clothes. We visited the Tokyo, a replica of France's Eiffel Tower, then strolled the Ginza, Tokyo's main shopping street. At night, it was most impressive. I've never seen a more brightly, colorfully lit street including the strip in Las Vegas. My most interesting experience was a trip to the Sony Building in downtown Tokyo. The interior of the building was designed like a spiral staircase. We circled around the interior viewing the various displays. Occasionally, we stepped up three or four steps. Before long, we were on the top floor. We had climbed seven or eight stories without realizing it.

During our walks, we philosophized about the war and various Army policies. About the war, as I remember, we had no question about the rightness of our cause or the necessity of America's involvement. We were in disagreement with the politicians about how the war was being fought. We thought that the military side of the war could be won first and then the hearts and minds of the people. Charlie wasn't winning converts through kindness, but rather through force and the fear of force. We felt the Korean way was the way to handle the Vietnamese: work with us in peaceful cooperation and we'll work with you in kind; fight us and we'll hit you and everyone associated with you with everything we have without quarter. This wasn't the popular view, we realized, but the folks expounding other approaches weren't being shot at. Besides, their approaches weren't working either. Rather, they were getting a lot of Americans killed.

We believed our government was supporting the wrong set of politicians. From what we could read in *Stars and Stripes* and weekly news magazines, Vietnamese leaders seemed more interested in power and riches than in establishing a democratic, capitalist society that would allow a peasant to own land and have upward mobility. If we were going to fight, we could fight for the system that believed as we did. It seemed to us that the South Vietnamese hierarchy was bent on maintaining the status quo; thereby, the upper economic class would continue to suppress the lower class without affording them an opportunity to enhance their economic condition. Still, we believed that a South Vietnamese government of any kind would be better than a Communist government. If the Communists won, a massacre of opponents would ensue.

We were particularly opposed to the misrepresentations we read in various publications. Of course, we didn't have first-hand knowledge of the big picture, but from what we had seen in our small part of the war, ARVN wasn't progressing nearly as well as our government leaders claimed. We had particular misgivings about the reported body counts. How could President Johnson make rational policy decisions based on such information? We did believe, however, that we had won our part of the Tet Offensive and that ultimately we and our South Vietnamese allies would prevail.

On the more personal side, we discussed such Army policies as the Up or Out Program for officers, accelerated promotions to captain, use of Category Four personnel (individuals scoring in the lowest category of the Army's Qualification Test), and the professional private. We agreed on the issues for the most part.

The Army's Officer Retention Policy gave an officer three opportunity to be promoted. If he was passed over a third time, he was released from active duty. We thought this unfair to the company grade officer who was good with troops, a good small unit leader, and satisfied with a captain's ranking. Some officers might not have the potential to be a higher-level staff officer or commander, but they could lead a company. We realized that duty with line units was for physically fit officers. But the officer should be allowed to continue so long as he could stay out front. When he no longer could, there were plenty of support jobs that could be filled by a concerned officer who knew what the infantryman, tanker, artilleryman, or engineer experienced and needed. Succinctly, the Army was big enough to find a job for an officer who was efficient at company level but didn't have the formal education or the planning and communicative skills for higher level positions. It was unfair and inconsiderate to use an officer for ten to twelve years and then turn him out to pasture, not because he was a poor officer or wasn't doing his job but rather because he didn't have higher command potential. This was particularly true when the Army could suspend the policy when company grade officers were in short supply. When convenient, like during a war, the Army found officers fully qualified but not selected, thus, getting around the up or out policy. If an officer was good enough to lead in combat, which is what the Army was about, he was good enough to lead during times of peace.

Moreover, we weren't in favor of the rapid promotion of lieutenants to captain. At that time, an officer could be promoted to captain with two years service. We thought this length of service didn't provide an officer with the experience to lead and administer a company. We did think that if a lieutenant filled a captain's position, he could be paid a captain's salary. We were also in favor of field promotions of lieutenants to captain. Who knew an officer better than his immediate superior?

We discussed the feasibility of majors commanding combat arms companies. It seemed a good idea to us. The British used majors to command their companies and majors commanded US Army aviation companies. Why not use majors? They'd be more experienced and mature. If majors commanded, what would we do with captains? Make them executive officers and staff officers. Of course, this would make captain a nothing grade, like the major rank was at the time, except in aviation units. Majors generally served as staff officers or action officers. They didn't lead troops. Thus, they were in an awkward position, assigned to duties that most leaders would rather not be assigned.

Another topic of discussion was the enlistment of Category Four personnel. Category Four personnel were the soldiers who scored in the lowest ranges of the Army's Qualification Test. During times of peace, the Army wouldn't enlist them. But the Army needed men and McNamara, the Secretary of Defense, had a program called project 100,000, whereby 100,000 Cat IVs, as the Army called them, were enlisted. I personally liked them. They did what they were told and gave you few problems. If they were handed a broom or mop, they'd work all day cleaning a floor without complaint. The more intelligent soldiers would ask a thousand questions about why the floor had to be mopped. I wouldn't want a Cat IV in leadership, planning, or decision positions. There was, however, a place for them in any unit. This conclusion led to our belief that line units could have duty or fatigue organizations made up of Cat IVs. The Cat IVs would do the menial jobs, so that the better-qualified soldiers could do more soldierly duties. This idea shouldn't be thought of as demeaning to the Cat IVs. Rather, it was the use of each individual to the best of his or her ability. Doing any necessity job wasn't demeaning. It was productive, useful, and I believe character building.

Along these same lines, we thought there was a place in the Army for the professional Private. We each knew men who didn't want responsibility and were happy being a rifleman or driving a jeep or truck. They were good at what they did. Their equipment was the best maintained because they knew their job. And for the most part they stayed out of trouble. I had served with one in Germany. He was a great soldier who could be relied on to accomplish any job given him. Not everyone is meant to be a sergeant major or general, but there's a place for anyone who wants to serve.

Our most strongly expressed opinion was that if the United States was going to provide money, weapons, equipment, and advisors to an ally, it should insist that it have authority over the allied army. We advisors had no authority and we had to wait to be asked for advice. It was true that our Vietnamese counterparts were more experienced than most advisors and some were excellent leaders. They, however, weren't generally successful. They weren't aggressive and they didn't get out front. There were a thousand excuses for this, but the fact remains that their adversary was doing better militarily with less. The Vietnamese could and should lead their army and fight their war, but advisors should have reported counseling sessions with their counterparts and there should be a procedure to have a commander relieved, based on the recommendation of an advisor. All the philosophic arguments against such an approach were believed to be so much hogwash. The ally accepted our taxpayer's money, our equipment and the death of our young men. They could damn well seek and consider our advice. This wasn't to say that we knew all the answers or that we shouldn't listen. To be ignored, however, was out of the question.

I should point out that I didn't consider Vinh or the 6th Cav as contributors to this situation. True, Vinh never asked me for advice and he wasn't as aggressive as I'd have liked. Still, I considered him a good officer and leader. Though initially I wasn't impressed with the 6th, I had changed my mind. The troopers were great. They could be better with better leadership. The same can be said of any unit.

Finally, the day came when our little group had to part. I was the first to go. The doctors decided that I was fit for return to Nam. A decision hadn't been made on the future of the others when I departed. I don't know their fate.

I boarded the C-141 with the intent of trying for a reassignment to the 11th Armory Cavalry Regiment (ACR) when I arrived in Saigon. I was proud of my association with the South Vietnamese and I was proud of their performance during Tet. No unit could have done better. I, however, considered myself a professional soldier and thought my career would be better served by serving with Americans. I wanted to lead, not direct supporting fires. I chose the 11th ACR because, from what I had read, I considered it: the top armor unit in-country. It was the fire brigade.

CHAPTER SIXTEEN

MY THO: 17 MARCH 1968

I went directly to the MACV Personnel Liaison Section at Ton San Nhut after deplaning. I told the NCOIC that I was returning from convalescent leave in Japan and that I wanted to be reassigned to the 11th ACR. I was told, "No change, you have to be out of country or in the hospital for over sixty days to be considered for assignment to a new unit." I didn't feel like fighting the problem. I was happy with my team and the 6th Cavalry.

I caught a bus for Kopler Compound to report in. I was assigned a room and told I could fly out the next day. While I was unpacking a few things, Major Evans walked in. He had been told that I was returning and came to Saigon to welcome me home and to arrange his flight home when he rotated. He'd be leaving in about a month. He had requested a circuitous flight through Thailand and Europe to the East Coast instead of flying to Japan and then the West Coast like almost everyone else. Few people knew that such flights were authorized, but leave it to my major to find a new wrinkle and to work it to his advantage.

The next morning, 17 March, I caught a Huey back to My Tho. When I stepped off the Huey at Dinh Binh airfield, none other than my old friend Major Ruff was waiting to board. He was all smiles. He was going home. The sorry rascal made it.

Things hadn't changed at Armor House. All my things, including the M-3 subs, were right where I had left them. Sergeant Neal was still alive and well. Lockett's replacement, Staff Sergeant Vann, had come on board. The only difference was that the searchlight crews had been transferred back to an American unit. I wouldn't be able to do anything about Sergeant Williams, the searchlight section leader who disobeyed my order during the battle for My Tho. Oh well, some people always get over.

That evening and the next few evenings were spent listening to war stories about the Squadron since I had been medevaced. Few Troop operations were being conducted. The Squadron had been busy while I was away. Each advisor had been wounded at least once. Lieutenant Lord was particularly vocal about one operation in which the Squadron had mistakenly gotten into a fire-fight with the 9th Division. "You ever seen .50 cal tracers coming at you? It's a hell of an experience, I tell you! I wanted to crawl into my helmet and stay," he said in wide-eyed disbelief.

Before my first operation, Vinh departed for Fort Knox to attend the Armor School's Advance Course. First Lieutenant Hong took over the Troop. On our first operation, I was impressed with Hong's professionalism. We spent the day roaming the paddies without finding anything more than a few VC flags. When we started back to My Tho, Hong, unlike Vinh, took a different route. He was in no hurry to be ambushed. The only unpleasant thing about the mission was that my headaches returned. I'd have to get used to the heat again.

The Squadron now regularly operated out of My Tho. Some operations were as a full Squadron, others were with two Troops. Few were of Troop size. Also, we changed our tactics. The Cav seldom looked for Charlie. We waited in My Tho or in an assembly area for the infantry to locate Charlie and call us in. This was a reversal of roles. Originally, the Cav (scouts) found the bad guys then called in the big guns, infantry and tanks, to finish them off. This was fine in the US Army, where the Cav was the lightweight that moved with stealth and the heavies were the combined arms task forces or the airmobile units. In the South Vietnamese Army, the Cav had the firepower and the infantry was the unit that moved with stealth. Despite the tactic, Charlie didn't want to fight. He was again playing hard to get and no major contacts were made.

The best thing about our new routine was that we were back in My Tho each night. I now had to be careful at the club. I couldn't badmouth the aviators about their nightly shower and sleeping between clean sheets. We were at the Seminary almost nightly to shower and watch a movie. It was no longer our lot to live like animals in the wild. Occasionally, we managed to get a movie at Armor House. War's not half bad when the enemy won't fight, you can't find him, and you have all the modern conveniences.

Sometime in late March, Captain Arthur went to an assignment with the Division staff and moved to the Seminary. Captain Seals replaced him. Seals was a career officer who would prove to be an asset to the team and become a good friend.

My routine returned to the nomadic wanderings of the Cav. The 18th of March was spent performing Troop maintenance and Sergeant Neal conducted a class on bore-sighting the 90 mm recoilless rifle. The next day we moved out on an operation at 0800 hours. The 2nd Battalion, 11th ARVN Infantry was attached. We were back in My Tho by 1600 hours. March the 20th was spent maintaining the tracks.

We moved out again on 21 March at O700 hours with the 32nd Rangers attached. The operation was completed by 1600 hours and we spent the evening at the Seminary's O-Club. The 22nd through 24th March was spent in maintenance in My Tho. On 25 March, we were again on operation under the operational control of the 11th Regiment. As usual, we completed our day's work by 1630 hours. This operation was a little different. We had a contact with 12 VC. We reported two killed and two wounded. There were no friendly casualties.

On the 26th and 27th of March, we were placed in operational reserve. This mission consisted of sitting in the paddies and waiting for the infantry to find something. We had no luck during these two days. Charlie stayed hidden. The next day was spent performing maintenance.

On 29 March we moved out at 0700 hours with 2nd Battalion, 11th Infantry. We fired on a group of suspected VC. I noted we possibly wounded two of the fleeing enemy. We picked up one suspect. On the 30th of March, we performed maintenance. The last day of March was spent providing security for some ubit. I didn't recall for what purpose or for whom.

Then on 1 April at 0630 hours, the entire Squadron moved out with the 32nd Rangers. The operation, which would circle above My Tho to the northeast, was planned for two days. The first day was uneventful—another ride in the sun. It was the dry season, which allowed us to laager (a circular formation with tracks facing out) in a rice paddy, out of sight of a village or a road. This was a new experience. We had never spent the night in the paddies. I was uncomfortable. Visions of a night attack by Charlie danced in my mind's eye. There was a beautiful sunset and the evening was quiet. I pulled out the little portable Zenith radio that Lockett, Long, and I had purchased four months earlier. I thought of Long's death premonition and saw Lockett lying in the road while I searched for AFN. I had survived, so far. Why? I found AFM on the dial as it began a broadcast of President Johnson's 31 March speech announcing a halt to the bombing of North Vietnam. I was crestfallen. The announcement couldn't have hurt me more if I had been hit in the chest with a sledge hammer. I thought we had won the Tet Offensive. I thought the Vietnamese were now fighting and doing well. I was proud of them and proud to be part of their struggle. Now with only a few words, my President had pulled the rug out from under me and had hung me out to dry. What's the use of fighting if your President want, it was Johnson who put us in this position, wouldn't provide all the support at his disposal! I called Neal and Vann to the command track and told them what I had just heard. They were speechless. I don't know if it was from shocked disbelief or agreement with the announcement. I was so angry and vocal that I hardly let them get in a word.

Fortunately, Charlie didn't attack. The next morning, we continued our search of paddies without success. At mid-afternoon, transmissions over the net began to jump. The infantry had located Charlie and he had decided to stand and fight. The tracks maneuvered to support the infantry. The tracks weren't firing, so I could clearly hear the mixture of M-16 and AK-47 fire as we moved through the dry paddies. Approaching a tree line, we began to receive mortar fire from Charlie.

"We're getting heavy fire from a bunker to our right, "I heard one of the infantry advisors report.

"We're pinned," I heard another report.

"We're receiving fire to our front, can't move," someone said.

"We're going to pull back and circle right," another reported.

"They're too well dug-in. We're pulling back to let the artillery work them over."

"Charlie One-six, this is Sierra Six, over," I heard Major Evans call.

"This is One-six, over."

"Roger, We're going to hold and bring the RF in from the south and the Rangers in from the north, break. They're going to link up on the east side of the canal. That'll put Charlie in a crescent, break. When they're set, we're going to push into the opening to drive Charlie to the east and into the blocking positions, over."

"This is One-six, Roger, over I replied.

"This is Six. While the infantry is making its move, we're going to try to hold Charlie in position with artillery, break. I have a Loche coming into your position. I want you to go airborne to see if you can better identify the VC positions and direct artillery, over."

"This is One-six, Roger, out." Well, there's a first time for everything. We have never had Loche support before. Wonder why he chose me to go. I had never directed artillery from the air.

"Charlie One-six, this is Lima Two-three in bound your position from the west, request smoke, over."

"This is Charlie One six, Roger, Two-three, wait. Smoke is out, over."

"Roger, One-six, I identify green, over."

"This is One-six, Roger Two-three, that's me. Come on in, over."

A few intermittent friendly artillery rounds were falling into the jungle as the chopper approached. Within seconds of landing, the Loche was airborne again. The pilot pulled maximum RPMs lifting off and banking hard to the South. I lost my orientation as the chopper climbed. It took me a few minutes to re-orient the map and get my bearings. The terrain looked different from the air.

Once airborne, the pilot contacted the supporting artillery unit.

"Romeo Lima Three-five, this is Oscar Two-one, over, the pilot called.

"This is Romeo Lima Three-five, over."

"Roger, Three-five, this is Two-one. I'm airborne vicinity five seven zero ahhh five niner zero to observe and direct fires on Objective Sabra, request safe fire line, over."

"This is Three-five. Stay east of line five six one ahhh five eight niner to five seven niner ahhh five seven one, over."

Suddenly, there was an explosion to our right and above us.

"Damn, that was an artillery round!" I said into the intercom. There was a shriek in my voice. I had to talk around my heart. The pilot screamed into the radio, "Three-five, three-five, check fire, check fire. We had an air-burst off my right rotor tip, over."

"Roger, check fire," replied the cool artillery man.

The pilot banked west and gained altitude.

"How did that happen?" I asked.

"I don't know must have been a bad fuse or a wrong fuse setting. I'll make a report when I get in," The pilot replied.

He was right by not making an issue of it. No one had time for that. They, whoever they were, could figure it out later. For me, I was ready to get on the ground. I didn't like the idea of being shot out of the sky, much less by my own artillery.

I had just gotten my heart back in my chest when I looked through the Plexiglas door window to see an F-4 swoop down and unload a bomb into the jungle. It was followed closely by a second jet firing its nose cannon.

My pilot was on the radio instantly to the FAC, "Falcon, this is Oscar Two-one, what you got going, over?"

"This is Falcon, I have four sorties coming in, over."

"This is Oscar, roger, out."

The pilot looked over at me and said over the intercom, "I may as well put you down. The air-strikes will take thirty, forty-five minutes. I don't have the fuel to stay around."

"Fine." I was ready. I wanted something solid under my feet. It was too crowded up here.

Back with the Troop, Major Evans told me that the Squadron would attack at 1600 hours. When the hour arrived, artillery tore into the jungle and the tracks moved forward across the paddies. "Don't forget to stop the artillery. You'll lose more than points on an ATT, "I thought. No one seemed to remember to request artillery or to stop it when they needed to during an ATT. It's not hard to remember artillery when you're playing for real.

"Romeo Lima Three-five, this is Charlie One-six, cease fire, cease fire, over."

"This is Romeo Lima, roger, cease fire."

"We're receiving heavy fire," I heard Lord say.

"We got a heavy system of bunkers to our front," Seals reported.

"We're getting some sniper fire," I chimed in.

"Tell your counterparts to have their crews watch their fire. We have friendlies directly behind Charlie," Major Evans called.

"Receiving mortar fire," Lieutenant Lord, the 2nd Troop's advisor, reported.

"The firing is getting heavier," Seals called.

"We're pulling back to let the gun-ships come in," Evans reported.

The tracks backed away from the tree line into the center of the paddies. Major Evans directed the gun-ships. The first gunship's whump-whump-whump thundered in my ears as it passed over head. As it passed over, its machineguns were chattering and then rockets went blazing downward. Little gray/white trails of death vanished into the trees. The second chopper came in and then the third and then the fourth. After the gunships had done their best to level the jungle, we charged forward again. Charlie's fire erupted into the tracks at a heavier volume than we had received on our first attempt. I didn't expect this. Charlie was supposed to run when the gun-ships came on station. There was no feeling of confidence. There was no lift in my morale. Heck, the gun-ships just made them mad. So much for gunships, they can't hit anything with those rockets anyway! Let's get the artillery back in here.

When the last chopper pulled off, Major Evans or someone called in the artillery again. Whoever it was must have been reading my thoughts. Charlie's fire began to subside. We pulled back again and waited for the artillery to stop. When the artillery finished with Charlie, Major Evans told us that we'd attack at dusk. "Damn, a night attack! Oh no! That ain't gonna be any fun at all," I thought. "That's Charlie's game. We won't be able to see anything in that jungle."

We sat for what seemed like ages.

"Sierra, Sierra, this is Sierra Six, Major Evans called. We answered in turn.

"This is Six. Charlie is moving out to the southeast." "Now how did they slip through two battalions of infantry," I thought. "We'll hold here for the night," Evans said, signing off.

I was relieved. I didn't want any part of thrashing around in the jungle at night. A night attack is one of the most difficult operations a unit must conduct. All manner of things go wrong. People step on booby traps. They go the wrong way. They get separated from friends. They shoot their buddies. Nope, best we leave night fighting to the infantry, Snake Eaters (Special Forces), and Rangers.

The night passed without incident as well as the next day. We rolled back into My Tho at 1700 hours to continue our routine daily operations.

The morning of 4 April we moved out at 0615 hours to escort artillery from Tan An to Long Dinh. We pulled maintenance from 0900 to 1500 hours and then moved to Bien Tri in Kien Hoa Province, arriving at 1900 hours. We spent the next day providing local security in Bien Tri. We remained in Bien Tri until 1530 hours on the 6th of April and then moved to coordinates 491314 to secure an artillery fire base. We must not have done much securing. We were back in Bien Tri for the night.

At 0730 hours on the 7th of April, we moved out on operation with the 235th RF Battalion. We picked up four suspects. At 1500 hours, we escorted an artillery unit to the My Tho ferry and returned to Bein Tri at 1530 hours.

The next day we were again in the paddies with the 235th RF Battalion before returning to My Tho. On the 9th of April, we were assigned a My Tho security mission. On the 10th, we moved out on operation at 0400 hours. There was no contact.

During 11 and 12 April, we remained in My Tho. I worked on the PPL (primary parts load, the repair parts carried by a unit) to identify shortages and problems within the system which slowed the flow of replacement parts.

We stayed in My Tho again on 13 April. During the day, we worked on weapons maintenance. That evening, several team members gathered on the officer's balcony at Armor House for a bull session. Major Evans was at the Seminary checking on his orders. Team members came and went. We discussed the war in general, its causes, and how well we were doing. We discussed such international issues as the devaluation of the French Franc, of which we knew nothing. While we pondered the issues, we watched a Spooky leisurely work over Charlie to the south across the My Tho River. We joked about the hell Charlie was catching and cheered on the Spooky. How unfeeling we had become! How ironic that we could sit joking and discussing issues totally unrelated to the war and calmly watch a rivulet of death pour down onto our adversary.

We also discussed our future plans. Lieutenant Lord was the only non-lifer (career soldier). He planned to return to Nashville to become a song writer. I thought he had a good chance to make it. He was the only person I had met that could sit down and write a report properly on the first attempt. He had a way with words and had a great sense of humor. At times, he'd have us all laughing our heads off about something that wasn't all that funny.

While I listened to the various conversations, I thought about why we were really in Vietnam. I knew the party line, but that was vague. What were the decision processes? Who really made the decisions? What was the real rationale? Why was Vietnam important to us other than to contain Communist expansion and to provide a political buffer zone? I decided that the next time I went to war I wanted to know the real reason and the real why. I'd major in Political Science when I got back home. The Army didn't care what I studied so long as I had a degree. Yes, Political Science was a good major for a career officer.

As the evening wore on, our group dwindled to four. Captain Seals and Lieutenant Lord got their heads together and became involved in their private world. I was left with Staff Sergeant Beck, Lieutenant Lord's senior NCO.

Beck was an interesting fella. I knew from prior conversations with Sergeant Neal that Beck was a German national and that he had served with the French in Vietnam. This was the first time I had an opportunity to talk with him and I was interested in him and his background.

"How did you wind up in the French Army?" I asked.

"In Germany after the war, I couldn't make a living, so I went to France and joined the Army," Beck answered simply.

"And you served in Vietnam with them?" I continued.

"Yeah, I served up north. Actually, several Viets in the Squadron and I were together."

"How would you compare the French Army with us?"

"There's more of a distinction between the officers and men. They are more disciplined and physical in training and the enforcement of discipline."

"Which do you think is the best?" I wanted to know.

"Both systems have their strong points," Beck replied evasively. I didn't push the point. It was a loaded question anyway.

"Well, how did you get in our Army?"

"When de Gaulle broke up the Legion, I went back to Germany. I had trouble finding a job. When I did find one, I'd be fired when they found out I'd served with the Legion. Finally, I worked my way to the States. Soldiering is what I know, so I joined the Army," Beck answered.

"You ever try to get a commission?"

"Yeah, but I couldn't get my citizenship, so I couldn't get into OCS."

Major Evans joined us. He had received his orders. He'd return home in his roundabout way in a few days. His replacement would be Captain Bell, who would soon be promoted.

I was sorry to see Major Evans leave. He was a good officer and leader. Also, I had come to regard him as a friend. I'd miss him. That was the Army. We all move on to bigger and better assignments and new friendships. Maybe I'd run into him again.

April 13 to 21, 1st Troop remained in My Tho. I spent the time showing Captain Bell around the Squadron and working on the PLL problem. We weren't receiving repair parts when we needed them. Sergeant Neal instructed the Troop's senior NCOs on the care and cleaning of the M-16. We went to the range and fired the rifle and the M-79 grenade launcher, nothing to write home about. Our evenings were spent at the Seminary's club.

On the 22nd, the Squadron moved out on an operation with attached infantry. Since Captain Bell hadn't been on a Squadron operation, he decided to go along and to leave me behind to monitor the radio. I followed the progress of the Squadron from reports to Captain Bell from the advisors. After each report, I posted the unit's position on a wall map in the Armor House's operations room. In the early afternoon, I overheard the Squadron make contact. I listened to the reports of the battle intently. I felt helpless and left out. I wished that I were there. Suddenly . . .

"Sierra Six, this is Charlie One-five, over." It was Sergeant Neal.

"This is Six, over," Bell replied.

"This is One-five. My X-ray's track took a hit. He's down, over." X-ray was a code name sometimes used for assistant. My ear became glued to the radio's speaker.

"This is Six, roger. How bad is he? Do you need a dust-off? over."

"This is One-five, I can't tell. The fire is too heavy to get to him. As soon as we recover the track I'll let you know, over."

I listened while 1st Troop made two attempts to recover Sergeant Vann's track. Finally, Neal came back on the air, "We couldn't recover the track but I managed to get X-ray back to my track. He's hit bad in the head and right shoulder. We need a dust-off, over."

"Sierra Base, this is Sierra Six, over," Bell called.

"This is base," I monitored. "I'll get the dust-off on the way, over."

I went on to confirm the Squadron's location and called in the medevac request.

Then I asked the big question, "Do you want me to come out." The reply was in the affirmative. I called the Division TOC and arranged for a chopper to take me out. Grabbing my rucksack, I headed for Binh Due airfield.

The chopper, hovering about a foot from the ground, set me down alone on a paddy dike about 200 hundred meters to the rear of the line of tracks. Just as I stepped from the skid, the pilot side slipped the aircraft to maintain his hover. I stepped into the paddy instead of onto the dike. I landed in the only water left in the otherwise dry paddy. As I climbed onto the dike, I thought, *Been in Nam six months and this is the first time to get my feet wet. During the dry season no less.*

The Huey lifted off and banked into the sky. I was alone. I shouldered my rucksack and headed across the paddy toward the tracks. I heard sporadic firing as I trudged across the open paddy. There was no cover. There was no concealment. Surely, Charlie is watching me. I watched to see bullets kick up dust around me. I knew that each step closer to the tracks would bring enemy fire. None came.

When I climbed onto the command track, the firing had almost stopped. Hong was sending two tracks forward for another attempt to recover the disabled track. This time they were successful. When the three vehicles were back within our lines, Colonel Thoan broke off the engagement and the Squadron returned to My Tho.

The reported count for the day was ten Cong killed. We captured one B-40, three AK-47s and one rifle. The Squadron suffered one killed and five wounded. Of course we had one badly damaged M-113. Who won?

CHAPTER SEVENTEEN

THRUONG GONG DINH: 2 MAY 1968

On May 1st, the 7th Division advisors were called to the Seminary to receive an operations order. This was a biggie. We had never been briefed before an operation. The 9th Division Liaison was there. The Air Force FAG was on hand. The artillery support officer was also in attendance. All the division staff advisors were there. This would be a division operation complete with code name, Thruong Gong Dinh. The area of operation would be Gho-Gao District, about twelve clicks east of My Tho.

The briefing followed the normal Army's briefing procedure. The G-2 advisor gave us an overview of the enemy situation. The G-1 advisor gave us the personnel picture. The G-3 advisor briefed the scheme of maneuver and prioritized air and artillery support. The G-4 advisor said the operation could be supported. We were all excited when we broke up. We had our act together. Charlie was in for a bad day. We wondered if he knew we were coming.

It might be well to point out that this was the first that I had heard of Operation Thruong Gong Dinh. I would learn some twenty years later that Thruong Gong Dinh was a major 9th Infantry Division and ARVN operation that extended from 1 March to 30 July 1968, 152 days. I had no idea that the 6th Squadron's operations during that period had been part of a larger campaign. This little point illustrates how isolated we advisors were and how little we knew about what was going on. We weren't informed about the big picture. We were just told when our units would move out, and we were expected to be with them. How can you give advice when you don't know what is going on and you're not asked to participate in the planning!

Back at the Squadron compound, we were briefed again by Colonel Thoan and provided operational overlays. The overlays were the best I had ever seen. They were each individually drawn. The craftsmanship, lettering, and drawing were perfect in every respect. I remember thinking I wish that the operation's sections of American units could turn out such good overlays.

At first light, we rolled out of My Tho into the rising sun. Its orange glow was almost blotted out by the dust raised by the rumbling tracks. Now this was what armor was all about, racing into battle on 210 horses, protected by aluminum armor. Not really, I'd have much preferred to be on a 52-ton tank, mounting a 105 mm cannon. But one had to work with what one had. Charlie couldn't match the tracks anyway, so they'd do.

Within the hour, we slowed and moved north into the dry paddies behind advancing infantry. We had hardly entered the paddies when the infantry made contact. We continued a slow pace forward. Charlie was delaying to the northeast. We were slowed more by the many dikes and narrow irrigation canals than by the effect of Charlie's fire. For the Cav, the operation became more of a bridging exercise than a search for Charlie.

As the morning wore on, it grew hotter and hotter. The troopers broke out umbrellas and slung up poncho flies from the radio antennas to protect themselves from the sun. We followed along, watching the curling smoke of burning huts and rice hay as the infantry pushed Charlie along. We bounced over dike after dike and bridged narrow irrigation canal after irrigation canal.

The techniques used to negotiate the canals were different during the dry season than those used during the rainy season. During the rainy season, canal banks were soft, which allowed a track to use its own power to gouge a slope into the exit bank or to be pushed over the bank by a following track. Once the lead vehicle was through the canal it pulled the next vehicle through. There were exceptions, as related earlier, but generally pushin' and pulling was the solution. During the dry season, canal banks were dry and hard. They wouldn't accommodate this method. Rather, they were bridged.

This terrain's irrigation canals were narrow and bordered on either side by narrow, raised banks. The banks, however, were beyond the five and a half foot spanning length of the M-113. When a track tilted forward over the bank, its nose fell short of the opposite bank and buried in the canal's bottom.

To traverse these canals was simple. We used our aluminum bridge spans to bridge the gap. Then, when the front of the track tipped forward, its front caught on the aluminum span and was pushed forward by the portion of track still on the rear bank. When the tracks caught on the opposite bank, they pulled the vehicle on across the canal.

The tactic was similar to that of a river crossing, only on a smaller scale. A platoon advanced to the canal and took up an overwatch position. One of its track crews laid a balk span section across the canal and called a waiting platoon forward. A trooper guided the tracks onto the span to ensure that the vehicle was centered on the span to keep it from tipping to one side and slipping into the canal. As the tracks of a platoon crossed, they moved forward and to one side to establish a perimeter. The next platoon across went in the opposite direction from the first platoon to from the other half of a crescent bridgehead. The rest of the Troop crossed, passed through the perimeter and continued the attack. The procedure was slow and repeated over and over. As a result, the infantry walked away from us.

A Ride in the Sun photo by Larry Cole

Bridging a Canal photo by Larry Cole

The monotony of the radio's squelch ringing in my ear was periodically broken by a report from an advisor.

"Sierra Six, this is Charlie Two-six, Phase Line Gold now, over."

"Roger, Two-six, out."

"Sierra Six, this is Charlie Three-six, over."

"This is Six, over. "

"This is Three-six, we're held up on a canal about one hundred meters east of Gold, over."

"This is Six, roger, out."

Flame Thrower in Action photo by Larry Cole

Air Strike photo by Larry Cole

And so it went, slow and monotonous. Then, near noon, Charlie decided to take a stand. The staccato of automatic weapons fire could be heard to our front. The tempo of the battle increased as we crossed a freshly scythed rice paddy. Suddenly, three huge field rats ran across the paddy in front of the tracks. Two troopers on the lead track sprung from their track and chased after the rats.

Everything stopped, the battlefield became deathly quiet. No one fired a shot. Lunch was about to be rounded up.

I watched in astonishment. I couldn't believe what was happening. I understood why our troopers stopped firing. They didn't want to shoot their buddies. But why had Charlie stopped? Our troopers weren't going to share their lunch. It'd remain, for me, one of the war's unanswered, comical mysteries. Two rats got away. One found its way to the pot.

After lunch, we continued our push. Progress was slow. There was no mad rush across the paddies like my platoons had done numerous times during training exercises in Germany. When one might be shot, one becomes a bit more cautious. By mid-afternoon, the infantry had pushed Charlie into his lair. He made the mistake of deciding to stand and fight. The infantry cornered him along a tree-lined canal about 500 meters to our front. From the sound of the battle, Charlie was giving as much as he received.

The Squadron stopped in the paddies to await air-strikes and to watch the show. The platoons were stopped behind dikes, which offered little protection for the tracks and no protection to the troopers sitting in the open. The command tracks lay back in the center of the paddies. Charlie must have been short of RPG's (another name for the B-40 rocket, the Soviet's light antitank weapon). We weren't drawing any fire. Or maybe he was too busy with our infantry to worry about us.

I was passed the task of directing the air-strikes. We sat in the open beside a large ditch next to a thatched hut.

"Charlie One-six, this is Raven Spotter, over."

"This is One-six, over."

"This is Raven, what you got for us, over?"

"This is One-six, we have dug-in infantry at coordinates six five four four five one, over."

"Roger, is that about fifty meters from the canal, over?"

"This is One-six, I don't know. I can't see the canal, over."

"Roger, I'll put a rocket in. Adjust from there, over."

"This is One-six, roger, out."

I looked up to my left and saw the small, silver O-2 lazily moving toward the tree line in a shallow dive. A tail of white undulating smoke shot from beneath its left wing. The rocket impacted short of where I wanted it.

"Raven, this is One-six, you're about two hundred meters short. Charlie is in the trees about where the tree line rises, over."

"This is Raven, roger. I'll give it another try, out."

The O-2 slowly circled around and made another run. This time his rocket was close enough for government work.

"Raven, this is One-six. That's the area. Give them the works, over."

"Roger, I have a flight of two. They'll be coming in north to south, over."

I watched the first F-4 scream in over the jungle in amazed envy. The Phantoms dispensed bombs and napalm on their strafing passes and then rolled lazily into the sky. I pondered how many deaths our combined effort caused.

Two flights of F-100s came in before Colonel Thoan decided to assault. When the last fighter streaked into the heavens, we began our slow roll forward. What a beautiful sight, fifty-one tracks bearing down on an enemy position with a devil's vengeance. Our volume of fire increased the nearer we came to the tree line. Again, the fight appeared one-sided. Reports from the other advisors shot over the net. Each Troop was receiving automatic weapons fire. I heard nothing. I was safe in the womb of my track's death chatter. I felt left out. We had hit Charlie's soft spot. I thought. Then in the distance, to my right, I heard several shots.

"Sierra Six, this is Charlie One-six, we're receiving sniper fire from our right," I said in an excited voice. I didn't think the Troop nor I was in any danger, but I wanted to appear to be as heavily engaged as the others. Not a good thing to do. I could have caused

Captain Bell to recommend an unnecessary reaction based on my report. All I received was a stoic, "Roger, out."

As I turned my attention back to the front, my track hit a dike and stopped. I looked toward the track on my left. It was also stopped against the dike. One of its troopers was crawling forward on one hand and his knees. In the other hand, he held a grenade. He let fly. The grenade landed Just on the other side of the dike. A black clad figure appeared from behind the dike. The track had stopped directly in front of a one-man bunker. The Gong was half out of his hole when the grenade exploded. He was bent backward by the blast. A good thing he hadn't had a RPG.

To my front, our newly acquired flame-thrower track cut loose with its deadly arch of flame. Surprise, Charlie! We have something new for you to worry about. I wished, however, that we had something that would penetrate the hardened clay bunkers in the dikes. Flame-throwers were fine if we could get close enough. We might lose some of our tracks moving in. A 106 mm recoilless rifle would be even better. We could sit back and blow the bunkers apart. Why close with the enemy if we didn't have to? I liked the idea of hitting at a distance from which I couldn't be personally engaged. Our lead platoons disappeared into the tree line. The firing ebbed. I looked along the dike to my front. Two dead VC lay half on the dike and half in the paddy. I hadn't seen them. I wondered if I had been their target.

Hong halted the command track at the dike. He must not have liked the idea of going I into the trees or he knew the battle was over. There was sporadic firing for a while. Then I overheard the FAC report that Charlie was withdrawing along a canal to the northeast. The command turned the battle over to the FAG to let the Air Force deal with the retreating stragglers.

When the firing stopped, we policed the battlefield. We searched several knocked-out bunkers. They were a macabre mess, torn, blasted, fumbled goo of clay and flesh where satchel charges had been used to destroy them. We pulled a Cong from one. It had collapsed on him. Covered with mud, he was a kid, not more than fourteen. Only a few minutes ago, however, he was as deadly a killer as any soldier in the war. The troopers questioned him with enthusiasm. They raised their voices and waved rifles and pistols in his face. They never touched him, though. He was either in shock, a well disciplined soldier, or scared half to death (maybe all three) because he didn't say a word.

I searched the area for souvenirs for my sons. I found two US O3s, the standard Army rifle during World War I. Charlie had been woefully outmatched if this was any indication of his weapons. Still, he made a determined stand. What was the Cong's secret? What hold did they have on their soldiers that compelled them to endure such hardship? Why would they stand in the face of such overwhelming power? Why did they keep coming back after loss after loss? I couldn't reach a conclusion, but one thing seemed certain. Modern technology couldn't stop, destroy, or totally defeat determined infantry. If we were to win, we had to beat Charlie at his own game: have a cause, get simple, and be disciplined. He survived on basics, stealth, and determination. He withstood our might. He evaded sophisticated detection devices straight from Buck Rogers. Still, he gave as much as he received. I might not agree with him but I had to respect him. He was cunning and resourceful. Most of all, he was disciplined and determined.

Nonetheless, this had been our day. It had been a good battle for us; any one-sided fight is. I hadn't fired a shot and as far as I knew I hadn't been shot at. I had again watched from the safety of my theater seat. The official report said that we killed 170 VC, captured 4, and seized 11 crew-served weapons. If the report included results from all units, maybe those were good figures. I think the KIA figures were high by at least one hundred.

The next two days were spent in My Tho. We performed maintenance on the vehicles and gloated over our great victory.

We were convinced that we were a part of the baddest unit in Vietnam. Without a doubt, we advised the best soldiers in the South Vietnamese Army. Charlie couldn't handle them. I had truly become proud of the cavalrymen. They had fought well. They were now aggressive. They were excellent soldiers when given a mission and were well led.

Barking dogs on the morning of 5 May awakened me. I lay on my stomach with my right arm hanging over the side of the bed. I heard the dogs but I didn't want to wake up. I was comfortable. I didn't have anything planned for the day. I had planned to sleep late. What were those dogs barking at? The thought had hardly passed when a thunderous explosion shook the house. Instantly, I was awake. I rolled onto the floor. "B-40s," I yelled hitting the floor. Captain Bell, who shared the room with me, hollered, "We're being hit. Get to the radio,"

I grabbed my M-3, which lay next to the bed, as we clawed on hands and knees toward the stairs. One explosion followed another. I didn't bother to count them. Glass and masonry flew through the dusty, smoke filled room. We slid down the stairs without trying to stand. In the radio room, Captain Bell raised the Division TOC.

"Tango Oscar, Tango Oscar, this is Sierra Six, we're under attack. Get us some help, over," Bell yelled excitedly.

I knelt next to the radio desk looking through the sitting room and out the front window and door.

"What size unit, over," I heard the duty officer ask.

"I don't know, just get us some help. We're being hit with B-40s, over," Bell barked over the radio.

"This is Tango Oscar, roger, I'll do what I can, out."

The explosions slacked and then stopped. Small arms fire could be heard in the other half of the house.

"I'm going to the other side to check the men," Bell said, heading for the stairs. The only connecting door between the two sides of the house was upstairs.

"Okay, I'll cover the front," I said, moving to the front window.

I saw a silhouette move across the front yard. I fired. Two or three rounds discharged then my weapon stopped. I applied immediate action (pulled the bolt to the rear) and fired again. Two more rounds fired and a stoppage. The figures continued to move across my front. I applied immediate action. "Now's no time for you to act up," I said out loud to the weapon. I fired at another silhouette. I fired two more rounds and a shortage. Oh no, what's the matter with this thing. Okay dummy, you haven't cleaned it since getting back. How many times have you told the men to keep their weapons clean? Now here you are in the middle of a firefight with a dirty weapon that won't work. A scene from an old war movie, *Battle of the Bulge*, flashed before my eyes. James Arness played the part of a rifleman who hadn't cleaned his weapon. He had placed it outside his foxhole and the bolt had frozen in place. When the Germans attacked, he was killed trying to get his weapon to fire. I was now in the same situation. Not thinking and not being prepared might cost me my life!

I had taped two other fifteen-round magazines to the one in the weapon. Something told me to try another clip. I pulled the magazine from the weapon, turned it over and inserted a new clip. A stream of bullets tore into the night when I squeezed the trigger. A shadow moved. I fired a long burst. Nothing moved. I checked the side window to my right. No one was there. Something moved to my front. I fired a long bust. Nothing moved. Where was Bell? Again, the house was rocked by B-40 fire. I rolled onto the floor and covered my head. My face, arms and legs were bleeding. The explosions continued. I was okay, they were only scratches from the glass. The explosions stopped. Where's Bell? I'd better go check on him.

I ran up the stairs, walked onto the balcony and entered the Cavalry Bar. Bell lay face down in the center of the room. A pool of blood surrounded his body. I walked over to him and looked down.

I knew he was dead. *Oh Christ, I pleaded, not him. He was one of the good ones.* Then I remembered him telling me not two days ago that he wouldn't get a minor wound. "If I'm hit, it'll be major. I don't think I'll be killed but I'll get a major wound." He was only half-right.

Before I could kneel down to check Bell's wound, Sergeant Neal called from the door which leads to the NCO's room, "We need a dust-off. Beck has been hit. I turned and walked back onto the balcony. Its wall had been blown away along with the sandbagged firing position we had prepared. Grenades lay strewn on the floor. I looked out over the generator shed in the front yard. Several men stood in the street. They wore American helmets. Thank God, ARVN has come to the rescue. There was a Ruff Puff outpost to the west on the edge of town. I turned and walked back downstairs to the radio.

"Tango Oscar, this is Charlie One-six, we need a dust-off. We have two casualties, over."

"This is Tango Oscar, roger. I don't know if we can get one in there. What's your situation, over."

"This is Charlie One-six, I think it's over, over."

"Roger, One-six, where do you want the dust-off, over?"

"This is One-six, we'll have to set it down in the street. There's no other place, over."

"Roger, One-six, I'll pass the word. Do you have anything to identify your position, over"

"This is One-six, I'll find something, over."

"This is Tango Oscar, roger, out."

I crept out into the front yard and crouched down behind one of our jeeps. I couldn't see anyone in the darkness. The Ruff Puff must be chasing Charlie. I called for Sergeant Neal. He came into the front yard from the other side of the house. Over the dividing wall, I told him to get an M-60. the Army's standard machine gun, set up at the southeast corner of his yard.

Back in the radio room, I found a green hand-held flare. I raised Tango Oscar on the radio and told him I had security out and that I had a flare to mark our position. Captain Seals and Lieutenant Lord came into the room. I sent them out into the front yard on the officer side of the house to set up a position. I waited for the chopper.

I heard the whump whump whump in the distance long before the pilot came up on the net. When his call came, his cool vibrating voice was as confident as a Being who couldn't be destroyed. He was in full control.

"Charlie One-six, this is Delta Oscar Three-zero, your net, over."

"This is Charlie One-six, I have you lima Charlie, over."

"Roger One-six, what you got for us, over?"

"This is One-six, I've got one KIA and one WIA, over."

"Roger, what 's the LZ like, over."

"This is One-six, you'll have to land in the street. There are no wires, over.

"Roger, how wide's the street, over?"

"This is One-six, I don't know. You'll just have to come in slow and check it out, over."

"This is Delta Oscar, roger, we'll give it a try. You'll have to guide us in, over."

I spent the next few minutes jockeying the chopper in. I had to work from sound and constantly remind myself to give corrections by direction instead of by left and right. My left may not be the pilot's left. When the chopper passed overhead, I told him to circle until I could pop the flare.

"Roger, One-six, I identify green, over."

"Roger, that's us. Come on in. There's no activity, over."

"Roger One-six, we're on our way. We'll have to do this slow. I'm not sure we'll fit, out."

I walked back into the yard. The chopper circled, descending ever so slowly, a few feet with each rotation. Finally, the chopper settled to the ground. What a job! Those pilots are the best and most fearless in the world.

"Neal, get Beck on board first," I called over the whump of the rotor blades. When Bell was carried out, I saw that he had been hit in the abdomen. His stomach had been torn away.

As the chopper lifted off, Neal and I walked back to the house. "Don't worry; we got him on the chopper. He'll make it," I said. We had the best medical service in the world. I had every confidence that if the doctors got him on the table alive, they'd save him.

We maintained our visual until the sun broke over the roof tops. With the first rays of light, I reconstructed the attack. For the first time, I realized that we hadn't received our normal guard mount from the Squadron the night before. What happened to them? Oh well, no need to dwell on that. I'll never get that story straight. I asked about Lord's and Seal's actions. They had rolled under their beds and covered themselves with mattresses when the first rounds hit. I don't recall what the NCOs did. The only thing they could have done is roll against the east wall of their room. They couldn't have gone downstairs. Charlie was on the stairs. After the first B-40 barrage, Charlie had entered the house through our theater at the southeast corner of the house. One Cong climbed the stairs, placed his rifle under the railing guarding the stair's opening and fired across the floor. Beck had rolled from his bed and slid under it. Charlie's fire caught him in the chest and abdomen. It was during this action that Captain Bell tried to check on the NGOs. As he traversed the bar, Charlie again fired B-40s to cover the withdrawal of his assault team. One round hit the front wall of the bar room. Its cone of fire shot forward, hitting Bell in the abdomen.

I checked out the vehicles. Their bodies had several shrapnel holes, but they all ran. Walking back into the house, I noticed the vertical concrete blinds that sat atop the half wall protecting the front door. The blinds had been almost shot away. I'd been shooting at a wall during the attack. There was just enough space between each blind's slat so that I could see movement. The blinds had protected our assailants. Anyway, they didn't try to force the door.

I checked the M-3's magazine that had been in the weapon when the attack began. The rounds had been in the magazine so long that the spring that pushed them up had lost its strength. There had been nothing wrong with the weapon. It had been the magazine. In the future, I'll have to remove the rounds occasionally and clean the magazines. Next time, I might not be so lucky. Laziness and stupidly almost cost me and the team dearly.

Twenty-twenty hind sight told me we shouldn't never been out on our own. One ups-man-ship was fine in the peace-time Army or outside a war zone. But in this case, it had cost the lives of two fine soldiers. We should have known we couldn't secure Armor Mouse in an area where houses were pressed against each other and there was no lighting. We couldn't see further than across the street. If we had all been awake and waiting, Charlie still could have been within B-40 range and hit us before we could react. No need to be cynical. We all wanted the best accommodations in Team 75. We all wanted independence from team headquarters. We wanted to flaunt our superiority at the other advisors. We had those perks, but they cost us in the end.

I rotated the team members to the Seminary for showers and breakfast when I thought it safe. I stopped by the medics to have my cuts cleaned and dressed, then had breakfast and showered. When asked if I wanted to keep the team at Armor House, I said without hesitation that I wanted to move to the Squadron compound. I was responsible now and I wanted security, not glamour. I no longer cared to maintain a macho image. The devil with living high and looking good. I wanted to get home to watch my kids grow up. If I had to live in an APC or a foxhole to survive, that was fine with me. No, the Armor House was definitely out.

I could have recommended that we relocate to the Seminary. No, I had an aversion to being close to the flagpole. The senior cav advisor would lose control of the team. We'd be tasked with added details to the benefit of the Seminary rather than the Cav Advisors. I wanted independence as well as security. The Seminary didn't offer both; the Squadron compound did.

Back at the house, I searched through the wreckage. Under the east carport, beneath the setting room window, I found a spent AK-47 brass shell. Now how did that get there? I wondered whom the round had been fired at. Was it me? From that position, I was the only target during the attack. How could he have missed from that distance?

The day was spent moving and cleaning the house. Colonel Thoan provided a detail and truck for both. We moved to the second floor of the Squadron's old officer's club located in the Squadron compound. The building was old and in poor repair. It'd have been condemned if it been in the States. I was concerned that the stairs would collapse under the weight of the advisors and our equipment. The floor swayed and had many loose boards. I could see daylight through the tile roof. So this was home?

That evening at the Seminary I was told that one dead Cong had been found in a field near the Ruff Puff outpost west of Armor House. He was wearing an American helmet. Disgust overwhelmed me. I had looked down on our attackers and had done nothing. There were grenades next to my feet and I hadn't used them. I could have gotten a few of them, but let them go without challenge. I was disappointed with myself for thinking they were ARVN.

Armor House Officer Side photo by Larry Cole

Armor House NCO Side photo by Larry Cole

Armor House Bar Room photo by Larry Cole

The next day we learned that Beck had died on the operating table. How ironic. He had seen and survived so much. He deserved better than to be killed while hiding under his bed. If you live long enough by the sword it will turn on you. The next day we would move to the Armor Compound and then into the Tan Hiep operation on 7 May 1968.

CHAPTER EIGHTEEN

THE "GOFER": MAY-JUNE 1968

When I returned from the 3rd Evac on 10 May, after the Tan Hiep operation, Cav Team had received a new senior advisor, Major Stephen Harrison. He was an older infantry officer. I don't recall the rationale, if there was one, for assigning an infantryman to the Squadron. Truly, it made little difference. We were more liaison or fire support officers than advisors.

Major Harrison was an old-line infantry officer with an Airborne and Special Forces background. He was on his second or third tour to Vietnam. He may have served several more short tours when Special Forces teams were assigned for short six month TDY tours, I'm not sure. He had been a general's aide two or three times and had been passed over for promotion. I found that curious. I had always heard that being a general's aide was a sure path to promotion. Harrison, however, was a bit of a good-natured renegade. He was a reserve officer, and had gotten into some mischief for which the general couldn't clear him. Whatever the reason, he hadn't been promoted. That was too bad, I found him to be an excellent officer. But who was to say that life was fair and the best rise to the top? I had met several officers that I believed well qualified for promotion who had been held in grade. I had also met a few officers that I couldn't fathom how they were commissioned, much less had been promoted to field grade rank. I couldn't point fingers, however, since there were officers who believed I couldn't pour sand from a boot with the directions printed on the sole, must less be a Captain in the US Army.

With Major Harrison on board, my lifestyle changed drastically. From his arrival until the end of my tour, events seem to run together, partly because they were administrative and routine and partly because the two were overlapping.

A few days after my return to the Squadron, Major Harrison told me that Team 75's senior advisor wanted to move me to the Seminary. He thought I should be offered the opportunity to get out of the field because I had been wounded so many times. He'd leave the choice to me, but he wanted to offer me a position in the TOC to keep me from harm's way until the end of my tour. I didn't have to think twice. I didn't want any part of the Seminary. I told Harrison that if it were all the same with him that I'd stay with the Cav. It was fine with him. He even offered to keep me out of the field. He'd go on all operations and I'd become the team's gofer. It was a deal, however, that wouldn't last long. No matter how good the intentions, the major would be called to a meeting or something would come up that required his attention and I'd be back on operation. That was okay by me. Actually, the way the arrangement fell out offered me one last memorable operation.

First, I became the team gofer. My days turned to roaming My Tho and having cold beer, Cokes, and sandwiches on hand for the advisors when the Squadron returned from an operation. I found the Navy mess hall and tried them. The food wasn't as good as I had been led to believe. I thought the Seminary's chow was better. I met the local Navy Seabee (construction engineers) detachment and arranged to be invited to their various parties. They were a great group and we got on well. My advisor buddies enjoyed the diversion from the Seminary.

My nights were spent lying in my bunk, staring through the cracks in the roof, listening to mortar rounds fall on My Tho, and wondering if the next round would land in the compound or on our billet. The Seminary ceased to be the big attraction. We now had the Seabee compound, a single two-story house on Hung Vuong Street, to visit once or twice a week. They were making the same mistake we had made. To my knowledge, however, they were never attacked—maybe because they were builders, not destroyers.

My first project was to set up the team's operations room in a small room provided by Colonel Thoan. This was no large project. I only needed to move in the desks and radio, put a map on the wall with a few charts, and we were in business. The biggest concern was getting screens on the door and windows. Maybe the Vietnamese could live without screens, but not Americans.

Next, I was tasked to write a report outlining the equipment needs of the Squadron. According to my notes, I recommended over Major Harrison's signature (he wasn't Armor, nor did he have the experience with the Squadron that I had, but he was the boss, and in the Army the boss signs reports regardless of who writes them) that we should be provided more bridging equipment and an M-113 recovery vehicle. Also, I wanted 106 recoilless rifles and a track with a dozer blade. The 106 recoilless was for bunker busting. The dozer was to assist in canal crossings.

It became evident that the upper room of the officer's club didn't fulfill our needs. We needed our own place. Major Harrison and I asked around and learned that the 9th Division was destroying some buildings. I was dispatched with the mission to find out how to get the team a house. I drove to Dong Tam one afternoon to locate some lumber and concrete or to find a way to abscond with a building that was being torn down. I took one of the M-3s I had picked up during Tet for trading material. I knew they'd come in handy. I drove around the base until I spotted an engineer crew tearing down a structure I thought would suit our needs. The buildings were small and nothing more than a wooden floor, three quarter wooden walls with screen enclosing the upper quarter to allow for ventilation, and corrugated tin roofs. One of them would be a start.

"Say, Sarge, What are you going to do with that lumber?" I asked.

"Sir, we're going to burn it. It's too much trouble to try to re-use," the sergeant replied.

"Say, I'm an advisor over in My Tho. We need a place to live. What will it take to get one of those off post?" I said. "No problem, sir, you tear it down you can have it," he replied. "It's less work for us."

I looked across the road and saw some concrete. "How about concrete?" I asked.

"That's a horse of a different color," he said. "I can't let you have any of that."

"Ah, come on, Sarge. Surely you have some extra."

"Well maybe," he replied, sensing that I knew the game and was willing to trade.

"I have this never-used sub. I'll trade for some of that concrete," I said, reaching into the jeep for the weapon.

He looked it over. "Well, I guess I could let you have a few bags."

"Great! I need to get a detail and a truck. I'll be back tomorrow. Will you be here?" I said.

"Yes, sir, I should be," he answered.

The next day with a truck detail and sub in hand I returned to tear down a building and to pick up the concrete. The deal went without a hitch. As I thought, we didn't have enough materials to build the size structure required to house the entire team. The bartering continued with different sergeants until I had what we needed.

We had the structural materials, but we still needed approval to build the house in the Squadron compound and the furniture and appliances to replace what we had lost in the attack on Armor

House and during our move. I'd have to go through channels to arrange those items. Going through channels was no big deal, but it was time consuming. Major Harrison said I could hand-carry the paperwork to speed up the process. I made a few telephone calls to learn the system and I was in business.

First, we had to come up with a set of plans and specifications for what we wanted to do. Then I had to draw a floor plan of the house and specify the site preparation requirements, such as backfill, sources of water and electricity, and barrier construction. Next, I had to come up with a justification for the construction. A separate request for each item of construction could be submitted, or a combined request could be forwarded. Either way, the total cost couldn't exceed three million piasters.

The request had to be presented in six copies. It could be in a letter format or on a DA Form 14-115. My notebook doesn't say which way we went. The request had to go to Corps at Can Tho for approval and then to USARV (US Army Vietnam, I think) for funding. Then back to Corps for purchasing and contracting.

I don't recall why all the red tape when we were going to scrounge the materials from Dong Tam anyway. Most likely it was because a land-use concurrence had to be attached to the initial request. Most certainly, good old Uncle Sam was probably going to pay for the use of the land. If he did, it was dumb on his part. His nephews were putting their lives on the line in the South Vietnamese's defense. They should be paying Uncle, not Uncle paying them. But that's not the way old Sam does things. His taxpayers have enough money to support the world. I wondered when we're going to stop paying people for the privilege of defending them!

Enough sour grapes. I really didn't care what had to be done. It all went toward my twelve months and it gave me something new to do and helped pass the time. As a result, I was in the air a lot between My Tho and Can Tho. I drove when I had to go to Saigon. I don't recall any problems in getting the approvals or the funding.

I did milk the exercise for all the travel time that I thought I could get away with. It helped pass the time.

Colonel Thoan was an excellent observer of the advisors. He quickly recognized my success in getting materials from Dong Tam. One day he approached me with a request. The officers and men needed a club or mess hall. They had no place to prepare their meals. Would I go to Dong Tam and scrounge enough concrete to build a club with kitchen? I had been in-country eight months and this was the first Vietnamese request for my help. Curiously, it wasn't for assistance in fighting but rather for help to improve their quality of life. It didn't take long for me to decide to help. My decision was based primarily on the assumption that the club would be used by all soldiers and their families instead of just the officers. The families needed all the benefits they could get. Also, the Squadron, in my view, had performed well over the past few months and had earned the facility. Finally, I guess, I was flattered to have finally been asked to do something other than ride on the back of an APC.

There was little problem in obtaining the necessary materials. The remaining M-3 subs came to good use. In no time, the club was built and operating. The troopers demonstrated a great deal of ingenuity in building the structure. With a few bags of concrete and some sand, they molded the concrete blocks and mixed the stucco by hand. They had few tools. None of them would have been considered modern by American standards, yet the building went up.

While I worked around the compound and watched the work on the club, I began to pay more attention to the people. I came to realize that they weren't as backward as I first thought. I can't recall any specific event that fostered this realization. Maybe it was seeing what the troopers could accomplish with so little. Maybe it was realizing that mothers allowed their babies to wander around the compound without diapers to prevent diaper rash. In the heat and humidity of the Delta, wet diapers exacerbated the age-old problem of keeping baby dry—no diaper, no heat rash. No heat rash, no crying baby. A poor solution in our view, but without automatic washing machines and air-conditioning, it was certainly practical. They merely adjusted their living habits to the environment, not the other way around. We might criticize their adherence to the siesta; but again, in the jungle and in the cities, without air-conditioning the heat was unbearable. Siesta kept the heat casualties down. We'd do the same or perish. Actually, the Army had adopted its version of siesta at Southern training facilities during the summer. When the combined heat and humidity reach a specified level, the installation went to a decreased training level to prevent heat injuries. The Army suffered numerous heat casualties and spent millions of dollars on research before it saw the error of its ways. The Vietnamese, Mexicans, and other Southern Hemisphere nationalities did it by instinct. Now who was the most intelligent and who could raise an eyebrow to ignorance?

Colonel Thoan's concern for his men and their families was manifested by two other projects. Mrs. Thoan worked relentlessly to obtain cloth for the Squadron's ladies to make clothing for their families. I didn't get involved in this project personally but I knew the effort was under way. Some of the advisors asked their families to send cloth. Also, Colonel Thoan wanted to get refrigerators for the families. He had the name of an American general in Saigon who controlled a large quantity of the desired items. During a lull in operations, Colonel Thoan asked Major Harrison and me to accompany him to Saigon to barter for the refrigerators.

The trip was an excellent aside to our war effort. Colonel Thoan was reported to be the son of Vietnam's Attorney General. Mrs. Thoan's family reportedly owned the Shell Service Station franchise in Saigon. I didn't confirm these rumors because I thought it impolite to ask the Thoans personally. Regardless of their status, they lived well. The home was small but well decorated with what appeared to be expensive furniture. They had a maid and a nanny for the children. Notwithstanding their apparent wealth, they seemed genuinely interested in bettering the lot of their countrymen. The country could have used a lot more citizens like them. Also, the Army could have used many more leaders like the colonel. He actually led his men on operation instead of sitting in My Tho or by directing operations from several miles to the rear.

We were in Saigon for three days. On our second evening, Colonel Thoan invited the American general, Major Harrison, and me to dinner at a Chinese restaurant in Cholon. We had a huge meal. I can't recall all the courses. There must have been a dozen. The only item that impressed me was the shark tail soup. It was my first experience with the soup and it was excellent. The Colonel must have put the bite on the general for the refrigerators, but I didn't hear. If he did, his offer wasn't high enough. We hadn't received them when my tour ended. Anyway, Major Harrison and I got a good meal and an enjoyable trip to Saigon for the effort.

The remainder of the trip was spent visiting the black market, visiting friends in Saigon, and visiting the 2nd Squadron stationed at a small installation north of Saigon. I don't recall what prompted our visit to the Squadron. It may have been that it was stationed at Tu Duc, the Vietnamese Armor School, which we wanted to visit. Whatever the reason, we dropped by to say hello to the advisors of our sister Squadron.

I thought we lived high until I saw how this team lived. It was billeted in a compound that would have rivaled the old quarters at Fort Sam Houston, Texas. The senior advisor was billeted in a white stucco house next to a tennis court. The billets sat along a tree-lined street straight out of an Andy Hardy movie. We marveled at the quiet luxury which was sharply contrasted by the living conditions of the troops at Tu Duc, which we visited later, and in My Tho. The French had taught the higher echelons of the Vietnamese Army how to live well if nothing else. We couldn't have had a hand in this.

Oh no, our Army was too austere for what I saw. Well, maybe these Vietnamese had Air Force advisors.

The black market was interesting. It operated openly. I could have bought anything I wanted or had enough money to purchase. I settled for a few Vietnamese items that would serve as souvenirs of the country, one of which was a gong.

In June, I went on R&R to Hawaii. As planned, I went with Jim Mosley. I drove up to Long Binh to meet Jim and then we drove to Tan Son Nhut to fly out. We met our wives at Fort DeRussy for a seven-day vacation.

Neither Nelwyn nor I remember much about our stay in Hawaii. It's been too many years. We went to the beach at both Waikiki and Fort DeRussy. We visited the International market. We rented a car and drove around the island. I enjoyed the cloud-covered mountains. We visited a botanical garden with a waterfall. We went to the Schofield Barrack's Post Exchange and drove up to the pass that the Japanese flew through to begin their raid on Pearl Harbor. We didn't go to Pearl Harbor or visit the memorial. I thought that would be too depressing. We visited Major Harrison's wife and family at Schofield Barracks. They had taken advantage of an Army policy which allowed dependents to remain in military quarters while their spouses were in Nam. We took in a Don Ho show. He was Hawaii's top entertainer at the time. Glenn Campbell was in town, but we didn't attend his show. He was just getting started and we didn't realize he'd become one of the country's top stars.

My most memorable experience was the night we and the Mosleys went to Fort Ruger, an old artillery post overlooking Honolulu, for dinner. It was the only activity we shared during the trip. We dined, danced, and looked down on the lights of Honolulu through the club's glass wall. The meal was excellent and the view breathtaking. The days flew by all too fast. Jim and I were soon on our way back to Charlie. I had just over two months left on my tour. What would they hold?

CHAPTER NINETEEN

GOING HOME: AUGUST 1968

Back in Vietnam the routine remained standard. My main task was to get the new Armor House built. Then one morning, the Squadron was called out on an unexpected operation. Colonel Thoan and Major Harrison were scheduled for a meeting with the corps and division commanders and their advisors that afternoon, so they couldn't make the operation. Politics before duty, you know. Major Kim, the Squadron XO, and I had to take the mission. Major Kim was an aggressive North Vietnamese who had fought with the French during the earlier war. He had lived outside Hanoi. Some of his family was still in the North. An affable person, he hated the Communists with a passion.

We moved out quickly and raced northwest along Highway 6A. When we reached its intersection with Highway Four, we ran into the rear of a civilian traffic jam. The traffic was stopped by a Communist roadblock a few miles up the road. At the head of the jam, we found a mine field consisting of several mounds placed in the road. The mounds could have contained explosive charges. Major Kim assessed the situation. He was in a hurry. He wanted at Charlie. It didn't take him long to decide that he was faced by a dummy mine field. Maybe a villager told him. Whatever the case, we drove through the roadblock after little hesitation.

The morning was beautifully silent as we pressed on toward Charlie. The montage of paddies presented a picturesque mosaic of rural Vietnamese life. We passed women treading an ancient irrigation water wheel. We passed papa sans working their wooden plows and their water buffaloes in a flooded paddy. The scene was straight from a travel folder. The morning was cool and the sky clear.

Off the road, we passed through some scattered trees. For the first time, I was concerned about booby traps. I searched each tree for trip wires or any sign of explosives. We were lucky. Charlie hadn't expected us and hadn't properly prepared our welcome. When we moved out of the trees, we came upon paddies filled with burial mounds. Their number and individual sizes was impressive and added a morbid reminder of what we were about. Sad, we couldn't even let the dead rest in peace.

The morning wore on. The operation had become another ride in the sun. It, however, offered more diversified scenery than I was accustomed to. I was enjoying the change. At siesta, we stopped in a village set in the center of the paddies. Major Kim and I visited the local chief to pay our respects and to share a cup of green tea. The formalities out of the way, we took our rest and waited for the heat to subside. When Kim was satisfied that it was time to move on, we mounted up and prepared to move out.

While the vehicles were jockeying into position, an old mama san came running up to the command track, spitting a torrent of Vietnamese and pointing to one of the tracks. Major Kim leaped from our track and ran to the APC, which the old woman had pointed out. He ordered the driver to lower the back ramp and then walked to the rear of the track. Shortly, a trooper leading a cow appeared from the cargo compartment. The soldier was terrified as he walked to the mama san. With much bowing, the cow was returned. The rope tethering the cow had hardly passed before Major Kim grabbed the soldier and threw him toward the dike in front of his track. From somewhere, a long, narrow switch appeared and Major Kim proceeded to give the trooper what for across his back and buttocks. The other troopers watched silently as the summary punishment was administered. Again, it wasn't the American way but it was effective. There was no doubt that the crewman had been caught red-handed. He was stealing from the people we were there to protect. There was no need for a lengthy wait to allow the lawyers to argue the finer points of law. There was no attempt at mitigation allowed. There was no excuse. There was no wait for the troopers to forget why the soldier was punished. Was he deprived of his human rights? Possibly, but he had deprived the villager of her rights to the possession and enjoyment of her cow. Unlike the first incident of corporal punishment I witnessed, this trooper's punishment wasn't too severe.

During the afternoon, the lead crews reported seeing Charlie withdrawing to their front. They fired on the fleeing enemy with little or no effect. They were too far away. The terrain turned against us. The paddies were crisscrossed with broad irrigation canals. The canals were wider than the ones we had encountered on the Thruong Gong Dinh Operation. We had to build modified H-span bridges with the aluminum balk spans. Constructing and dismantling the bridges were time consuming allowing the Cong to walk away from us each time we crossed a canal. For all our supposed speed and mobility, we couldn't close with our quarry.

Fortunately, two sections of American scout Loches were operating south of My Tho. They hadn't been able to find anything to work on so their leader offered his services to the division. The division duty officer in turn offered them to the Squadron.

When the choppers came on station, I directed them toward our last sighting of Charlie. In no time, the scouts had Charlie in their sights and went to work. The rest of the afternoon was spent coordinating our efforts to keep the pressure on our fleeing adversary. The scouts reported where Charlie went to ground and then pulled off. We moved toward the sighting. When Charlie saw the tracks bearing down on him, he was in a quandary and confused. Would he stand and fight the Cav or would he run and take his chances that the choppers had left the area? He decided to run. As soon as we saw the distant black specks move into the paddies to escape us, I called in the scouts. Though out of sight or sitting in the paddies to our rear, the choppers could move in and pounce on Charlie with their mini-guns before he could get to the next hedgerow. The Loches were having a great day until they ran low on fuel.

After the choppers pulled off, we headed back to My Tho. It had been an interesting day. My pride in armor's ability to keep up with infantry had been tarnished a little. Charlie had walked away from us. With our best efforts, we couldn't catch him. But I had learned a new tactic. Armor working with helicopters was a potent force. I didn't record the results of our efforts, but the body count was high that day thanks to the Loches. Why hadn't we used the tactic before, probably because ARVN didn't have the choppers or possibly because the American choppers were held back to support American units. Would the tactic be used again? Probably not, but hopefully!

My days in the paddies came to an end in September. It was time to get ready to go home. I spent my time running errands for the team and traveling to Saigon to arrange for orders, register the rifles I had picked up for my sons, and generally to pass the time.

On my trips to Saigon, I had been keeping track of the reconstruction of the Tan An Bridge. One of the larger bridges in the Delta, Charlie had blown it a few months before I arrived in-country. I was told a canoe filled with explosives had been floated down the canal and into the legs of the bridge. The explosives were then command detonated, felling the bridge's center span. A pontoon bridge had been built as a by-pass to keep the traffic and produce flowing into Saigon. I wanted to cross the main span one time before going home. I got my wish on my last trip. Unfortunately, ARVN couldn't secure it. I was still on leave before reporting to the Armor School when I heard on the evening news that Charlie had again felled the bridge.

One evening at the Seminary, I was told of a disturbing event. I was talking with Major Anderson, the new G-1 advisor and administrative officer.

"You'll never believe what happened last night, Cole", Anderson started.

"What's that?" I was always interested in a good story.

"Last night, after curfew, we heard shots from up the road," Anderson continued. "We sounded the alarm, but the firing stopped and nothing came down the road." At the time, anything that moved after dark was considered VC and open game. The policy was necessary but resulted in some civilian trucks, whose drivers pushed to the limit, being shot up by jumpy Seminary guards.

"So?" I questioned.

"Well, the colonel started running around, organizing a patrol to check out the shots."

"So?"

"He was only asking the staff officers to go. He was going to lead it."

"What! A full colonel leading a combat patrol?" I said.

"That's right," Anderson said with a smile.

"And with senior staff officers?" I asked.

"That's right," Anderson replied.

"Did you go?" I asked.

"No, he asked me to, but I told him I had work to do," answered Anderson.

"So, what happened?" I asked.

"The colonel got six officers together and moved out across the road," Anderson said.

"They run into anything?" I wanted to know.

"Naw, they only went about fifty meters up the road and turned back. They weren't out thirty minutes," Anderson said.

A big "mmmmm," was my only reply.

"When the colonel came in he told me to write them all up for a Silver Star, Anderson said looking me in the eye.

"You're kidding?" I said in surprise.

"No. That's what happened, honest," he said.

"What did you say? What did you do?" I asked.

"I said I wouldn't do it."

"And you're a career officer? You want to kiss your career goodbye? I asked.

"No, but I couldn't go along with that. "

"Good luck," I said.

Not the most glamorous story coming out of the war. I only relate it because it sheds light on the attitudes of some of the senior officers. They wanted an opportunity to further their careers. Medals helped toward that end. If a medal opportunity didn't come to them, they made their own opportunities. I believed the story then and still do. I ran into Anderson at Fort Knox a few months later and asked him if he had had any trouble from the colonel over refusing to write up the awards. He told me the colonel pressed him a few days and then dropped the issue.

In early September, the Squadron received nine 106 mm recoilless rifles. All right! Just what we needed. Maybe my earlier report had been useful. Charlie could no longer hide, in relative safety, in his rat holes bored into the hard clay dikes. The 106s could easily blow the entire dike away.

The 106 had been developed by the Army as a light anti-armor weapon for the infantry. It was too large to be hand-carried, so it was mounted on a jeep. Its size, however, wasn't practical for the infantry and it had been replaced by the LAW and the 90 mm recoilless rifle, which could be hand carried.

True to the Army system, the team's first requirement was to submit a report of where the new weapons could be placed in the Troop TO&E (Table of Organization and Equipment). As I saw it, we had two choices. We could put them in the support platoon with the mortars or in the line platoons.

My recommendation, again over Major Harrison's signature, presented the following rationale. If they were in the support platoon, we couldn't use both mortars and 106s at the same time. If we were at mortar distance, we were too far back and out of sight for the 106s. If we were at 106 range, we were too close to use the mortars. And, of course, one crew couldn't fire both weapons simultaneously. Also, if a support platoon track were knocked out, we'd lose two systems.

If we placed the 106 in the line platoons, they'd be up front where they could be used against bunkers. If in the line platoon, the Troop could increase its shock effect. We could assault under the combined fires of the mortars and the recoilless rifles. This would allow a Troop to put maximum fires on an objective. That's the name of the game and would hopefully result in fewer friendly casualties. If Charlie got lucky and hit a 106 track, we lost only one weapons system instead of two. We'd lose one or more .30 cal machine guns if they were placed on a line track, but that was fine. A 106 was more useful against a bunker than a .30 cal.

From the above, it should be obvious that my recommendation was to place the 106s in the line platoons. In a tanker's mind, there was no question about where the weapons should go, but the infantry senior advisor needed justification. My recommendation was approved. With placement approval, Colonel Thoan asked me where the weapon should be mounted on a track. I was shocked. In-country eleven months and now I could give some advice.

Mounting the 106 presented two problems. It had a tremendous back blast. We couldn't place it forward on the track without endangering the crew and closing the cargo hatch. Also, the sight, traversing handle, and elevation handle was on the left side of the weapon.

With these restrictions, we had only one place to mount the weapon—the right rear of a track. We'd have to remove the right side machinegun. That was all right; as I said, the 106 was a good trade off for a .30 cal machine gun. The loader would have to stand outside the vehicle, but that was okay too. The range of the 106 was great enough that the track shouldn't be subjected to accurate enemy fire. Also, the back deck of the weapon's carrier would have to be lowered straight out from the vehicle to give the loader a platform from which to work. The Vietnamese were too short to stand on the ground and load a weapon mounted on top of an M-113.

We mounted one weapon and took the track out into the paddies to test fire it. I got the call to give a class on how to sight and fire it. I had fired a 106 one time in OCS. It was a simple weapon to operate. The gunner used a modified .50 caliber spotter rifle to lay the main gun on target. The .50 cal round was designed to offer the same ballistics as the 106. The gunner sighted the weapons using the elevation and traversing handle until he thought he was on target. He then pulled out on the elevation handle knob to fire the spotter round. He adjusted the spotter round until it sailed into the target, then he pushed in the knob and the 106 fired.

My class covered bore-sighting, zeroing and firing the weapon. It was an informal class by Army standards but I got the points across. After the class, we fired. The results were outstanding. The gunners hit their targets and gaping holes appeared in the dikes.

Unfortunately, I never saw the weapons used in combat. Captain Seals told me later at Fort Knox that the Cav put them to good use after I rotated. My time finally came. I was going home. As I looked back on my tour, I realized that it hadn't been half bad. The only bad time I had was during my first month when I was getting acclimated and learning to live on the road. After I arranged a place to sleep and learned where to get a good supply of C-rations, the remaining months on the road hadn't produced unbearable physical hardships. I hadn't had to walk the paddies. I hadn't had to sleep on the ground in the rain. I hadn't had to sit all night in an ambush position. I hadn't had to fight leeches and snakes as well as Charlie. I hadn't been caught in the paddies, out-manned and out-gunned with no support. I hadn't been left alone when the Troop withdrew. My beret was off to the light infantry who had to suffer most of these conditions.

I had come to appreciate the Vietnamese people and the ARVN soldier. Both could endure unwarranted hardship and make do with very little. I was particularly proud of the Cav. They had done well. They had done everything asked of them. They hadn't backed up and they hadn't, in my opinion, lost a battle. I was willing to serve with them under any future conditions. I can easily brag about their accomplishments and their bravery under fire.

My only regret was that I hadn't been able to advise or to be of more assistance to Vinh and Hong, the way I wanted. Perhaps I could have been more forceful. But I didn't want to come on too strong with combat veterans. I was told to be patient. Possibly I was too patient. As I looked back, however, most of the things I wanted to try were eventually tried--some worked and some didn't.

During my year, I had come to some conclusions about how we should have conducted the war. First, I had decided that the United Sates couldn't win the war for South Vietnam unless we completely took over the government and war. Since we weren't there to do either of these, we could have become involved only if the South Vietnamese government established policies that were compatible with the beliefs of Americans and with the desires of the South Vietnamese people. If the American system of justice and human rights were at odds with what the South Vietnamese wanted, we shouldn't have gotten involved. Likewise, if the South Vietnamese government wouldn't support a democratic, capitalist system directed toward the general welfare of the people, we should not participate in their effort to maintain power.

A related consideration was the Army's leadership. If the leadership wouldn't aggressively pressure the war, we should have withdrawn. I believed that the ARVN soldier was as good as any soldier. His leadership, however, was lacking in most cases. Colonel

Thoan was an exception, as were a few other leaders. There were excellent ARVN units, as future battles would demonstrate; however, they were too few. Once the Army's leadership demonstrated a desire to support the government and was found to be free of corruption, we could have supported the Army with the best we had, just as if it were an American Army. It'd have been better to provide dollars and equipment instead of lives!

To ensure that the leadership was adequate, American advisors should have had a greater role in planning and supervision of funds at all levels. There should have been a system that required an advisor and a commander to have "footlocker sessions" to discuss tactics and procedures. If the advisor were less experienced, these sessions would afford him the opportunity to learn and express opinions. Each officer should submit reports on these sessions. If a host commander was found lacking, there should have been a procedure whereby the advisor could have had him relieved--not a popular view. We can't insult an ally by telling them that they are ineffective. Rather, we had to suffer through pushing more men and dollars into the grinder.

In this same vein, I wouldn't send non-combat-experienced people to advise combat veterans. The veteran isn't going to listen to an inexperienced advisor no matter how well grounded the advisor was in theory. This may have been difficult in the early stages of the war, but when I arrived on the scene we had plenty of veterans to serve with the Vietnamese. The point is, don't send an advisor with less experience than the person he's to advice.

Next, I held to the theory that first we beat them and then we win their hearts and minds. Again, not a popular view then or now. If it worked with Japan, it should have worked with Vietnam. I don't mean to infer that we should have waged a campaign of genocide. Rather, we should have met force with force. Simply, if we received fire from a village, we should eliminate it. If the villagers didn't support Charlie, he wouldn't be there. I had heard the argument that the villagers couldn't stop Charlie. In some cases, maybe so, but mostly I believed they supported Charlie because they feared him more than us. I'd point out, however, that those who espoused other views weren't getting shot at or side-stepping booby traps.

I'd have recommended a modified Strategic Hamlet Program, where we established democratic enclaves and work out from them. We wouldn't move forward until each enclave was well established with a democratic government and a capitalist system that would provide the community services expected of a modern society. How this plan differed from the Strategic Hamlet I don't know. I wasn't schooled in that program. What little I knew of the program seemed workable. The problem was that the South Vietnamese couldn't or wouldn't defend the hamlets.

I thought that our tours were too short. Don't get me wrong. I didn't want to stay longer. I had a family and I wanted to be with them. But I considered myself a soldier; I'd have stayed if ordered. I wasn't, however, going to volunteer. I had just learned my job and had just gained the confidence of my counterpart. In short, I was just becoming effective when I rotated. We should have committed for the duration. As it was, we relearned old lessons over eight years in four different battle zones. As a result, we fought twenty-four one-year wars. On the other hand, the Viet Gong and North Vietnamese fought one twenty-nine-year war, including their struggle with the French.

Finally, I'd have gone to the source of the problem, North Vietnam. I'd have thrown everything we had at the North short of nuclear weapons. Americans unaware of how the war was fought might think that we did just that. Of course, I didn't participate in the air war of the North. But, from what I read, I knew that we were fighting with one-half an arm. Later, conversations with pilots who flew in the North confirmed my belief. We tied our hands so as not to kill civilians. Those civilians, however, were supporting a supply and war machine that was killing Americans. They should have been made to see the error of their ways. Conventional warfare is total war involving all the resources of a nation; therefore, all elements of a warring country are subject to retaliation.

This isn't to say that the war would have turned out differently had these changes been made. The war was far too vast and diverse for a few policy changes to totally affect the outcome if the South Vietnamese didn't want to fight. Charlie, on the other hand, was willing to die and the civilians of the North withstood great tribulation from our bombing for their cause. I must, also, admit that I'm uncertain that anyone had the capability to withstand the pressures experienced by our bush grunts for much over a year. But Charlie withstood the pressures with far less support than we Americans and ARVN had. It is only to say that I believe we could have done better and might have won had we used all our resources. We could have learned our lessons and applied our knowledge better and more consistently. We wouldn't have had to retrain men and relearn valuable lessons each year. Even with our faults, however, I thought that we were winning and that the war would soon be won.

About two days before I left the Squadron, Major Kim called me aside and offered his thanks for my service and offered me a few North Vietnamese souvenirs, among which were a compass and a North Vietnamese belt buckle. There was no going-home party. Parties weren't in our Team's tradition. Major Harrison, Captain Rogers (my replacement) and I had a few drinks at a local bar and that was that.

The trip back to the world was uneventful. I had some problem with exchanging piasters or something at Ton Son Nhut. Whatever the problem, it caused me to almost miss my plane. You'd think I'd remember all the details about something that serious, but I don't. I only remember running around the airport to straighten out the problem and breaking out into such a sweat that I soaked my khakis through from shoulders to ankles.

Several friends were on my flight. We landed at Travis Air Force Base and caught a taxi into San Francisco International Airport. We laughed and joked during the drive into Frisco. The cab driver sat stoically at his steering wheel. He didn't seem to care for our levity. I guess returning GIs were nothing new to him. He had heard it all. At the airport, I got my shoes shined and bought a ticket on the first flight to Texas. I called my wife and waited for the plane.

The flight was a milk run. We flew over the Grand Canyon and stopped at every airport between California and the Midland-Odessa, Texas airport. The plane wasn't crowded and no one spoke to me. I didn't expect them to.

My wife and our good friends, Peggy and Gene Purser, met me at the Midland-Odessa air terminal. They were old high school buddies that we had double-dated with. There was no fanfare. I didn't expect it. What was to celebrate? The war wasn't over. We hadn't won. The only thing to celebrate was that another Nam advisor was safely home. The only thing to look forward to was another tour in Nam. Luckily, for me it never came.

APPENDIX ONE

WEEKLY REPORT 2–9 DECEMBER 1967:

1. DAILY ACTIVITIES (OMITTED).

2. MAINTENANCE:

    a. The tracks in the Troop are beginning to show wear from lack of second echelon maintenance. In the past week two tracks have been deadlined due to lack of power. Two more tracks are having the same type problems and will soon have to be deadlined. This would bring the troop strength down to nine vehicles.

    b. The advisor's jeep is in bad need of maintenance. The gears jump out of gear and the vehicle has no power. I believe it needs a new clutch or needs to have the clutch adjusted.

3. GENERAL:

    a. On the night of 4 Dec, when the Troop went to the relief of an ambushed truck convoy, artillery illumination was called for. When the area was illuminated, we were better illuminated than the possible VC positions. Although, the rice paddies were well illuminated we could not tell if there was movement in the tree lines.

I felt the illumination was giving the VC an advantage and not us. Because the vehicles were stationary and in the open, darkness was our best concealment. When we illuminated we lost this concealment and snipers began firing at us from the south side of the road. Personally, I will not call for illumination unless I am using C-47s or I am very closely engaged and need light to identify friendly troops. The searchlights would have been better to use in the situation just covered.

b. After having taken part in four small ambushes, I am convinced that the best way to neutralize the ambush is to dismount a number of men, after gaining fire superiority, and assaulting the ambush site. At the present time all we are doing is firing into the ambush site and them moving out after a time. When we do this, all the VC has to do is lie behind a paddy dike and wait for us to leave. We can fire all night and as long as the VC stays down they have no problem.

c. During the two months I have been here I have come to the conclusion that the only way to effectively take an objective is by total envelopment. If infantry is attached they should cross canals behind the objective to cut off withdrawal routes and then search the objective. When no infantry is attached a squad from the Troop should cross the canals to set blocking positions and then search the objective. The method we are now using allows the VC to cross canals that the tracks cannot cross and wait in safety until we leave the area. Attached overlays A, B & C [overlays have been lost) will show what I have in mind with infantry attached. The objectives are the same as objectives 4 & 5 on the operation of 6 Dec.

4. MORTARS:

   a. During the ambush on 4 Dec this team had its first opportunity to observe the mortars in action. It was found that Vinh does not know how to use the mortars in this type of situation and that the mortars are slow in reacting. When Vinh decides to employ the mortars he called them to the ambush site before allowing them to fire. This was a waste of time and only allowed the VC more time to withdraw. He should have left the mortar in place and used indirect fire.

   b. Once the mortars were employed it was found that the crew did not use the traversing mechanism. To traverse the mortar the crew moved the track rather that the traversing mechanism. This again caused a waste of time and was an ineffective method to engage a target.

   c. When the mortars engaged the target they fired as if they were firing at a point target rather than an area target. It was felt that the best method to cut off the VC's withdrawal and to properly search the wood line was to use the traverse and search method. This method would have cut off the VC's withdrawal route and would have saturated the area slowing the VC down so that our dismounted personnel could have caught up with them. Also, once the VC reached the wood line Vinh continued to use his machineguns. This was a waste of ammunition.

   d. Here again Vinh ran the whole show. He tried to direct the fire of the mortars, again adding confusion to the situation. He had mortars and machineguns firing and a dismounted element assaulting the ambush. If he would have given a mission order to each element and then supervised from a central point he would have better control. As it is now, no one makes a move until Vinh is beside him to direct him.

5. REMOUNTING MORTAR:

a. At the present time the mortars are mounted facing forward. This allows the mortar to go into operation quickly, but cuts down on the range and creates a safety problem. With the mortars mounted in their present manner the area around the muzzle is very dangerous. The only place that the men have to prepare a round for firing is in the front of the track. To do this with any speed the excess charges have to be dropped to the floor. As the 8 mm mortar has a bad habit of having burning charges fall off when it is fired, one of these charges might fall into the area where the men are preparing ammo, causing an explosion and the loss of a track. Also, with the mortar firing to the rear of the track the platoon leader could sit on the top of the track next to the TC's hatch and direct fire. As it is now the platoon leader is on the ground in back of the track. He does not have the observation point that he would get be being elevated. Also, he could be closer to the mortar making it easier to communicate with the gunner.

b. I feel that it might be worth considering dismounting the mortars when we are in a stationary location such as P-16. This will take some thought and discussion before a decision can be made as to advising to do this. If we do this, the reaction time will be quicker at short ranges around your position. On the other hand your move-out time could be cut down should you have to move. However, training would greatly offset this.

6. USE OF A SQUAD:

I have talked Vinh into training an eleven-man squad to be used to search when infantry is attached, to flank ambushes, and accompany the searchlight on patrols and ambushes. It will take some time to train them, but once trained I believe we will see great dividends.

7. INTERPRETER:

I now have Vinh interested in training so long as I give the instruction. To do this I need an interpreter. Vinh has been interpreting, but we can only give classes when Vinh has time to help. If I had an interpreter I could give more classes and get more done.

8. DISMOUNTING:

This team has started dismounting on objectives and at any other time I feel our presence might set a good example for the Vietnamese. So far I feel that this is paying off. I have found that the Vietnamese are willing to follow us so far and will better search objectives when we are on hand to advise them. Because Long and Lockett [named changed) have assisted greatly in this effort and because they have come under fire two times while being dismounted and advising I would like to put them in for the Army Commendation Medal w/v [for valor) device. I feel that they deserve at least this much. I also feel that the other teams could follow the example we are setting. I say this because we have let the other teams know what we are doing and they say we are crazy and it is not our job to dismount. They also say they stay on the tracks. I think an award to Lone and Lockett might help to encourage them [the others) to do the same. I do not feel that their action is deserving of a higher award because the contacts were not heavy.

9. HOUSE MEETING:

The question has again arisen as to when you are going to have a house meeting.

APPENDIX TWO

WEEKLY REPORT 14–20 JANUARY 1968

21 January 1968

SUBJECT: Report of Weekly Activities, 14–20 Jan 68

TO: Senior Advisor
     6th Armored Cavalry
     APO San Francisco 96359

1. SUMMARY OF TROOP ACTIVITIES:

14 Jan--Unit Strength was 101 men and 13 tracks. The Troop provided road security at P-21 from 0830 to 1900 hours. The unit moved to 047446 at 1900 hours for the night. No activity.

15 Jan--Unit Strength was 101 men and 13 tracks. The Troop moved to P-20 at 0830 to provide road security. At 1945 hours the Troop moved to P-21 for the night. No activity.

16 Jan--Unit strength was 102 men and 13 tracks. Troop provided road security from P-20 to P-21 from 0800 hours to 2000 hours. The headquarters platoon had mechanical training of the M-16 rifle. The unit moved to 108458 at 2000 hours for the night. No activity.

17 Jan--Unit strength was 102 men and 13 tracks. Troop provided road security from P-20 to P-21. The 1st and 2nd Platoons received mechanical training on the M-16 from 0800 hours to 1100 hours. The 3rd and support platoons received mechanical training on the M-16 from 1400 - 1600 hours. The unit remained at 108458 for the night. No activity.

18 Jan--Unit strength was 105 men and 13 tracks. The Troop provided road security from P-19 to P-20 and from P-21 to P-22 CP remained at 108458. One platoon had light contact at 1600 hours at 129459. No casualties. Unit moved to 119458 at 2000 hours for the night. No other activity

19 Jan--Unit strength was 102 men and 13 tracks. The unit provided road security from P-20 to P-21 until 2000 hours, then moved to 128459 for the night. No activity

20 Jan--Unit received mortar fire at 0035 hours. After being fired on the unit moved to P-20 for the night. U.S. casualties was one KIA and four wounded. Vietnamese casualties were seven KIA and three wounded. Unit strength was 92 men and 13 tracks. Unit returned to 128459 to police up at 0730 hours. The Troop provided road security from P-20 to P-22 until 1800 hours. At 2100 hours the Troop moved to P-20 for the night.

3. GENERAL

    a. Counterpart has continued to show a willingness to employ the searchlights in missions other than local security. However, due to a full moon the searchlights were not able to be used other than during the first few hours of darkness. On 14 Jan one light was used on an ambush, but due to the moonlight proved to be of no use.

b. While the platoons are providing road security they are wasting a great deal of time that could be used for platoon type training. At the present time the men are sleeping, cooking or playing cards once they get into position. This is most unsatisfactory. The platoon leader could leave a guard on each track and give classes to his remaining men during the hours of 0800 to 1100 hours and 1400 to 1700 hours. Some of the subjects that could be taught are reporting of intelligence information, first aid, commo procedure, ground guiding, maintenance of weapons, maintenance of gas mask, and mortar adjustment.

c. Overall maintenance of weapons in the Troop is unsatisfactory. Weapons are not properly cleaned after firing causing them to jam, in many cases, when they are next fired. Generally, the gunners clean their weapons by running a patch down the bore and pouring gasoline or a mixture of gasoline and oil over the receiver assembly. This problem has been brought to counterpart's attention, but no corrective action has been taken by him that I can see.

d. I have been reluctant to comment on how well counterpart accomplishes his mission of road security until I had a good long look at his method. Now, I believe that I can say that his method is unsatisfactory. When he is assigned a section of road to secure (say from P-20 to P-22) he will send each platoon to an assigned position at a certain time and they will not move from these positions until he calls them in to the CP location at night. This means that at most only 2000 meter or a 9000 meter area is secured. Of course, the area security depends on the terrain, but generally a platoon can secure only 500 meters of highway. This is if the troops are doing their job. In most cases they are not. They play cards or sleep. If the platoons were to change locations a couple of times a day, they could cover all of their area of responsibility for that day and not just 500 meters of it.

e. Night security and displacement remains to be a problem. Security is limited to possibly five guards for the Troop at night, half of these sit down or sleep. I have suggested that a sergeant of the guard be appointed, to counteract this, but no action has been taken. As for displacement, the Troop continues to park bumper to bumper beside the road. The losses to an assault or mortar attack would be staggering. A good example of his not using disbursement was the night of 20 Jan. On this night he had nine tracks positioned in less than a 100 meter perimeter around the Esso Station at P-20. If one mortar round had hit the 55 gallon gas cans beside the station, he would have lost at least three tracks. If rounds would have come into the area as they did on the morning of 20 Jan our losses would have been high.

APPENDIX THREE

VIET GONG BATTLE PLAN

Research after the Battle for My Tho indicated that the VC 261 B Battalion initiated the battle with its assault on the Ranger Compound on 30 January. The 261 A and 263 Battalion attacked across the Boa Dinh Canal. The 261 A battalion turned east to attack the bus station, traffic circle, and Catholic Church. This was the battalion that met 1st Troop at the traffic circle and along Hung Vuong Street. The 263 Battalion continued south to the west of the city's reservoir. This battalion fought the US 9th Division. The 514 VC Battalion attacked the Binh Due air field from the west.

# WORLD AHEAD *press*

Self-publishing means that you have the freedom to blaze your own trail as an author. But that doesn't mean you should go it alone. By choosing to publish with WORLD AHEAD PRESS, you partner with WND—one of the most powerful and influential brands on the Internet.

If you liked this book and want to publish your own, WORLD AHEAD PRESS, co-publishing division of WND Books, is right for you. WORLD AHEAD PRESS will turn your manuscript into a high-quality book and then promote it through its broad reach into conservative and Christian markets worldwide.

IMAGINE YOUR BOOK ALONGSIDE THESE AUTHORS!

We transform your manuscript into a marketable book. Here's what you get:

BEAUTIFUL CUSTOM BOOK COVER
PROFESSIONAL COPYEDIT
INTERIOR FORMATTING
EBOOK CONVERSION
KINDLE EBOOK EDITION
WORLDWIDE BOOKSTORE DISTRIBUTION
MARKETING ON AMAZON.COM

It's time to publish your book with WORLD AHEAD PRESS.

Go to www.worldaheadpress.com for a Free Consultation

www.ingramcontent.com/pod-product-compliance
Lightning Source LLC
Chambersburg PA
CBHW020348170426
43200CB00005B/90